Theorizing Masculinities

RESEARCH ON MEN AND MASCULINITIES SERIES

Series Editor:
MICHAEL S. KIMMEL, SUNY Stony Brook

Contemporary research on men and masculinity, informed by recent feminist thought and intellectual breakthroughs of women's studies and the women's movement, treats masculinity not as a normative referent but as a problematic gender construct. This series of interdisciplinary, edited volumes attempts to understand men and masculinity through this lens, providing a comprehensive understanding of gender and gender relationships in the contemporary world. Published in cooperation with the Men's Studies Association, a Task Group of the National Organization for Men Against Sexism.

Volumes in this Series

Other series volumes in preparation

Theorizing Masculinities

Edited by
Harry Brod
Michael Kaufman

Published in cooperation with the Men's Studies Association,
A Task Group of the National Organization for Men Against Sexism

SAGE Publications
International Educational and Professional Publisher
Thousand Oaks   London   New Delhi

For information address:

SAGE Publications, Inc.
2455 Teller Road
Thousand Oaks, California 91320

SAGE Publications Ltd.
6 Bonhill Street
London EC2A 4PU
United Kingdom

SAGE Publications India Pvt. Ltd.
M-32 Market
Greater Kailash I
New Delhi 110 048 India

Printed in the United States of America

Library of Congress Cataloging-in-Publication Data

Main entry under title:

Theorizing masculinities/edited by Harry Brod, Michael Kaufman.
     p. cm.—(Research on men and masculinites series: 5)
    "Published in cooperation with the Men's Studies Association, a task group of the National Organization for Men Against Sexism."
    Includes bibliographical references and index.
    ISBN 0-8039-4903-0.—ISBN 0-8039-4904-9 (pbk.)
    1. Men's studies—Philosophy. 2. Masculinity (Psychology).
    3. Men—Psychology. 4. Men—Attitudes. 5. Sexual orientation.
    6. Feminist theory. I. Brod, Harry, 1951- . II. Kaufman,
    Michael, 1951- . III. Men's Studies Association (U. S.). IV. Series.
    HQ 1088.T55 1994
    305.32—dc20   94-7490

95 96 97 10 9 8 7 6 5 4 3 2

Sage Production Editor: Diane S. Foster

Contents

Foreword

"Hate between men comes from cutting ourselves off from each other," wrote the great Viennese philosopher Ludwig Wittgenstein (1980, p. 46). "Because we don't want anyone else to look inside us, since it's not such a pretty sight in there." This fifth volume in the Sage Series on Research on Men and Masculinities invites us to look "in there," inside the definitions of masculinity. The essays in this volume tell us less about *what* to think about masculinity and more about *how* to think about it.

Ironically, virtually all the authors are, themselves, men. For decades, it was feminist women who had been theorizing about the meanings of masculinity—and with good reason: Men's efforts to live up to some vaguely defined notions of masculinity had some disastrous consequences for women. Institutionally, women lived in a world in which men held virtually all the positions of power. Interpersonally, individual women felt powerless to effect the kinds of changes in their lives they wanted.

Feminism thus proposed a syllogism: Women were not in power and did not feel powerful; men were in power and therefore must feel powerful. But this symmetry between women's powerlessness at the aggregate, social level and at the individual, interpersonal level, however, was not matched by an equally symmetrical relationship for men to the idea of power. Sure, it was empirically quite true that men occupied virtually all positions of power, and thus it could be accurately said that men were *in* power. But this power did not translate to a feeling of *being powerful* at the individual level.

In fact, when the feminist analysis was presented to men, they often would respond as if the speaker were from another planet. "What do you mean men are in power?" they would ask incredulously. "I have no power at all. My wife bosses me around, my kids boss me around, my boss bosses me around. I'm completely powerless!"

This helps to explain why many men seem to be looking for power rather than reveling in their experience of it—the enormous resonance among men of those disingenuous antifeminist arguments for "men's rights"; the lure of contemporary men's retreats that provide men an encounter with deep, powerful masculinity through ritual, drumming, and chanting; or even those Wall Street yuppies eating power breakfasts in their power ties.

This volume brings to interested readers a new generation of theorists of masculinity, thinkers who theorize masculinities from the inside, as it were, from that disjunction between the aggregate social power of men and men's individual experiences of powerlessness. To be sure, they do not legitimate those individual experiences as somehow empirically true because they are truly felt. Individual experience must always be placed within its appropriate social and historical context. But these theorists take the disjunction as a starting point, and often a framing device, for theorizing about men.

In so doing, they raise inevitable questions. Questions such as "which men" are to be theorized? A wide variety of the essays deal with different configurations of masculinity based on differing social locations. What analytic perspectives shed the most revealing light on the construction of masculinities? Some authors theorize masculinities from the center and others theorize from the margins. Some theorize from the relations between or among men, some from the relationship between women and men, and still others in the specific relationships between heterosexual men and homosexual men. Some utilize Marxian or Freudian themes, while others employ distinctly postmodern analytic principles to make men sensible.

By creating these new lenses through which to view masculinities the editors of this volume invite us to fashion a new angle of vision on the construction and meanings of masculinities. They join in the wider feminist project of making masculinities visible—even, at times, to men themselves. In this way they contribute to the project outlined by James Baldwin (1962, p. 21), himself no stranger to feeling marginalized by traditional configurations of masculine power: "We, with love, shall force our brothers to see themselves as they are, to cease fleeing from reality and begin to change it."

MICHAEL S. KIMMEL
Series Editor

References

Baldwin, J. (1962). *The fire next time*. New York: Dell.
Wittgenstein, L. (1980). *Culture and value*. Chicago: University of Chicago Press.

1

Introduction

HARRY BROD
MICHAEL KAUFMAN

Each of us has previously written or edited two books on men and masculinities: Harry Brod's edited volumes *The Making of Masculinities: The New Men's Studies* (1987) and *A Mensch Among Men: Explorations in Jewish Masculinity* (1988) and Michael Kaufman's edited volume *Beyond Patriarchy: Essays by Men on Pleasure, Power, and Change* (1987) and his book *Cracking the Armour: Power, Pain, and the Lives of Men* (1993). But neither of us has coedited a book before. That we feel the need to do so now is certainly testimony to the growth of the field and the growing difficulty of one person being capable of encompassing within one's purview the wide range of topics needing to be addressed. Perhaps it is also indicative of the cooperative culture that is emerging in profeminist men's work, in both intellectual and organizational efforts.

Though we have found through working together that our views of politics and scholarship are at least compatible, if not in many areas identical, we had each set somewhat different agendas for our earlier books. *The Making of Masculinities* intended to delineate a scholarly field of inquiry, interrogating different disciplines and approaches for new feminist understandings of masculinities. Though primarily written by men, it had some women contributors, too. *Beyond Patriarchy* aimed to be a more direct political intervention by men, many of them academics to be sure, but nonetheless men engaging in a more direct encounter with contemporary culture to further a feminist agenda for change. Though both books were committed to both scholarship and activism, they made different choices about foreground and background.

In this book we wanted to retain and further develop what we thought best about our choices of focus in our earlier books. We wanted to keep a simultaneous focus on both scholarship and activism and, indeed, to explore their interconnections around the thorny issues involving feminist work on men, performed mostly, but not exclusively, by men. Fortunately, another one of our aims for this book dovetailed perfectly with this one. We wanted the book to represent a sort of state-of-the-art look at theorizing masculinities in what seemed to us a new, second wave of work in this area. Brod had ended his introduction to *The Making of Masculinities* with the words "My greatest hope for this volume of essays in the new men's studies is that it be a stepping stone for a newer men's studies." One of the hallmarks of this "newer men's studies," we believe, is precisely a greater awareness of the relationship between theory and practice in both activism and scholarship. Many of the chapters in this volume explore these issues.

One thing that should not be surprising is that most of the contributors to this volume are men who have been active in the profeminist men's movement. For some this has meant the organization of activist groups working on issues of men's violence, supporting women's freedom of choice on abortion, or challenging homophobia and developing a gay-affirmative culture. For others it has meant such activities as taking antisexist initiatives into the school system. It has meant working to develop umbrella groups or coordinating organizations doing political action in all the countries we come from, and it often means working in men's support groups. In some cases it has meant encouraging the development of a scholarship by men that is committed to research, writing, and teaching that is profeminist, gay affirmative, and dedicated to the enhancement of men's lives.

Perhaps this interest in the relation of theory and practice dates us, accurately for the two editors and for most of the contributors as well, as children of the 1960s. After all, the 1990s often seems an intellectual era in which the world of theory all too often takes on a life completely inaccessible to all but a handful of people and in which the love of clever word play seems to have more attraction than using our knowledge to analyze the problems that surround us in order to effect social change.

The real issue, though, is that the existence of the chapters in this volume results not from the contemplation by men of feminist ideas in the abstract, but rather, in the case of those of us who are male, from our encounter with these ideas in the context of our own processes of change, perhaps from our experiences in men's support groups, perhaps from looking at our own ideas and behavior, perhaps from being challenged in relationships, friendships, and work, or perhaps from our experiences doing public education work to reach other men. In all these things, we have been confronted with the necessity of:

- Learning to listen to the voices of those groups whose presence and knowledge have been suppressed, as a result of their color, sex, sexual orientation, class, and so forth
- Looking at our lives and experiences as the lives and experiences of men, rather than maintaining the patriarchal arrogance that our lives are the lives of generic human beings
- Seeing how we and our brothers get hooked into the privileges and psychological life of a patriarchal society
- Feeling the enormous weight of homophobia and heterosexism in our lives, regardless of our own sexual orientation, and feeling similarly the dynamics of other forms of oppression
- Identifying the sticking points that make change so difficult
- Sensing the diverse experiences and diverse articulations of sexism among our brothers of varying classes, races, sexual orientations, ages, physical appearances and abilities, ethnicities, religions, and nationalities

And so the notion of committed research is not research committed to a single doctrine or the production of ideas that will get our women friends nodding in appreciation. Rather it is a recognition of diversity: of the need for diverse lines of inquiry and of diverse perspectives on a range of experiences within the broad framework of feminist analyses. For the male contributors, the sense of commitment within our research is also a recognition that any theoretical challenge is a personal challenge for the simple reason that the objects of analysis are our own lives as men and the intricate relations of power into which we have entered with the men and women around us. In practical terms this means drawing on examples from our own lives—something we always do in terms of our own processes of inquiry, something we sometimes do in terms of the presentation of our ideas in these articles. It means grappling with our responsibility to challenge an oppressive status quo—in the realm of ideas, in relation to the structures and institutions in which we find ourselves, and in our personal lives—while avoiding the pitfalls of a politics of guilt and blame. All in all, we hope that the nature of our commitment to change does not saddle us with a set of preconceived assumptions that must then be proved, but rather that our intellectual inquiries will be freed from the dogmas, the prejudices, and the common sense notions handed down to us from the millennia of patriarchal life and culture.

Our title highlights other issues we wish to explore. This is a book about the methods, frameworks, and approaches for the theorization of masculinities. It is concerned not so much with documenting new empirical findings but with raising questions about what it really means to theorize masculinities through diverse modes and methods. How does one *really* go about placing men and their institutions at the center of an analysis without replicating the patriarchal biases of previous studies of men? A number of the authors here, and many others, have for quite some time now insisted that the difference lay in *how* one theorized men and masculinities, that the new studies we were producing and looking for were about men *as men*, rather than as generic human beings whose gender went unnoticed and untheorized or at least undertheorized.

Such studies are further differentiated from earlier and nonfeminist ones, and from much of the more popular contemporary genre of books about men, because they incorporate the fundamental feminist insight that gender is a system of power and not just a set of stereotypes or observable differences between women and men. As soon as we enter into studies of masculinities as studies of relations and manifestations of unequal power and the internalization and reenactment of those relations, a wide range of difficult questions emerges. Such questions are the object of the essays in this volume.

Among these questions, although perhaps often more implicit than explicit, is the question of how the fields of women's studies, gay studies, and studies of people of color, as well as new and traditional approaches to the studies of class, can enter into the study of men as men. What can be the impact of the many new methodologies generated in these and other fields that place at the center of analysis persons and practices previously taken for granted?

One aspect, therefore, of an emerging second wave of critical studies on men and masculinities is the clear recognition that theorization concerns the elaboration and articulation of relations of power. The mention of sexual orientation, color, class, and so forth points to the other term in our title, highlighting that this volume is also about *masculinities*, not just about *theorizing*. The second aspect of a new wave of critical men's studies is the ever-growing recognition that we cannot study masculinity in the singular, as if the stuff of man were a homogeneous and unchanging thing. Rather, we wish to emphasize the plurality and diversity of men's experiences, attitudes, beliefs, situations, practices, and institutions, along lines of race, class, sexual orientation, religion, ethnicity, age, region, physical appearance, able-bodiedness, mental ability, and various other categories with which we describe our lives and experiences.

Although we reject the establishment of any hierarchy of oppression or insight among various subgroups, it is nonetheless the case that as the discourse about masculinities has emerged, gay studies has come to occupy a very central place. It is important to understand the nature of the special status of gay studies within men's studies and its attendant rationales both because of the importance of gay studies itself and because examining this issue will help to understand the more general problem of what is involved in fully integrating the study of one category, such as gender, with others, for example, race, class, and so forth. Although some argue that integrating diversity is a move toward political accommodation that takes one away from scholarly standards, we believe it is a matter of making necessary commitments that are both scholarly and political. Scholarship here remains committed, but not doctrinaire.

One approach maintains that what is involved in seeing gay studies as central to men's studies is a structural claim about the social construction of masculinities, a claim that heterosexism is more fundamental to the dynamics of sexism than is, for example, racism or classism. Another approach, in contrast, holds that an epistemological rather than structural claim is in evidence here, the idea being not that issues of sexual orientation are necessarily any more central to understanding gender than are issues of, for example, race or class, but that gay men are socially situated in such a way that they have particularly noteworthy insights into the social construction of masculinities across the board, and therefore their perspectives must be especially highlighted. Still another view of the matter holds that the special role of gay studies in men's studies is neither structural nor epistemological but rather historical. On this line of reasoning gay perspectives merit special consideration because various historical forces have put gay issues on the contemporary agendas for change as well as for scholarship in a particularly crucial and pivotal way. This approach yields a more explicitly political rationale.

In the work of any one individual one often, of course, finds these three perspectives present in various variations and combinations. From various perspectives and for various sorts of reasons, then, the centrality of gay studies within men's studies emerges neither as a case of granting most favored status to one group nor as a shunting aside of other concerns, but rather as a necessary component of any inquiry into men and masculinities.

Although we too set out to produce a book from a perspective that gave extensive coverage to gay studies within its consideration of men's studies, we found that when we assembled the chapters in this volume we did not have as substantial a representation of gay studies as we had hoped for. We attribute this to the way academic publishing has become institutionalized. Gay studies had established its own journals, conferences, caucuses, homes in various scholarly presses, and the rest of the apparatus of academic publishing significantly prior to what has come to be called men's studies. These venues have by now established a prior claim and loyalty among gay studies scholars. Thus, although we found an enthusiastic response to our solicitation of chapters from scholars who identify their work as being in men's studies or gender studies or the critique of masculinity or whatever other appellation finds favor in their eyes, we found scholars who identified with the field of gay studies repeatedly telling us that other journals or books already had claim to their current work. We regret we were therefore not able to include more of their work in this volume, despite our commitments to integrating gay and straight men's studies.

We found the same phenomenon at work in other groups we wanted to have well represented in this volume. For example, although a number of the chapters concern other cultures, they are written by scholars from the Anglophone cultures with which we are most familiar—the authors all currently work in the United States, the United Kingdom, Canada, or Australia. Although there is some representation of racial diversity, there is not as much as we would have liked, nor is there the number of women contributors we had hoped for, again often because scholars in these areas had their respective communities making the same prior claims on their efforts as we found among gay studies scholars. Our efforts have made us aware how far we still are from realizing the type of inclusive scholarship we would find ideal. Our hope is that this book becomes part of a dialogue among all these communities in order to establish more inclusive and integrated communities of theorists and activists.

It remains to provide the reader with a guide to the chapters that follow. This book is divided into two parts. Though all the chapters partake, to one degree or another, of our dual project of engaging both in a sort of metatheoretical discussion about how one theorizes masculinities and in an actual examination of certain configurations of masculinities, the chapters in the first part, which we call "*THEORIZING* Masculinities," emphasize the former, while those in the second part, which we call "Theorizing *MASCULINITIES*," emphasize the latter. In the first part of this book, the reader will find critical examinations of the conceptualizations of masculinities in various fields, primarily within psychoanalysis, social science, anthropology, history, sociology, and Marxism, while in the second part one will find critical considerations of, among other topics, feminism, postmodernism, homophobia, the mythopoetic men's movement, black English masculinities, Mexican immigrant men, steelworkers, profeminist men, Superman, and the military.

R. W. Connell's "Psychoanalysis on Masculinity" traces the history of thinking about masculinity in psychoanalysis, looking at the development of Freud's own views, especially regarding the classical formulation of the Oedipus complex, Adler's concept of masculine protest, Jung's archetypal theory, critical debates triggered by Klein and Horney, the Frankfurt school, and more recent radical and feminist psychoanalytic theories.

Scott Coltrane's "Theorizing Masculinities in Contemporary Social Science" attempts to synthesize micro- and macroapproaches to the study of gender, reflects on recent debates about essentialism, looks at cross-cultural studies of father-child relationships and women's status in nonindustrial societies, and considers current methodological debates about feminism, postmodernism, and standpoint theories in the sciences as they impinge on questions about profeminist men's studies.

Don Conway-Long's "Ethnographies and Masculinities" examines anthropological studies of men, focusing on concepts of honor and shame in the Mediterranean, alternative sex-gender systems in the Pacific, the role of ritual, and the practice of daily lives.

Harry Brod's "Some Thoughts on Some Histories of Some Masculinities: Jews and Other Others" reexamines the concept of "masculinities" and uses an examination of Jewish masculinity to consider the dynamics of analyzing nonhegemonic groups of men.

Jeff Hearn and David L. Collinson's "Theorizing Unities and Differences Between Men and Between Masculinities" argues for an explicit theorization of both "men" and "masculinities" as categories that are produced by men and that describe certain men, their relations, discourses, and practices. The chapter emphasizes the need to recognize both unities and differences among men and masculinities, thereby providing a framework for considering different types of men without diluting attention to the power of men.

Michael S. Kimmel's "Masculinity as Homophobia: Fear, Shame, and Silence in the Construction of Gender Identity" looks critically at the treatment of men in classical social theory and conventional histories. He argues for new conceptualizations of masculinity as power relations, as the flight from the feminine, as a homosocial enactment, and as homophobia, the latter itself then considered as a cause of sexism, heterosexism, and racism.

Michael Kaufman's "Men, Feminism, and Men's Contradictory Experiences of Power" develops his notion of men's contradictory experiences of power and uses this as an analytical tool for understanding the possibility of men's embrace of feminism.

In Part Two, David H. J. Morgan's "Theater of War: Combat, the Military, and Masculinities" observes that war and the military traditionally have had the strongest associations with masculinity and the wider gender order. In these sites the male body is linked to the body politic. Although modern societies have not eroded the links between masculinity, the military, and violence, they have, however, rendered these linkages more complex, multistranded, and contradictory. This chapter makes the case for a more finely tuned comparative analysis, exploring the boundedness of military cultures and the pervasiveness of military values in order to disentangle some of these complex strands of interconnection.

Mairtin Mac an Ghaill's "The Making of Black English Masculinities" critically examines how a group of young Afro-Caribbean male students negotiate their masculinity within the context of an English secondary school. He focuses on interactions between white male teachers and the subcultural responses of a highly marginalized and alienated group of young black men, exploring how their different perspectives help to shape black student masculinities.

Pierrette Hondagneu-Sotelo and Michael A. Messner's "Gender Displays and Men's Power: The 'New Man' and the Mexican Immigrant Man" argues that images in popular media and scholarly writings of the lives of class-privileged white men, including the mythopoetic men's movement and the "New Father," and of Mexican immigrant men distort the realities of these men's lives through race and class biases. The chapter argues that a critical/feminist sociology of men and masculinity should decenter and problematize hegemonic masculinity by proceeding from the standpoints of marginalized and subordinated masculinities.

David S. Gutterman's "Postmodernism and the Interrogation of Masculinity" examines the implications of postmodern conceptions of subjectivity on theoretical and political challenges to normative masculinity. It discusses the ways that the question of gay male gender identity and the deconstructive efforts of profeminist men illustrate the contingency of masculinity and address potential strategies for social change.

Arthur Flannigan-Saint-Aubin's "The Male Body and Literary Metaphors for Masculinity" interrogates some of the contradictions of the phallic metaphor of masculinity by suggesting an alternative *testicular* or *testerical* metaphor, an example of which can paradoxically be found in the character of Superman/Clark Kent.

Michael S. Kimmel and Michael Kaufman's "Weekend Warriors: The New Men's Movement" challenges the theoretical framework of the most widely known book about men to appear in recent years. It takes issue with the anthropological, psychological, historical, and political assumptions of Robert Bly and other writers and activists working within the mythopoetic framework.

This volume, then, explores a number of the emerging themes, concerns, and debates in the critical study of men and masculinities. Included among these is first, as previously discussed, the relationship between critical theorization and the practical activities of challenging patriarchal structures, behaviors, and identities. Another is the conflict between using versus critiquing traditional disciplines and structures of knowledge— that is, the extent to which inherited academic discourses and disciplines themselves perpetuate patriarchal theory and practice versus the extent to which they can be used as analytical tools of subversion.

Third is a tension between those who stress the need to integrate diversity to produce a more inclusive theory versus those who suggest that a recognition of diversity requires abandoning the quest for a single grand theory of masculinities. A related issue is which, if any, masculinities— including subordinated masculinities—are more central to the theorization of masculinities or, alternatively, does any privileging reproduce structures of dominance and hierarchy?

A final concern to which we draw attention is the status of men's subjectivities and the continuities and discontinuities between men's structural positions in hierarchies of power and men's own felt experiences.

Theorizing Masculinities, as a whole, does not attempt to resolve any of these conflicts and debates. Indeed, a number of its chapters only implicitly explore these tensions. We hope, though, that in its totality *Theorizing Masculinities* is a contribution to understanding not only how we can understand the diverse identities and practices of half of humanity but also how we can contribute toward ending domination by men.

Acknowledgments

Several of the brief summaries of the chapters are drawn from abstracts provided by the authors themselves, for which we thank them. We would particularly like to thank Michael S. Kimmel for first suggesting we edit this volume and for his invaluable assistance in all stages of its production.

References

Brod, H. (Ed.). (1987). *The making of masculinities: The new men's studies*. Boston: Allen & Unwin.

Brod, H. (Ed.). (1988). *A mensch among men: Explorations in Jewish masculinity*. Freedom, CA: The Crossing Press.

Kaufman, M. (Ed.). (1987). *Beyond patriarchy: Essays by men on pleasure, power, and change*. Toronto: Oxford University Press of Canada.

Kaufman, M. (1993). *Cracking the armour: Power, pain, and the lives of men*. Toronto: Viking Canada.

2

Psychoanalysis on Masculinity

R. W. CONNELL

Psychoanalysis has a paradoxical position in discussions of masculinity. The Freudian movement made the first serious attempt at scientific research on masculinity and explanation of its major patterns. Yet its findings have been largely neglected in the current revival of social-scientific interest in masculinity. As all who have read Freud's texts know, psychoanalysis was the product of an incisive intelligence and a profound commitment to science. Yet psychoanalysis gave birth to the confused irrationalism that now shoulders aside all claims of science in popular discussions of the "deep masculine."

Psychoanalysis on the one hand has enriched almost every current of radical thought in the 20th century, from Marxism, surrealism, and existentialism to anticolonialism, feminism, and gay liberation. On the other hand, it has evolved into a medical technology of surveillance and conformity, acting as a gender police and a bulwark of conservative gender ideology.

My intention is to explore these paradoxes by tracing the history of psychoanalytic ideas about masculinity (with some attention to their connections to psychoanalytic practice) from Freud's first formulations up to the present. Given the diversity within psychoanalysis, this can only

AUTHOR'S NOTE: This chapter began in a project undertaken 10 years ago with Tim Carrigan, whose help I gratefully acknowledge. Pam Benton and Mike Donaldson have provided more recent criticism and help. The initial work was supported by a grant from the Australian Research Grants Committee. There are, of course, many ways of approaching psychoanalysis. I have described mine in an essay on Freud (Connell, 1983), arguing for a social and dialectical view of psychoanalysis.

be an outline history. But I hope there is enough detail to establish that despite bizarre twists in the story, psychoanalysis remains a vital resource for the understanding of masculinity, and that some of the best leads it provides are found well back in its history.

Classical Psychoanalysis: The Oedipus Complex

Freud did not set out to do research on gender. He was a doctor, with a middle-class practice in Vienna, specializing in what were taken to be disorders of the nerves. He sought a psychology able to account for "neuroses" and a means of treating them. Within the cultural ferment of the turn-of-the-century European intelligentsia, however, his medical reasoning led to revolutionary conclusions: to a sweeping theory of sexuality, to the concepts of repression and the dynamic unconscious, and to the method *psychoanalysis,* hyphenated as it used to be spelled in English, that was both a remarkable tool of research and a debatable method of therapy.

All of this brought him, step by step, to the issues of gender that in other forms were being heatedly debated in advanced political and cultural circles. By the application of the new method Freud, more than anyone else, showed the artifice within the apparently natural characters of women and men, and made an inquiry into the way they were composed both possible and, in a sense, necessary.

Freud nowhere wrote a formal account of masculinity, though he wrote two dubious papers on femininity. To an extent, then, I have to reconstruct an inarticulate current of thought. Yet the materials are abundant, because Freud never stopped wrestling with issues about gender. One can distinguish three moments in the evolution of his ideas on masculinity.

The first was contained in the initial statements of psychoanalytic methods and concepts. *The Interpretation of Dreams* (1900/1953a) set out Freud's basic principles: the continuity between normal and neurotic mental life, the concepts of the unconscious and of repression, and the language of interpretation that allowed unconscious mental processes to be read through dreams and symptoms. The Oedipus complex, "the fateful combination of love for the one parent and simultaneous hatred for the other as a rival" (Freud, 1931, p. 229), was introduced only in a guarded manner in this book. But in the next few years it was proclaimed the key moment in psychosexual development. What precipitated the oedipal crisis, for boys, was identified as rivalry with the father and terror of castration. These ideas were crystallized in the Little Hans case history

(1909/1955a). Freud now had a definite idea of a formative moment in masculinity, and the dynamics of a formative relationship. The "Rat Man" case history (Freud, 1909/1955b) confirmed these ideas and showed how the father complex played out in an adult obsessional neurosis.

The *Three Essays on the Theory of Sexuality* (1905/1953b), an abstract of early psychoanalytic thinking and the classic of modern sexology, offered the idea that humans were constitutionally bisexual, as a way of thinking about sexual inversion. Homosexuality, Freud argued, is not a simple gender switch: "A large proportion of male inverts retain the mental quality of masculinity." So there is an important distinction between the choice of a sexual object, that is, the structure of one's emotional attachments, and one's own character traits. (This distinction is still not always grasped in discussions of gender.)

In the second and third essays Freud offered a narrative of psychosexual development from infancy to adulthood, suggesting among other things that boys' and girls' sexuality diverges sharply only in adolescence. The explicit comments on masculinity were few, but there was a strong implicit argument. The general theme of the *Three Essays* was that adult sexuality is constructed by a long and conflict-ridden process, in which original elements are combined and transformed in extraordinary ways. The process may take unexpected turnings (perversion), seize up (fixation), or fall apart (regression) at any step along the way.

It follows that adult masculinity, as an organization of character around sexual desire, must be a complex, and in some ways precarious, developmental construction. It is not given a priori in the nature of men, as European culture generally assumed. It is not wholly defined by the active/passive polarity that Freud initially saw as underlying sexual and mental life, which in due course became the basis of Adlerian and Jungian theories of masculinity.

What I might call the architectural approach to gender, a focus on the process of construction, reached its peak in the longest and most polished of Freud's case histories, the "Wolf Man" study. This recorded the analysis of a Russian aristocrat that lasted from early 1910 to the eve of the First World War, and its central themes concern masculinity. It marked a second stage in Freud's thinking on the subject.

Freud introduced the issue of masculinity near the end of a long chapter on his patient's famous dream about white wolves, while reflecting on the early history of the little boy's sexual development. He toyed with an equation between activity/passivity and masculinity/femininity, suggesting that the latter was usually superimposed on the former at about the oedipal stage. But he noted that in the crisis of the boy's emotional relation to his father, the feminine aim in relation to the father was repressed because of the fear of castration: "In short, a clear protest on the part of his masculinity!" (Freud, 1918/1955c, p. 47).

A pre-oedipal narcissistic masculinity was thus revealed, strong enough to force the repression of the strongest current in the boy's desires. Through a long argument, far too complex to summarize here, Freud pursued the psychological consequences of this archaic current of emotion, of the homosexual desire repressed in the oedipal crisis itself, and of an identification with women and jealousy of the mother that coexisted with the other currents.

In this case study Freud went a long way beyond the formulas of the *Three Essays*. Here he produced the first really detailed map of the contradictions and fissures within an adult man's personality. He showed an adult heterosexual masculinity underpinned (and undermined) by several contradictory layers of unconscious emotion. This case study stands as a challenge to all later research on masculinity. No account of the subject will do that has not absorbed the Wolf Man's lessons about the tensions within masculine character and about its vicissitudes through a life history, the turnings, strategies, and negotiations involved.

To recognize Freud's genius as a clinical observer is not to say he grasped the theoretical consequences of everything he saw. The Wolf Man study was accompanied by a frustrated worrying at the idea of masculinity/femininity. Freud kept coming back to the active/passive polarity although obviously dissatisfied with it. He remarked about this time that the concepts of masculinity and femininity "are among the most confused that occur in science" (1905/1953b, p. 219, n. 1, added to the text in 1915). This comment was followed by a distinction between psychological, biological, and sociological concepts of masculinity/femininity. But he could not get these definitions together.

The Wolf Man study itself reveals the underlying problem Freud could not resolve. The narcissistic masculinity predating the oedipal crisis implies a powerful cathexis of male genitals, but there is nothing in the particular case that would account for this. Ultimately the boy failed to acquire the consolidated masculinity to which he was, so to speak, patriarchally entitled—the failure that brought the grown man to Freud's door as a patient.

Both the failure and what it was a failure in are social. The particular configuration of the Wolf Man's childhood milieu, a scene of elusive desires and attenuated relationships, made it impossible for him to settle on an acceptable object of desire. But the issues go far beyond one household. Castration anxiety, indeed the whole oedipal constellation, rests on a *cultural* exaltation of masculinity and overvaluing of the penis. This was clear enough to Adler at the time and is basic in modern feminist psychoanalysis. But Freud was engaged then in a polemic against Adler's ideas, and indeed the point was made difficult to see simply by the way he set up the analysis as a clinical case study. The medical approach both gave him the materials of the problem and prevented its resolution.

The Wolf Man study and the theoretical reflections it spurred, but did not resolve, were the closest that Freud came to spelling out a theory of masculinity. There was, however, something more to come, a moment in the development of his ideas when another perspective on masculinity became possible, even half-emerged.

This chance was provided by the structural theory of personality he developed in the years around 1920, particularly by the concept of the superego. This, in his mature theory, is the agency in personality that judges, censors, and presents ideals. It is formed in the aftermath of the Oedipus complex by internalized parental prohibitions (Laplanche & Pontalis, 1973, pp. 435-438; Silverman, 1986).

Freud initially used this concept to fill out his narrative of individual development and character formation. But he began to see it as having a gendered character, being crucially a product of the child's relation with the father. The mechanisms that produce it, he concluded, are clearer and more decisive in the case of boys than of girls; this became a key idea in his late writings on femininity. Most striking, in *Civilization and Its Discontents* and other late writings about culture and religion, he began to see a sociological dimension in the concept of the superego: "Civilization, therefore, obtains mastery over the individual's dangerous desire for aggression by weakening and disarming it and by setting up an agency within him to watch over it, like a garrison in a conquered city" (Freud, 1930/1961, pp. 123-124).

This line of thought remained speculative; Freud never became acquainted with the methods of social research. But its implications are profound. For here is the germ of a theory of the patriarchal organization of culture and the mechanism of its transmission between generations through the psychodynamics that construct masculinity. To develop the idea would be to tilt further toward social determinism than Freud ever did. Later writers on masculinity have moved exactly in that direction but have mostly abandoned Freud's theorizing about the superego.

So Freud opened more doors than he walked through. But the leads he gave for the analysis of masculinity were remarkable enough. Beginning with conventional, essentialist ideas about a masculine/feminine, active/passive polarity in emotional life (a conception he could never quite shake off), he moved on to provide a method for the investigation, a guiding concept for it, a first map of the development of masculinity, and a warning about the limits of the idea. I will finish this discussion with some notes on each of these.

The method "psycho-analysis" itself means intensive study, one person at a time. It involves the decoding of personal meanings in an extraordinarily fine-grained way. (Freud, unlike many Freudians, did not go in for prepackaged symbolism.) It requires a strenuous balancing of concern for the person and critique of what the person says—an affectionate and curious skepticism balanced by a sense of the pain and poetry of life.

This has not proved an easy stance to sustain. In medical psychoanalysis it has usually been converted into a formula of professional detachment, in which the answers are in principle known in advance. Consequently, the method has ceased to be a means of discovery. In psychoanalytic cultural and social theory, the method has been dropped and only the interpretive formulas kept. Theorists debate the Law of the Father or the significance of sublimation without two cases to rub together.

The concept of the unconscious is still far from universally accepted; Freud's formulations of the idea hardly represent the state of the art now. What his formulations did, however, was signal the presence of powerful motives and defenses that cannot be easily acknowledged. This is important in getting past concepts of masculinity as simple rationality or simple self-interest; psychoanalysis makes one aware of how complex personal "interests" may be. Modern analyses of homophobia depend on this point. With the idea of the unconscious, Freud introduced a concept of layers in personality, which can be in contradiction with each other—indeed, usually are. Each personality is a shade-filled, complex structure, not a transparent, homogeneous whole.

The map Freud offered was his account of psychosexual development, centering on the Oedipus complex, a map he kept updating and redrawing to the end of his life. This map was not the list of "stages" that later child psychology took psychoanalysis to be (which I learned, as an undergraduate, like a litany: oral, anal, genital, latency . . .). It was, rather, the script of a drama, with characters (body parts, family members, parts of the mind), a plot line (pre-oedipal attachments, the oedipal crisis, identification), and a good deal of suspense about the denouement. Freud was highly aware of the different paths the plot could take because people arrived as his patients when their dramas had in some way gone awry. This led him directly to the view that different adult personalities were the outcomes of different paths of development, not different starting points. For this reason he rejected the notion of *qualitative* difference between homosexual and heterosexual people, such as the concepts of biological difference and a "third sex" that were being produced in his day by Magnus Hirschfeld and others in the early homosexual rights movement (Wolff, 1986).

This sense of immense variety in adult outcomes being produced by the complex combination and recombination of a few initial ingredients also underpinned the point Freud most insistently made about masculinity: that it never exists in a pure state, as the whole being of a man. Femininity, too, is always part of a man's character, whether in the form of bisexual object choices, a passive aim in sexuality, or identification with the mother. It was a strong sense of the truth and importance of this insight, I think, that kept Freud playing with the idea of constitutional bisexuality long after it had ceased to perform a useful function. It was this critical and disturbing insight that was thrown out with the bathwater when later, more conservative, psychoanalysts explicitly abandoned the theory of bisexuality.

The Road Not Taken: Masculine Protest

Freud's early psychoanalytic writings were received with a mixture of enthusiasm and hatred that is hard to grasp today. He was both vilified as a kind of pornographer and hailed as a medical genius. Within a few years a movement had formed around him, whose core members were doctors who had adopted his therapeutic methods. Associations were founded, journals launched, congresses held. This movement became the medium of theoretical debate over Freud's ideas. It also rapidly became (partly in response to the vilification from outside) a means of social control, insisting on orthodoxy as the price of membership. The intellectual history of psychoanalysis therefore became a history of splits.

The first of these involved Alfred Adler, a socialist doctor who had become convinced of the importance of social factors in disease before meeting Freud and who became for a time his most active supporter. Adler was president of the Psychoanalytic Society in Vienna at the time of his clash with Freud in early 1911. Some minutes of the key meetings survived, giving off a strong odor of unspoken anger, whether personal or political is not clear (Jones, 1958, pp. 148-149). At all events the occasion of the split was a series of papers read to the society by Adler, and it is a remarkable fact that the centerpiece of these papers was a theory of masculinity.

Adler's argument started from the opposition of masculinity and femininity that was found in the *Three Essays*. Adler, too, treated this as a basic polarity in mental life. He differed immediately, however, in stressing that the feminine side of the polarity is devalued by the culture. Children of both sexes, being in a position of weakness vis-à-vis adults, are thus forced to inhabit the feminine position; they necessarily develop a sense of femininity and doubts about their ability to achieve masculinity. The "childish value judgments" formed about this masculine/feminine polarity persist as a central motive in later life.

Submission and striving for independence coexist in the child's life, setting up an internal contradiction between masculinity and femininity. "This usually initiates a compromise"; in normal development some kind of balance is struck. The adult personality is thus a balance under tension.

But if there is weakness (and Adler had the idea that neurosis often was triggered by some physical inferiority or other), there will be anxiety that motivates an exaggerated emphasis on the masculine side of things. This "masculine protest," in Adler's famous phrase, is central to neurosis. It is basically a matter of *overcompensation* in the direction of aggression and restless striving for triumphs.

In his vivid sketches of the masculine protest, Adler was not drawing a sharp distinction between neurotic and normal. He saw the masculine protest as active in normal mental life, neurosis breaking out only when it failed to be gratified and turned sour.

It was not far from here to a critique of masculinity itself. Though the masculine protest as such was a feature of women's life as well as men's, in women's case it was overdetermined by their social subordination. In men's case it could become a public menace. Adler took a highly critical view of hegemonic masculinity and men's domination of women, cued by the feminist and socialist critiques of women's subordination. For instance, in discussing children's uncertainties about their sexual roles, he remarked: "To this is added the arch evil of our culture, the excessive pre-eminence of manliness. All children who have been in doubt as to their sexual role exaggerate the traits which they consider masculine, above all defiance" (Adler, 1956, p. 55).

As an account of the sources of neurosis, this had moved a long way from Freud's libido theory. Adler rejected Freud's biologism. In an argument that anticipated Sartre, Adler criticized the theory of repression as mechanistic, suggested that drives are constituted in personality in variable ways, and saw the Oedipus complex as only one form that might be taken by a larger dynamic—"a stage of the masculine protest."

Freud vehemently rejected this view as an unwarranted simplification of neurosis, and on this point Freud was certainly right. Adler left the Society, taking part of its membership with him. The break was a serious loss for both sides. Orthodox psychoanalysis from that point on became an increasingly closed system, resistant especially to the issues of social power that Adler had emphasized.

Adler, for his part, lost touch with Freud's marvelous sense of the intricacies and contradictions of mental life. He was still to do very interesting writing about politics and psychology, including a sketch of a psychology of power, important work on education, and an early and perceptive socialist critique of Bolshevism (Adler, 1928, 1956). His book *Understanding Human Nature* (1927/1992) had a statement of a psychoanalytic case for feminism that was clearer than any found elsewhere until the 1970s.

But he never did theoretical work of such quality again. The idea of the masculine protest was gradually domesticated as the abstract idea of "striving for superiority," diluting the sexual politics. Adler himself became, like other Freudian dissidents, the father-figure of a small cult and the author of an increasingly woolly though warm-hearted system that went under the name of "Individual Psychology." During the 1920s Adler pushed left-wingers out of his movement in a search for respectability, as orthodox psychoanalysis did on a grander scale. (The story can be traced in Ellenberger, 1970; Sperber, 1974.) The critical theory of masculinity sketched in his early papers was never developed.

Toward the Archetypes

Adler has been mostly forgotten; not so the next dissident to leave Freud's camp. Carl Jung was even more prominent at the time: The president of the International Psychoanalytic Association and a noted ʌ and experimental psychologist, he was widely regarded as s successor (Wehr, 1987). His alternative psychoanalysis has remained the most influential.

The conceptual issues between Freud and Jung at the time of their break had nothing to do with the theme of masculinity, but Jung had already begun to explore that question in a long article on "The Significance of the Father in the Destiny of the Individual" (1909/1961). Its main line was an orthodox Freudian argument about the importance of the family constellation around the child in shaping later emotional life. Jung offered, in a short case history of an 8-year-old boy, a beautiful study in ambivalence and the layering of motives in masculine development—the themes that Freud was shortly to paint on the larger canvas of the Wolf Man study.

Years after the split with Freud, Jung came back to these themes, but now in a very different mood. He was system building, and the masculine/feminine polarity, as Freud and Adler had found, is seductive to system builders. In *The Relations between the Ego and the Unconscious,* one of the key statements of his new system, Jung plunged in. He distinguished between the self constructed in the exchanges between a person and the social environment, which he called the *persona* (Greek for *mask*), and the self constituted in the unconscious by the process of repression, which he called the *anima*. These tend to be opposites; the opposition is to a large extent a gender opposition. Public masculinity means private femininity.

> No man is so entirely masculine that he has nothing feminine in him. The fact is, rather, that very masculine men have—carefully guarded and hidden—a very soft emotional life, often incorrectly described as "feminine." A man counts it a virtue to repress his feminine traits as much as possible, just as a woman, at least until recently, considered it unbecoming to be "mannish." The repression of feminine traits and inclinations naturally causes these contrasexual demands to accumulate in the unconscious. (Jung, 1928/1953, p. 187)

Disregarding his own careful qualification, Jung swept on to explain why masculine men have a feminine interior: because of this repression, because of the influence of women in adult life, and—another piece of Jung's system building—because of the influence of inherited, archetypal images of women. The archetypes in the collective unconscious, originally introduced in arguments such as these to explain the paradoxes of emotional life, in due course became the main theme of Jungian argument about gender.

Jung applied these ideas in an interesting exploration of the emotional dynamics of patriarchal marriage. He suggested that to the extent a man identifies himself with a strong, authoritative masculine persona, "he becomes inwardly a woman," compensating the outward show with "feminine weakness," and this can result in moral subordination to his wife. This was the most subtle part of Jung's analysis. His attempts to extend the analysis to women—assigned an *animus* while men had an *anima,* in a mirror-image argument—were crude in the extreme.

In this and other writings (e.g., Jung, 1982), Jung picked up the Freudian theme that was troubling many psychoanalysts at the time, the presence of femininity within masculinity, and gave it a popular face. He gave it a label ("anima and animus") and an easily understood explanatory formula (development of masculinity equals repression of femininity and vice versa). He presented this familiar opposition as rooted in timeless truths about the human psyche, through the theory of archetypes.

If Freudian concepts without Freudian methods have been common in recent cultural theory, Jungian concepts without any methods at all have dominated recent speculation about masculinity. Archetypes are fatally easy to find, in the absence of the discipline originally provided by clinical case study. Jung's own later books ranged enthusiastically through esoteric arts and world religions in search of archetypes. Followers have scoured mythological systems in search of gods and goddesses who will do as archetypes of modern psychological traits. I do not know whether to laugh or cry when confronted with texts such as "The Mythic Male" (Bethal, 1985), an erratic hunt through Greco-Roman myths, taken completely out of their contexts, for male gods who personify different "modes of masculine consciousness." The phenomenally successful *Iron John* (Bly, 1990) is a Jungian work exactly in this vein, except that Robert Bly finds his myth and most of his archetypal figures in a folktale retold by the Grimms rather than more conventionally in the pages of Ovid. However, he, too, ignores the cultural origins of his tale and scrambles its interpretation with ideas about "Zeus energy" and even wilder borrowings from oral cultures.

Equally influential was Jung's treatment of the masculine/feminine polarity as a universal structure of the psyche. Here Jung's influence, initially progressive, has been increasingly reactionary. The polarity at first provided a way of calling for a balance in mental and in social life between masculine and feminine influences. Jung, indeed, was the first person to propose what might be called masculinity therapy, which became popular in the 1970s (Solomon & Levy, 1982). He argued that "a certain type of modern man," accustomed to repress weakness, could no longer afford to. To change, it was necessary to distinguish oneself from both persona and anima. In a very interesting passage Jung suggested techniques for talking to one's anima, as if to a separate personality, and educating it (Jung, 1928/1953, pp. 199-208).

But if this launched the idea of men "getting in touch with their femininity," repopularized 40 years later, it did so at a high price. With both femininity and masculinity seen as archetypal structures of consciousness, no *historical* change in their constitution is possible. All that is possible is a change in the balance between them. In modern Jungian writing this produces an interpretation of feminism, the political movement, not as an attempt to contest the oppression of *women* but as a reassertion of *the feminine*. It assumes that in recent history the feminine has been dominated by the masculine, not that women have been dominated by men.

This is why Jungian theory has become central to the current antifeminist reaction among formerly progressive men. For this formula immediately yields the idea that modern feminism is *tilting the balance too far the other way* and suppressing the masculine. This is exactly what a whole series of Jungian writers have been arguing (Bly, 1990; Corneau, 1991; Kaufman & Timmers, 1985-1986; Tacey, 1990). The idea is enthusiastically received in the North American "men's movement" as an explanation for men's troubles with feminist women. Bly's very influential criticism of "soft men" who have caved in to feminism and lost the deep masculine is based precisely on this Jungian formula of archetypal balance.

Because Jung's original texts are now little studied, the roots of this argument in the early history of psychoanalysis are forgotten. It is worth recalling those roots to see what has been lost. Jung based his analysis on a metapsychological opposition, which Freud was gradually working his way past. Jung's formulations lost most of the subtlety and complexity in Freud's maps of psychosexual development, a loss reflected in the crudity of recent Jungian concepts of masculinity. By locating the basic determination of gender in the racial unconscious, the supposed depository of the archetypes, Jung turned completely away from the path toward social and historical understanding that had been pointed out by Adler.

Clinical Psychoanalysis and Its Taming

In the 1920s an increasingly visible split developed between those to whom psychoanalysis remained a method of individual therapy, and who therefore stayed within a medical or at least clinical framework, and those to whom psychoanalysis was a powerful general psychology able to inform cultural analysis of all types. In this section I will sketch the development of ideas about masculinity in the clinical tradition.

By the end of the 1920s gender issues had become a problem among orthodox psychoanalysts as well as an issue between them and dissidents. A small controversy about the issue of masculinity developed in technical psychoanalytic journals. It would be an exaggeration to speak of a feminist psychoanalysis, but women were more prominent in the second generation of analysts and there were some feminist strains in their thinking. The cultural milieu of Weimar Germany, increasingly the center of gravity for psychoanalysis until Hitler took power, had its differences from that of Hapsburg Vienna.

Debate was launched by Melanie Klein (1928) in an article on the "Early Stages of the Oedipus Conflict." What Klein uncovered was not the pre-oedipal masculinity that had surfaced in the Wolf Man case, but something even more unexpected: a pre-oedipal femininity in boys. She went so far as to talk of the "femininity-phase" as a normal part of development, characterized by both identification with the mother (wish for a child, etc.) and jealous rivalry of her. The theme of femininity within masculinity was taken up by Felix Boehm (1930), who stressed the frequency with which boys and men identify with women and show currents of envy and jealousy toward the mother. Like Klein, he postulated an early feminine phase of development—"the male is first of all a little girl"—heavily overlaid later but never without its effects in the psychology of men.

There is a certain air of surprise about these articles, as if their authors were somewhat disconcerted by what they had found. Freud himself was plainly bothered at this time by the issue of gender; these years saw not only his continuing efforts to unpack the active/passive dichotomy but also his articles on female sexuality and femininity. The issue was soon pushed further.

In an article crisply titled "The Dread of Women" Karen Horney (1932) noted both the pervasiveness of this theme in mythology and psychology and the insistence with which men deny it. She traced both facts to aspects of boys' sexuality that were missed by Freud's focus on fear of the castrating father. For Horney, fear of the mother is more deep-seated and more energetically repressed. The vagina itself, she argued, is the symbolic center of the process. The boy's typical reaction to feelings of inadequacy is to withdraw libido from the mother and focus it on his own self and genital, reactively strengthening his phallic narcissism—and preparing the ground for castration anxiety. Later reactions among men are fueled by these emotions, among them the tendency to choose socially inferior women as love objects and the practice of actively undermining women's self-respect to support "the ever precarious self-respect of the 'average man.' "

This article by Horney was the high point of the critique of masculinity in classical psychoanalysis. It had obvious flaws. It postulated a biological heterosexuality to prove the little boy's knowledge of the vagina, and gave no reason (any more than Freud had done) why the boy's experience with his mother should be generalized to the whole universe of women. Nevertheless the debate crystallized two key points: the extent to which masculinity is a structure of overcompensation and the fundamental connection of the making of masculinity with the subordination of women. The feminist edge to Horney's argument is obvious.

In the following generation clinical psychoanalysts briskly retreated from these positions. The retreat was not accidental; it was bound up with the whole institutional and political history of psychoanalysis at this time. Psychoanalysis in the German-speaking countries was virtually wiped out by the Nazis in the 1930s, who considered it "Jewish science." Many practitioners emigrated to the United States. There, for a variety of reasons—including their precarious position as immigrants, the local analysts' base in a conservative medical profession being increasingly integrated with the corporate world (Starr, 1982), and the impact of McCarthyism—the movement shed its sexual and cultural radicalism. As Marcuse (1955) noted, psychoanalysis moved far to the right in the generation between 1930 and 1960. It became for the most part a technique of normalization, concerned with adjusting the unhappy individual to the demands of social reality, rather than with questioning the terms on which that reality was constructed.

To say that psychoanalysis is a technique of normalization is no metaphor: The practice has a social effect. One can see this in cases in which psychoanalysts have reported the whole course of a treatment. I will give a French example, the analysis of a psychotic 14-year-old boy by Françoise Dolto (1974). Like the best of Freud's case studies, and those of Laing (discussed below), this gives a vivid account of the strained emotional interior of a whole family. The psychoanalyst intervenes by explaining the law of the father to the boy and pushing him toward the oedipal crisis, which he has never had. The analytic cure thus involves the reinstatement of what orthodox psychoanalysis defines as the normal type of masculinity.

This social practice gave more than symbolic meaning to the way psychoanalysts' shift to the right affected their thinking about gender issues and about masculinity specifically. The developmental path to adult heterosexuality, which Freud had seen as a complex and in many ways fragile construction, was increasingly seen as the unproblematic *natural* path of development. All others were deviant and signs of pathology. Marriage itself could be seen as a sign of mental health, and phallic aggressiveness a desired outcome of therapy for men. Psychoanalysis thus came to medicalize every type of gender dissent from the hegemonic pattern in middle-class white American culture. Most conspicuously, it medicalized homosexuality, which was declared inherently pathological by conventional analysts in the 1950s and 1960s, clearly the product of "disturbed parent-child relationships" (Bieber et al., 1962). The result was a long series of efforts to "cure" men of their homosexuality, in which psychoanalysts found themselves aligned with the purveyors of electric shock treatment and other professionals who abused gay people.

The immensely detailed critical history of psychoanalytic ideas about male homosexuality by Kenneth Lewes (1988) shows that this naturalizing of one "healthy" path of development and pathologizing of all others required a basic shift in the conception of the Oedipus complex. To Freud and the early analysts the Oedipus complex was *necessarily* traumatic, with no exceptions, and its passing was necessarily disruptive. That was basic to their sense of the fragility of adult masculinity. As Lewes observes, classical theory saw the Oedipus complex as having a range of outcomes, *all* of them neurotic in some sense. Human sexuality involves a traumatic encounter with culture, hence the sense of tragedy in Freud's cultural criticism. The nontragic, normalizing medical psychoanalysis of the 1940s and afterward lost the capacity for a critique of masculinity that classical theory had provided.

As Marcuse noted, this loss of critical edge was widespread in psychoanalysis at the time. A prime example of what he called Freudian "revisionism" was the work of Erik Erikson, perhaps the most influential psychoanalytic writer of the midcentury. Erikson (1950) departed from Freud's libido theory not on logical but on historical grounds. At the end of the 19th century the management of sexual impulses might have been a formative issue in development; but in the circumstances of mid-20th-century life, the crucial issues had to do with establishment of ego-identity. Erikson's work had immense influence on child and adolescent psychology and on popular psychology at the time. The concept of "identity" became a catchword, and his model of stages in human development became the basis of educational as well as therapeutic programs. In due course the concept of identity as the focus of emotional development also provided the basis for a new model of gender.

This was developed by Robert Stoller (1968), whose work centered on a remarkable development in gender practice, the invention of the "transsexual." The creation of this social category has been traced by Dave King (1981), who shows the interplay of a medical technology of "sex reassignment," journalistic fascination with "sex changes," and psychiatric categories for gender marginality. The invention of the surgical techniques created a need for psychological assessment of who should be allowed to go under the surgeon's knife, and this led to a research concern with gender identity. Stoller's study of transsexuals and of little boys who seemed to be on a path toward femininity led him not toward the classical psychoanalytic view of gender as a contradictory structure, but to the conviction that there was a noncontradictory, unitary *core gender identity* laid down in the first years of life. This was established by the pattern of emotional interaction between parents and children, and it was powerful enough to override the physical facts about the body if they were discordant. Transsexualism for men was thus psychologically defined not as the *desire to be a woman,* but as the *belief that one already was.*

Though built on the lurid gender contradictions of transsexuals' lives, this too was a normalizing theory. It located identification with women not in the unconscious of all men, but in a specific aberrant group. Boys affected by bad mothering—"the malicious male-hater" is one of Stoller's categories for describing the women in their lives—may be "rescued" by intervention to normalize family relationships. Given such views among the psychiatrists, one can imagine what gender ideology is like among the surgeons. It is not surprising to learn from nonmedical researchers such as Anne Bolin (1988) that males wanting sex reassignment surgery take great care to conform to the *doctors'* beliefs about appropriately feminine dress and behavior. Not much contradiction will be left hanging out.

The concept of core gender identity has had wide influence since it was propounded by Stoller, as a theory of normal gender development as well as a theory of aberration. It has influenced recent psychoanalytic writing about child development (Tyson, 1986) and about homosexuality (Friedman, 1988) and recent anthropological discussions of masculinity (Stoller & Herdt, 1982).

This has come a long way from Freud. Robert May (1986), indeed, seriously questions whether this is a psychoanalytic view at all. May argues that Erikson's concept of identity is really a meliorist ego psychology and goes on to show that the concept of gender identity in the work of Stoller and others has lost essential insights about conflict, fantasy, and the unconscious.

Clinical psychoanalysis in the United States, both with and without libido theory, thus evolved a normalizing psychology of gender whose main effect in practice was to reinforce social convention and whose main effect in theory was to define departures from hegemonic masculinity as actual or potential pathologies. Because this definition of healthy masculinity is given from outside the science, that is, by the dominant gender order, no theoretical consensus is required—and none exists. When the American journal *Pyschoanalytic Review* put together a special issue "Toward a New Psychology of Men" (Friedman & Lerner, 1986), it was noticeable that there was no new psychology in it. Rather, several established perspectives—gender identity, Jungian, classical Freudian, and object-relations—sat beside each other without interacting. That seems to be the state of ideas about gender in the clinical psychoanalytic tradition as a whole. I think this incoherence has a lot to do with the historic failure to develop the openings that Adler and Horney offered toward social analysis. Let me turn, then, to the wilder shores of nonclinical, unofficial psychoanalysis where the social has been a central theme.

Radical Psychoanalysis

Adler's attempt to merge Freudian theory and social radicalism perhaps came too soon, but war and depression spurred new attempts. The most spectacular was made by Wilhelm Reich, the only person, as far as I know, to have been thrown out of both the international communist movement and the international psychoanalytic movement. In the 1920s and early 1930s he was at the cutting edge of psychoanalysis and one of the leaders, alongside radical Adlerians, of a move to turn it into a form of social action. His attempt to develop a program of sex education and therapy in working-class Vienna and Berlin (Reich, 1972) is one of the most fascinating episodes in the history of psychoanalytic practice.

In the brilliant essay on "Ideology as a Material Force" that opened *The Mass Psychology of Fascism,* Reich (1933/1970) took up Freud's question of the social function of sexual repression and connected it with the creation of a social order that was not only an exploitative class society but also an "authoritarian patriarchy." Patriarchal marriage and family provided its organizational frame. Psychoanalysis revealed that "the interlacing of the socio-economic structure with the sexual structure of society and the structural reproduction of society take place in the first four or five years and in the authoritarian family" (Reich, 1933/1970, p. 30). The family is, in effect, the factory of the authoritarian state.

From this promising beginning Reich developed an analysis of fascist movements as the culmination of repressive tendencies in capitalist society. He offered a remarkable analysis of fascism's appeal to women through a reactionary ideology of the family, which deserves to be better known. But this and other lines of thought drew him away from the little Hitlers ruling inside the "authoritarian family." The nearly simultaneous rejection by his comrades both in psychoanalysis and in revolutionary politics undermined the synthesis between them that he had sought. As Reich's mind became more and more filled with thoughts of blue-tinged cosmic orgone energy (Rycroft, 1971), gender became less and less of a puzzle to him. His later writings have nothing of interest for the analysis of masculinity.

The theme of the authoritarian family was, however, picked up by the Institute for Social Research, the famous "Frankfurt school." In exile in Paris after the Nazi takeover of Germany and trying desperately to explain what had happened there, theorists of this group drew psychoanalytic and Marxist ideas together in the volume *Studies on Authority and Family* (Horkheimer, 1936). This was the point of departure for Erich Fromm's famous book *The Fear of Freedom* (1942), which set out a historical typology of personality structures centering on the "mechanisms of escape" from the anxieties set up by the great historical changes producing individuality and alienation. Fromm offered, in effect, a historical typology of masculinities. One of the escape mechanisms, "authoritarianism," combined masochistic and sadistic traits; Fromm saw this as being characteristically produced in the German lower middle class and a reason for their support for Nazism. The other mechanisms, "destructiveness" and "automaton conformity," were nowhere near as vividly described; but the latter had a continuing career in American social criticism, as Riesman's (1950) "other-directed character," Mills' (1951) "cheerful robot," and Marcuse's externalized superego (1964).

Even more influential was the research undertaken after the Institute's second flight, to New York, published in *The Authoritarian Personality* (Adorno, Frenkel-Brunswik, Levinson, & Sanford, 1950). The underlying idea was that fascist movements managed to tap hidden psychological predispositions with roots in the emotional dynamics of childhood. The key pattern identified was a combination of conformity to authority from above and aggression toward those below. These traits were traced back to harsh and loveless parenting, dominance of the family by the father, sexual and emotional repression, and highly conventional morality. The threads were teased out in great detail through clinical case studies as well as projective testing and attitude surveys. The book was notionally about generalized types of personality and attitude, but it was in practice a discussion of men. Indeed, *The Authoritarian Personality* marked an important moment in research on masculinity, comparable to the Wolf Man case study 30 years before. It provided the first detailed clinical picture of a type of masculinity linked to the social and political setting in which it was constructed.

If the hypotheses so patiently investigated by the Frankfurt school were right, this was a masculinity particularly involved in the maintenance of patriarchal ideology—marked by hatred for homosexuals and insistence on the subordination of women. But it was not the only show in town. *The Authoritarian Personality* analyzed this character type in contrast to a "democratic character" that could resist the appeals of fascism. Inadvertently, therefore, the research documented different *types of masculinity,* distinguished along lines other than the normal-versus-pathological categories of clinical psychoanalysis. In this light, the arguments of mainstream psychoanalysis could be seen as accounts of the tensions in one specific pattern of masculinity, rather than in masculinity in general.

This was a theoretical step of considerable importance. But it was not followed up. The Frankfurt school dispersed, and its most famous inheritor in the next generation, Juergen Habermas, had no interest in gender. Discussion of *The Authoritarian Personality* sputtered out in technical debates over personality measurement and Cold War attacks on its politics (Christie & Jahoda, 1954).

Neither Reich nor the Frankfurt school questioned the classic conception of libido. But this was directly challenged in the "existential psychoanalysis" proposed in France by Jean-Paul Sartre. In *Being and Nothingness* (1943/1969) Sartre rejected the idea of libido as a necessary basis of personality, suggesting rather that libidinal determination was a mode of being that the person *could* take up. Sartre saw "empirical psychoanalysis," as he called the Freudian tradition, as too mechanical, insisting that what was specifically human was the process of constituting oneself by choice and commitment. He replaced the concept of the unconscious with an argument about the different ways self-knowledge is organized. The "mystery in broad daylight" could be understood by a method that Sartre called existential psychoanalysis. The core of this was tracking down the life history to establish the constitutive commitments that had ramifying effects through the rest of the life. Sartre's emphasis on method was remarkable, given that most reworkings of psychoanalysis marginalized the issue.

It was Simone de Beauvoir who applied existential psychoanalysis explicitly to questions of gender in *The Second Sex* (1949/1972). Hardly a treatise on masculinity, the book was nevertheless instructive for masculinity research. It showed how the method could be used to delineate a range of ways of life *within* the broad gender categories. De Beauvoir's brilliant essays on various types of femininity transcend the typologies of more orthodox psychology, which persistently have a static, accomplished character—as if setting up the typology had closed off the historical process that produced it. Existential psychoanalysis in her hands showed gender as a developing engagement with situations and structures, including the consequences of previous choices.

What this could mean for studies of men is shown in the early work of the Scottish psychiatrist R. D. Laing. In his famous study of schizophrenia, *The Divided Self*, Laing discussed the striking case of "David," a student whose studied eccentricity—swishing around with an opera cloak and cane, for instance—seemed to be going a bit too far. Probing, Laing found a whole life that had been composed of playing parts—the good child, for his mother; the precocious schoolboy, for his teachers; after his mother's death, the little housewife, for his father. A gender subtext came out. The dramatic roles David rehearsed in front of his mirror were always women's roles, the clothes he dressed up in were his mother's, and he found himself unable to stop playing the part of a woman. His struggle against this commitment was what led to his fantastic get-up and extravagant manner: "This 'schizophrenic' role was the only refuge he knew from being entirely engulfed by the woman who was inside him, and always seemed to be coming out of him" (Laing, 1965, p. 73). The struggle to escape from his female personae had led him to set up a whole series of other personae that now formed, in Laing's terminology, an elaborate false-self system.

In this and other texts (Laing, 1969; Laing & Esterson, 1970) Laing gave wonderful accounts of the internal politics of the family. However, he never developed the clues his own work offered to the analysis of gender. He came to believe conventional therapy did more harm than good and soon became the central figure in the British antipsychiatry movement, which criticized the very category of schizophrenia and tried to create communal modes of personal healing. Nor did Sartre turn to gender relations in his later theorizing (Sartre, 1976), which offered powerful abstract models for connecting personal practice with large-scale social dynamics, but worked out the details only for the dynamics of class.

Apart from these cases and Sartre's own vast study of the novelist Flaubert, *The Family Idiot* (1981-1989), the methods of existential psychoanalysis have remained for the most part unused. I think this is profoundly unfortunate, because they offer the best chance in the psychoanalytic tradition to overcome mechanical and categorical ideas of gender. In Laing's studies the contradictions of gender are not mechanical. They are produced socially, but they become contradictions precisely by being taken up as incompatible courses of action, with the person being committed to two (or more) at once. It was this dynamic that had the power to tear apart David's control of his emotions; his defense, the false-self system, has parallels in other masculinities recently studied (Connell, 1991).

Much better known in current research on gender is the work of Jacques Lacan, a contemporary of Sartre, whose structuralist psychoanalysis has had a powerful influence on cultural studies and on feminist theories of gender in France and Britain (Roudinesco, 1990; Turkle, 1978). It has not led explicitly to a theory of masculinity, but certainly has an implicit one.

Where object-relations and identity theories played down the Oedipus complex, Lacanian theory not only reasserts it but takes it as the model of cultural processes in general. Oedipal repression becomes the constitutive moment of language or of the social. The phallus becomes the point of reference of every semiotic system. Masculinity is, in effect, written outward from the oedipal knot into the realm of communication and social order as a whole. Femininity, by contrast, may become the principle of disorder in the sense of being the negation of this phallocentric ordering of meaning, as it seems to do in Luce Irigaray's (1985) writing and in literary theory influenced by her. Men's homosexuality, too, can be read as the refusal of the oedipal path of sexual development, as in the influential work of Guy Hocquenghem (1978).

The articles by Klein, Boehm, and Horney discussed earlier not only marked the peak of interest in masculinity in classical psychoanalysis but also were part of a shift of interest among psychoanalysts toward the earliest years of childhood. Klein herself, by the 1940s, was a recognized leader of this movement. It was pursued in the following decades by the object-relations school of psychoanalysis, which laid emphasis on the direct social relations of child rearing. John Bowlby's (1951) famous "maternal deprivation" thesis was an early product of this work, with the ideological effect of pressuring mothers to stay in the home with their infants—a prime example of the way psychoanalysis served to police the gender order.

It is ironic, then, that object-relations theory should become the main basis for the openly feminist psychoanalysis that developed in the United States in the 1970s and 1980s—and specifically for its account of masculinity. Here a major change in theorizing about masculine development came to fruition. In classical theory the drama had centered on the *oedipal entry into masculinity,* whether the key agent was the father (Freud) or the mother (Horney). This emphasis was carried on by Lacan, for whom the symbolic father was central. In the arguments of Nancy Chodorow (1978) and Dorothy Dinnerstein (1976), the drama centers on *pre-oedipal separation from femininity,* with the focus unquestionably on the mother.

Chodorow's book was called *The Reproduction of Mothering,* but it contained an account of masculinity that has had a large impact on recent thinking (McMahon, 1993). The division of labor in child care meant that boys, like girls, had a woman as primary love object and object of identification. The construction of masculinity proceeded through the disruption of this identification, resulting in a character structure emphasizing boundaries between people and lacking that need to complete oneself in relations between people that led women toward mothering. Chodorow's argument developed an ideal-type of masculine and feminine development. Dinnerstein's argument, based on clinical work, gave greater emphasis (like Horney) to *fear* of the mother in the pre-oedipal period. Dinnerstein saw the reaction against femininity as a powerful underlying motive in men's hatred of women and men's violence in the public world from which women were excluded.

These claims have been much debated. There is, I think, force in Ian Craib's (1987) argument from within object-relations theory that approaches like Chodorow's tell us little about the internal organization of masculine personality. This parallels the criticism of gender identity theory made previously and recalls my earlier point about the fading of Freud's concept of the superego. But there is no doubt about the political significance of this work. Here the radical cultural potential of psychoanalysis has come to the surface again.

Conclusion

Psychoanalysis offers to modern thought on masculinity a uniquely rich method of investigation, some illuminating general principles, and an immense variety of specific hypotheses and insights. These do not come without cost and risk.

The method, based on the clinical case study and Freud's "talking cure," yields massive quantities of evidence for investigations of gender. Pop psychologies of masculinity are based on a parody of this method, the anecdote purporting to summarize a "case." I should therefore emphasize that the genuine case study—whether classical, Jungian, or existential, whether short or long—is a *discipline* of inquiry. The investigation produces evidence that has to be interrogated; interpretations are subject to challenge by fresh evidence. It is difficult and time-consuming work. Psychoanalytic interpretations reflect the complexity of the people being studied; they do not seek to reduce personalities to simple formulas.

Long before social constructionism became influential in discussions of gender, psychoanalysis had offered a picture of adult character as constructed through a long, necessarily conflict-ridden, process. This process produces a layered and contradictory structure. If social researchers on masculinity learn any one thing from the Freudian tradition, it should be this. Freud's concept of the unconscious, though immensely influential, is only one way in which this layering and contradiction can be represented. Sartre and Laing have provided another, in their analyses of contradictory commitments and practices.

Recognizing a conflictual process of construction, psychoanalysis further recognizes that the process can follow different paths. Indeed, this was fundamental to Freud's understanding of the neuroses as constructed from the same materials as "normal" mental life, put together in a different way. Psychoanalytic research has provided rich documentation of the diverse paths the construction of masculinity can take, both within the one society (as in the psychoanalytic work of the Frankfurt school) and between societies (as in the cross-cultural study of alternative nuclear complexes by Anne Parsons [1964]). The idea of multiple masculinities that is familiar in recent social research finds a precise meaning, and some of its strongest evidence, in psychoanalysis.

Psychoanalysis is often read as a theory of the individual, and Freud certainly dreamed of foundations in biology; but in truth it is a social science. Psychoanalytic case studies are all about the relationships that constitute the person, the prohibitions and possibilities that emerge in that most extraordinary and complex of social processes, the raising of one generation of humans by another. Psychoanalysis does not provide an alternative or a supplement to social theories of masculinity; it is engaged in social analysis from the start. Psychoanalysis forces one to recognize that the social is present in the person—it does not end at the skin—and that power invests desire in its very foundations.

Yet the understanding of the social in most psychoanalytic work is severely limited (and in some instances, such as the Jungian tradition, practically absent). Questions of social structure and large-scale dynamics are often very remote. Those psychoanalytic formulations that are clearest about questions of social dynamics, or even make use of social-structural concepts—such as Adler's and Horney's work in the early decades, the Frankfurt school, and more recently Laing's work on the family and feminist object-relations theory—are the most fruitful sources for the analysis of masculinity.

Given these principles, psychoanalysis provides a tremendous range of hypotheses, suggestions, insights, and guesses about the making of gender and the working of gender relations. Freud's idea about the importance of castration anxiety, Adler's argument about overcompensation, Jung's suggestions about the gender dynamics of marriages, Horney's and Dinnerstein's arguments about the importance of boys' fears of the mother, the Frankfurt school's ideas about the impact of family power structure and societal alienation, Chodorow's ideas about emotional separation, Lacanian arguments about the oedipal ordering of symbolization, are all useful lines of thought. To treat one of them as the a priori framework for a theory of masculinity would be to misuse psychoanalysis (in a way unfortunately typical of its applications in the social sciences). But deployed in the detail of cases (which need not be only individual life histories, for as Dollard's [1937] classic study of race relations showed, psychoanalysis can also be deployed in the study of collectivities and institutions), these ideas will greatly enrich understanding of the social dynamics towards which we grope with terms such as masculinity.

Freud did not succeed in founding a science, in his own sense of a positivist science of the mind. He founded something more ambiguous, and more interesting: an enterprise of scrutiny and theory that has the capacity to be both an ideology and technology of social control and a means of cultural critique and personal discovery. Both sides of psychoanalysis show in its tangled encounters with issues of masculinity. I think Freud's invention is an essential aid in understanding men's gender and gender politics, but is never enough on its own. It is an instrument that needs to be used with precision, on the right kind of material, in full awareness of the social mysteries that create the mysteries of desire.

References

Adler, A. (1928). Psychologie der Macht [Psychology of power]. In F. Kobler (Ed.), *Gewalt und Gewaltlösigkeit* (pp. 41-46). Zürich: Rotapfelverlag.

Adler, A. (1956). *The individual psychology of Alfred Adler: A systematic presentation in selections from his writing.* New York: Basic Books.

Adler, A. (1992). *Understanding human nature.* Oxford: Oneworld. (Original work published 1927)

Adorno, T., Frenkel-Brunswik, E., Levinson, D. J., & Sanford, R. N. (1950). *The authoritarian personality.* New York: Harper.

Beauvoir, S. de. (1972). *The second sex.* Harmondsworth, UK: Penguin. (Original work published 1949)

Bethal, M. (1985). The mythic male: Spectrum of masculinity. *Colorado Institute of Transpersonal Psychology Journal, 2*(2), 9ff.

Bieber, I., et al. (1962). *Homosexuality: A psychoanalytic study.* New York: Basic Books.

Bly, R. (1990). *Iron John: A book about men.* Reading, MA: Addison-Wesley.

Boehm, F. (1930). The femininity-complex in men. *International Journal of Psycho-Analysis, 11,* 444-469.

Bolin, A. (1988). *In search of Eve: Transsexual rites of passage.* South Hadley, MA: Bergin & Garvey.

Bowlby, J. (1951). *Maternal care and mental health.* Geneva: World Health Organization.

Chodorow, N. (1978). *The reproduction of mothering: Psychoanalysis and the sociology of gender.* Berkeley: University of California Press.

Christie, R., & Jahoda, M. (Eds.). (1954). *Studies in the scope and method of "The authoritarian personality."* Glencoe: Free Press.

Connell, R. W. (1983). Dr. Freud and the course of history, *Which way is up? Essays on sex, class and culture* (pp. 3-16). Sydney: Allen & Unwin.

Connell, R. W. (1991). Live fast and die young: The construction of masculinity among young working-class men on the margin of the labour market. *Australian and New Zealand Journal of Sociology, 27*(2), 141-171.

Corneau, G. (1991). *Absent fathers, lost sons: The search for masculine identity.* Boston: Shambhala.

Craib, I. (1987). Masculinity and male dominance. *Sociological Review, 34*(4), 721-743.

Dinnerstein, D. (1976). *The rocking of the cradle, and the ruling of the world.* New York: Harper & Row.

Dollard, J. (1937). *Caste and class in a southern town.* New Haven, CT: Yale University Press.

Dolto, F. (1974). *Dominique: Analysis of an adolescent.* London: Souvenir Press.

Ellenberger, H. F. (1970). *The discovery of the unconscious: The history and evolution of dynamic psychiatry.* New York: Basic Books.

Erikson, E. H. (1950). *Childhood and society.* London: Imago.

Freud, S. (1931). Female sexuality. In *The complete psychological works of Sigmund Freud: Standard edition* (Vol. 21, pp. 221ff). London: Hogarth.

Freud, S. (1953a). The interpretation of dreams. In *The complete psychological works of Sigmund Freud: Standard edition* (Vols. 4-5). London: Hogarth. (Original work published 1900)

Freud, S. (1953b). Three essays on the theory of sexuality. In *The complete psychological works of Sigmund Freud: Standard edition* (Vol. 7). London: Hogarth. (Original work published 1905)

Freud, S. (1955a). Analysis of a phobia in a five-year-old boy. In *The complete psychological works of Sigmund Freud: Standard edition* (Vol. 10, pp. 1-149). London: Hogarth. (Original work published 1909)

Freud, S. (1955b). Notes upon a case of obsessional neurosis. In *The complete psychological works of Sigmund Freud: Standard edition* (Vol. 10, pp. 151-249). London: Hogarth. (Original work published 1909)

Freud, S. (1955c). From the history of an infantile neurosis. In *The complete psychological works of Sigmund Freud: Standard edition* (Vol. 17). London: Hogarth. (Original work published 1918)

Freud, S. (1961). Civilization and its discontents. In *The complete psychological works of Sigmund Freud: Standard edition* (Vol. 21). London: Hogarth. (Original work published 1930)

Friedman, R. C. (1988). *Male homosexuality: A contemporary psychoanalytic perspective.* New Haven, CT: Yale University Press.

Friedman, R. M., & Lerner, L. (1986). Toward a new psychology of men: Psychoanalytic and social perspectives [Special issue]. *Psychoanalytic Review, 73*(4).

Fromm, E. (1942). *The fear of freedom.* London: Routledge & Kegan Paul.

Hocquenghem, G. (1978). *Homosexual desire.* London: Allison & Busby.

Horkheimer, M. (Ed.). (1936). *Studien über autorität und familie* [Studies on authority and family]. Paris: Alcan.

Horney, K. (1932). The dread of women. *International Journal of Psycho-Analysis, 13*, 348-360.

Irigaray, L. (1985). *This sex which is not one.* Ithaca, NY: Cornell University Press.

Jones, E. (1958). *Sigmund Freud, life and work,* (Vol. 2, 2nd ed.). London: Hogarth.

Jung, C. G. (1953). The relations between the ego and the unconscious. In *Collected works: Vol. 7. Two essays on analytical psychology.* London: Routledge & Kegan Paul. (Original work published 1928)

Jung, C. G. (1961). The significance of the father in the destiny of the individual. In *Collected works: Vol. 4. Freud and psychoanalysis* (pp. 301-323). London: Routledge & Kegan Paul. (Original work published 1909)

Jung, C. G. (1982). *Aspects of the feminine.* Princeton, NJ: Princeton University Press.

Kaufman, J., & Timmers, R. L. (1985-1986). Searching for the hairy man. *Women and Therapy, 4*(4), 45-57.

King, D. (1981). Gender confusions: Psychological and psychiatric conceptions of transvestism and transsexualism. In K. Plummer (Ed.), *The making of the modern homosexual* (pp. 155-183). London: Hutchinson.

Klein, M. (1928). Early stages of the Oedipus conflict. *International Journal of Psycho-Analysis, 9*, 167-180.

Laing, R. D. (1965). *The divided self: An existential study in sanity and madness.* Harmondsworth, UK: Penguin.

Laing, R. D. (1969). *Self and others* (2nd ed.). London: Tavistock.

Laing, R. D., & Esterson, A. (1970). *Sanity, madness and the family: Families of schizophrenics* (2nd ed.). Harmondsworth, UK: Penguin.

Laplanche, J., & Pontalis, J.-B. (1973). *The language of psycho-analysis.* New York: Norton.

Lewes, K. (1988). *The psychoanalytic theory of male homosexuality.* New York: Simon & Schuster.

Marcuse, H. (1955). *Eros and civilization: A philosophical inquiry into Freud.* Boston: Beacon.

Marcuse, H. (1964). *One dimensional man: Studies in the ideology of advanced industrial society.* Boston: Beacon.

May, R. (1986). Concerning a psychoanalytic view of maleness. *Psychoanalytic Review, 73*(4), 579-597.

McMahon, A. (1993). Male readings of feminist theory: The psychologization of sexual politics in the masculinity literature. *Theory and Society, 22*(5), 675-695.

Mills, C. W. (1951). *White collar: The American middle classes.* New York: Oxford University Press.

Parsons, A. (1964). Is the Oedipus complex universal? The Jones-Malinowski debate revisited and a south Italian "nuclear complex." *Psychoanalytic Study of Society, 3,* 278-326.

Reich, W. (1970). *The mass psychology of fascism.* New York: Farrar Strauss & Giroux. (Original work published 1933)

Reich, W. (1972). *Sex-Pol: Essays, 1929-1934.* New York: Vintage.

Riesman, D. (1950). *The lonely crowd: A study of the changing American character.* New Haven, CT: Yale University Press.

Roudinesco, E. (1990). *Jacques Lacan & Co.: A history of psychoanalysis in France, 1925-1985.* Chicago: University of Chicago Press.

Rycroft, C. (1971). *Reich.* London: Fontana.

Sartre, J.-P. (1969). *Being and nothingness: An essay on phenomenological ontology.* London: Methuen. (Original work published 1943)

Sartre, J.-P. (1976). *Critique of dialectical reason: Vol. 1. Theory of practical ensembles.* London: NLB.

Sartre, J.-P. (1981-1989). *The family idiot: Gustave Flaubert, 1821-1857* (3 vols.). Chicago: University of Chicago Press.

Silverman, M. (1986). The male superego. *Psychoanalytic Review, 73*(4), 427-444.

Solomon, K., & Levy, N. B. (Eds.). (1982). *Men in transition: Theory and therapy.* New York: Plenum.

Sperber, M. (1974). *Masks of loneliness: Alfred Adler in perspective.* New York: Macmillan.

Starr, P. (1982). *The social transformation of American medicine.* New York: Basic Books.

Stoller, R. J. (1968). *Sex and gender: On the development of masculinity and femininity.* New York: Science House.

Stoller, R. J., & Herdt, G. H. (1982). The development of masculinity: A cross-cultural contribution. *American Psychoanalytical Association Journal, 30*(1), 29-59.

Tacey, D. J. (1990). Reconstructing masculinity: A post-Jungian response to contemporary men's issues. *Meanjin Quarterly, 49*(4), 781-792.

Turkle, S. (1978). *Psychoanalytic politics: Freud's French revolution*. New York: Basic Books.

Tyson, P. (1986). Male gender identity: Early developmental roots. *Psychoanalytic Review, 73*(4), 405-425.

Wehr, G. (1987). *Jung: A biography*. Boston: Shambhala.

Wolff, C. (1986). *Magnus Hirschfeld: A portrait of a pioneer in sexology*. London: Quartet.

3
Theorizing Masculinities in Contemporary Social Science

SCOTT COLTRANE

Life is not determined by consciousness, but consciousness by life . . . circumstances make men just as much as men make circumstances.

Karl Marx, 1846/1978a

Not, then, men and their moments. Rather moments and their men.

Erving Goffman, 1967

Living a century apart and working at different levels of analysis, Karl Marx and Erving Goffman made unique contributions to the under-standing of social life. Although their works are rarely mentioned to-gether, these passages resonate with each other and raise two issues that deserve the attention of scholars who study gender. The first is that both men used what is now called "sexist" language. Both subsumed all of humanity under the term *men*, effectively minimizing the experiences of women and ignoring the importance of gender in men's lives. One might excuse their linguistic transgressions because they were following social customs, but one ought not lose sight of the fact that gender, though considered elsewhere in their writings, was of secondary importance to them. In that sense, these two theorists teach by negative example and remind scholars that they are breaking new ground by explicitly focusing on gender when studying men.

On a second issue, the models of society presented by Marx and Goffman highlight the importance of social structure at the macro- and microlevels. Social structure is the patterned repetition of the same types of events happening over and over again, involving many different people spread out across many different locations (Collins, 1988). Marx's and Goffman's ideas about social structure have fallen out of fashion in the recent postmodern turn toward discourse analysis and historical particularity, but their insights into the dialectical nature of social processes and their emphasis on systemic patterns of social relations have much to offer contemporary gender scholars. The macrohistorical view from Marx reminds one that individual choice is constrained by material circumstances, especially the unequal distribution of wealth and access to the means of production. The microinteractionist view from Goffman is a reminder that routine social experiences shape consciousness and define individual identities. Both theorists conceived of complex reciprocal relationships between structure and agency, but both ultimately gave priority to patterned systems of social relations. For Marx, "men" made history, but not under conditions of their own choosing. Rather, historically variable social and economic conditions shaped peoples' consciousness and constrained their actions according to identifiable patterns (Marx, 1851/1978b). For Goffman, men and women actively engaged in impression management, but they were held hostage to routine ritual observances and the collaborative production of selves (Goffman, 1967).

Few would argue that Marx privileged social structure over individual choice, but Goffman, too, gave precedence to the structure of situations. He conceived of "moments" as historically situated events that followed a loosely patterned sequence, carried normative prescriptions, and, most important, created an emergent sense of self. More than most social scientists of his day, Goffman acknowledged the importance of individual initiative in shaping society, but his fundamental assumption was that moments created "men" rather than the reverse. Although he did not attempt an explicit study of masculinity, Goffman began to write about gender before he died in 1982, and his analytical scheme, coupled with some of Marx's insights, provides the foundations for a promising microstructural approach to the study of gender (Goffman, 1977, 1979). In this chapter, I emphasize the continuing heuristic value of the concept of social structure and suggest that a microstructural approach to the study of masculinities can help guide one through some difficult epistemological and political dilemmas.

Marx and Goffman were criticized for departing from the accepted research protocols of their times, but they both advocated empirical research that seems rather scientific and conventional by today's standards. In contrast, many recent critical scholars advocate abandoning conventional sociological approaches to the study of gender on the grounds that these methods tend to favor a masculinist individualism, mask diversity, and perpetuate inequality. Conventional social science has favored the interests of dominant men and slighted the influence of gender, but the call for its abandonment carries some dangers of its own. A more reformist strategy would acknowledge the sexism of past research, but continue to use a range of objectivist and subjectivist methods to document patterned regularity in systems of inequality. Underlying this position is the belief that the critical insights of Goffman and Marx can be coupled with conventional social science methods to further the understanding of men and masculinities. Toward that end, I describe some of the epistemological issues raised by recent gender scholarship and suggest how a microstructural analysis of masculinities might be both politically and intellectually satisfying. Rather than focusing on one specific issue in detail, this chapter surveys potential and actual problems in the field and closes with a few suggestions for ways to incorporate men's standpoints into gender studies.

Past Research on Men and Masculinity

Research on men is as old as scholarship itself, but a focus on masculinity, or men as explicitly gendered individuals, is relatively recent (Morgan, 1981). As the women's movement was gaining momentum in the 1970s, men began writing about how boys were socialized to be tough and competitive and how men had trouble expressing their emotions (Goldberg, 1976; Nichols, 1975). Often confessional, therapeutic, and ignorant of the power dimension of gender relations, this style of research on men continued through the 1980s and into the 1990s. Some writers focused on their personal experiences caring for a child (Clary, 1982), or on middle-aged men's longing for their fathers (Osherson, 1986), and many emphasized how men suffered from confining masculine stereotypes and were misunderstood by women (Farrell, 1986). These popular books helped men develop their sensitivities, but paid little attention to those who suffered at the hands of dominant men's privileged position.

Recent best-selling authors in this tradition include Robert Bly (1990) who blends mythical storytelling with pop psychology in a celebration of tribal male bonding. Books like this posit timeless natural differences between men and women, and although these authors often portray themselves as part of a progressive men's movement, their writing often resembles the antiwoman rhetoric of reactionary men's rights activists (Coltrane & Hickman, 1992).

In response to, and in support of, the women's movement, a different group of men scholars and activists adopted an explicitly feminist perspective in their early explorations of masculinity. The defining feature of this approach to men's studies was its attention to men's power over women (Pleck, 1977/1981; Sattel, 1976). During the 1980s, critical studies of men became more sophisticated and scholars developed concepts such as "hegemonic masculinity" to highlight the multidimensional and socially constructed aspects of male dominance (Connell, 1987). Recent scholarship on men uses insights from feminist theories, highlights diversity in masculinities, includes a focus on gay men, and promotes an understanding of what Kaufman (1993) calls "men's contradictory experiences of power" (Brod, 1987; Hearn & Morgan, 1990; Kaufman, 1987; Kimmel & Messner, 1989). Many current scholars use postmodern critiques of value-free social science, apply critical Marxist and feminist standpoint epistemologies, and attempt to move beyond older structuralist theoretical frameworks (Jackson, 1990; Messner, 1990; Seidler, 1989).

At the risk of oversimplification, there are thus two conflicting styles of men writing about masculinity: One celebrates male bonding and tells men they are OK, and the other focuses on issues of power using academic feminist interpretive frameworks. The former approach sells many books and receives much media attention. The latter approach, of which this volume is an example, focuses on the contradictory meanings and experiences of manhood and aligns itself with the women's movement. Of concern in this chapter, however, is the observation that neither approach makes extensive use of conventional social science methods to bolster its arguments.

For most profeminist academics, the choice to forsake positivist social science is intentional, for the traditions that spawned it are held accountable for a ubiquitous style of masculinity that is detached, unemotional, authoritarian, and prone to violence and destruction (Easlea, 1981). Nevertheless, critiques of "masculinist" social science leave unanswered some difficult questions about how to study men. For example, how does one determine what are masculinist research methods, and on what basis should they be rejected? Similarly, what counts as "feminist" research, and how is this determined? If men want to study masculinity using feminist insights, can they avoid reproducing patriarchal consciousness simply by adopting a style of discourse common among women's studies scholars? These questions plague contemporary male scholars researching men, even if the reasons for and the implications of their methodological choices remain unarticulated. For those who celebrate masculinity and tend to avoid issues of power and dominance, these epistemological questions are typically of little concern. But for profeminist men studying masculinities, these questions remain critical.

Goals of Feminist Men's Studies

Criticism of male scholars who focus on "men's studies" or call their work "feminist" has come from different quarters. In the tradition of patriarchal dominance, some colleagues (mostly men) find gender studies superfluous and suggest that conventional academic subjects are more worthy of scholarly attention. Feminist colleagues also question men's intentions when they focus on gender, and some worry about the potential patriarchal usurpation of women's studies' initiatives (Canaan & Griffin, 1990; Jardine & Smith, 1987; Reinharz, 1992). Given a discouraging and sometimes hostile academic environment, why, then, would men want to study masculinity from a feminist perspective? The short answer is that gender is too important to ignore and that feminist theories explain more about gender than other theories.

Although there are many different reasons for studying gender and a variety of theoretical and methodological approaches to its study, one key feminist assumption has inspired much research. In a very general sense, gender carries undue importance in the social world, and its salience tends to reinforce men's power over women. Most feminists agree that gender is socially constructed and that its form and relative importance are subject to change. Many, like Judith Lorber, the founding editor of *Gender & Society,* promote the idea that women and men ought to be socially interchangeable: "The long-term goal of feminism must be no less than the eradication of gender as an organizing principle of postindustrial society" (Lorber, 1986, p. 568). Paradoxically, one of the ways to work toward this long-term political goal of reducing the importance of gender is for scholars to call attention to it. Many feminists thus focus on gender as an analytical category in the study of women's lives, but do so, ultimately, to reduce its importance in everyday life.

For men to concur that gender should be unimportant in everyday life, however, opens them to criticism because men have often blithely assumed that gender could be ignored, or at least argued that competence, rather than mere biology, provided them with special privileges. Historically, men's experiences have been universalized, allowing them to overlook discrimination against women and legitimate male dominance (Kimmel, 1990). Many profeminist men avoid this regressive potential by highlighting gender and paying attention to men's overt and subtle exercise of power. By placing gender at the center of their analyses, they attempt to overcome past tendencies to view men as generically human. By linking the ways that men create and sustain gendered selves with the ways that gender influences power relations and perpetuates inequality, feminist men's studies support and compliment the critical perspectives of women's studies.

Because gender is one of the most important organizing principles of societies throughout the world, and because male scholars have too often ignored its influence on men, an explicit focus on masculinities is clearly warranted. Nonetheless, highlighting gender in the study of men carries some risks of its own. Sometimes academic claims about the importance of gender are addressed by adding "sex" to a long list of competing independent variables. When this is coupled with the pressure to publish statistically significant differences (rather than similarities), one ends up with widely reported sex differences that are relatively meaningless. Other researchers use clinical reports, interpretive methods, and ethnographic techniques to contrast the lives and perceptions of men with those of women. The findings of difference that emerge from these studies tend to legitimate taken-for-granted assumptions about dissimilarity and reinforce the importance of gender in everyday life. Thus, the use of gender as an analytic category can work against the political goal of reducing its salience. I am not suggesting that one ignore gender because of this risk. Gender carries so much weight in most social and institutional settings that it needs to be studied explicitly, even at the risk of overemphasizing its importance. Nevertheless, it is useful to consider the political implications of adopting research methods or embracing theories that stress gender differences.

Essentialist Claims About Gender

Despite research and theories to the contrary, most people continue to conceive of gender differences as innately given, reflecting some underlying essential dichotomy between men and women. Early feminist scholarship, whether it focused on women or men, assumed that biological sex differences could not account for the social meaning of gender or the relative distribution of power and prestige between and among men and women. In the 1980s, academic discourse frequently moved "beyond" debunking the false unity of sex and gender, as if popular essentialist notions had already been transformed. It might seem "old" to continue to argue against the innateness of masculinity or femininity, but the distinction between sex (biological) and gender (social) deserves frequent repetition. The assumption of natural and God-given differences between men and women is so firmly embedded in habits of thought and social institutions that to focus on difference instead of similarity carries political risks.

The tendency to essentialize gender differences is not limited to the political or religious right, or even to men. Some contemporary women writers celebrate gender differences that are characterized as fundamental and timeless. For example, some French feminists (Irigaray, 1981), cultural and eco-feminists (Griffin, 1978), neoconservative feminists (Elshtain, 1981), and biosocial feminists (Rossi, 1985) conflate sex and gender by positing universal sex differences based on females' reproductive functions and putative closeness to nature (Stacey, 1983). A similar essentialist argument about men can be found in Robert Bly's *Iron John*. Bly worries that modern men have lost touch with their "Zeus energy" and recommends all-male retreats and rituals to restore the natural order (Bly, 1990). The form of community that Bly conjures up with visions of Zeus energy, however, has misogynist overtones. Women in ancient Greece, for all its democratic ideals, were relegated to the home and prohibited from participating fully in public life. This points to one of the central flaws in mythopoetic and other essentialist approaches to gender: They reduce historically and culturally specific myths and practices to universal psychological or biological truths, thereby ignoring the social structural conditions that produced them. One should question the assumption that reinstituting ancient male initiation rites will heal modern men and rescue a declining culture. In fact, reenacting ancient chest-pounding rituals on a grand scale would probably increase gender antagonism rather than promoting some idyllic balance between fierce men and yielding women. Accepting the notion of a natural masculine fierceness and an inborn "need" for masculine validation reaffirms gender difference and carries the very real danger of perpetuating violence against women and other men.

Robert Bly's account is only one among many that invoke images of fundamental, timeless, and natural gender differences stemming from biological sex. Many of these accounts rely on biblical passages or call up primordial images of tribal societies to verify their version of natural gender differences. Authoritative males and nurturing females from ancient times come to stand for some underlying masculinity or femininity that supposedly resides deep within humans. Unfortunately, this imagery resonates so closely with Western culture's gender ideology that most people accept the tribal portrayals as evidence for the inevitability of patriarchal power and feminine frailty. This is a fundamentally false assumption based on an inaccurate reading of human history and a profound misuse of biological and anthropological evidence. For instance, feminist anthropologists, biologists, and historians of science have demonstrated how an oversimplified "Man-the-Hunter" interpretation of human evolution based on sociobiology (Tiger, 1969; Wilson, 1975) ignores important evidence in its quest to rationalize women's domesticity (Bleier, 1984; Haraway, 1978).

Using Comparative Research
to Refute Essentialist Claims

To evaluate essentialist claims about masculinity or male dominance, it is helpful to rely on the concept of social structure and attend to cross-cultural variation in the organization and expression of gender. Early versions of comparative research on women sought to locate the "origins" of gender inequality by looking at so-called primitive peoples (Engels, 1891/1978). Like natural law theorists before them, these scholars were prone to fabricate a past in order to justify their vision of the future. Later researchers attempting to understand the position of women in nonindustrial societies have generally concluded that male dominance was widespread, but that women's subordination is not a unitary phenomenon that appears the same at all times and in all places. Rather, the status of women appears to be multidimensional and subject to change due to a variety of factors (e.g., Blumberg, 1984; Chafetz, 1984; Leacock, 1981; Ortner & Whitehead, 1981; Sanday, 1981). Although comparative cross-cultural studies of gender are fraught with epistemological difficulties, they are one of the few reliable and convincing ways to refute popular essentialist theories of gender.

There are two basic ways to evaluate theories using comparative cross-cultural research: extensive and intensive approaches (Ragin, 1987). Extensive approaches tend to compare whole cultures, societies, or nations; typically include a large number of cases; reduce social phenomena to variables; seek patterns of association via statistical analyses; and are good for testing universals (as well as generating some false universals of their own). The emphasis in extensive comparative research is usually to identify cross-cultural similarities between different instances of general outcomes and to isolate structural correlates of social phenomena. Though not necessarily required, extensive comparative research also tends to use quantitative data and statistical analysis. Much extensive comparative research is nomothetic, seeking causal explanations for why observed phenomena occur. For some, the goal is to test competing theories and determine "laws" of social organization. Others have less grandiose goals and use extensive comparative research more inductively. In these cases, researchers are attempting to isolate which social features might be idiosyncratic; which structures, ideologies, or associations might be historically or culturally specific; and which might be considered common features of the general social phenomenon under study.

Intensive comparative studies, in contrast, contain just a few cases and tend to be idiographic, relying on thick description of historically specific occurrences. This small-scale case study approach seeks to interpret specific instances of some phenomenon and is an excellent means of identifying cross-cultural difference (though it is prone to overgeneralizing from atypical cases). Intensive comparative studies are attuned to historically situated phenomena and because they are more detailed than extensive comparisons, they pay more attention to the specific contexts of social practices. In the late 1980s and early 1990s historians, anthropologists, and increasing numbers of sociologists (including most feminists) tended to favor the intensive approach to comparative studies (cf. Kohn, 1989). Intensive and extensive comparative approaches can coexist, and the distinction between them is sometimes blurred, as when intensive researchers refer to similar "types" of cases (Kandiyoti, 1991) or when extensive researchers use detailed illustrative examples (Coltrane, 1992).

There is no "right way" to do cross-cultural or comparative research, and both of the approaches outlined help to explicate social structures. Intensive studies are in some ways more fundamental, because secondary analysis of the extensive sort depends on initial detailed ethnographies or historical case studies. Intensive comparative studies are especially useful for showing how some individuals or groups depart from a falsely universalizing conception of gender, but they are open to the claim that the few cases selected are atypical. Extensive comparisons can isolate cross-cultural variation among many different societies and can link that variation with specific sets of social structural conditions. The heuristic value and political import of such linkages should not be underestimated. When one documents cross-cultural and historical variation in gender relations and can isolate the conditions under which various divisions of labor and distributions of wealth and prestige occur, one is better able to understand how gender systems operate and how gender shapes peoples' everyday lives. Perhaps even more important, with large-scale comparisons and causal explanations, one can argue convincingly that gender is socially constructed and be in a better position to transform gender relations to make them more equal. My own research provides an example.

Father-Child Relationships and Women's Status

In two extensive comparative studies of nonindustrial societies, I isolated some of the conditions under which men tend to dominate women. Coded data on about a hundred societies were used in each study, including cultures from all major geographic regions of the world and representing societies ranging from small-scale hunter-gatherers to populous feudal agrarian states. One study looked at men's ritualized displays of manliness—boastful demonstrations of strength, aggressiveness, and sexual potency of the type idealized by Robert Bly (Coltrane, 1992). This study also looked at the conditions associated with other micropolitical aspects of gender relations, such as women deferring to men by bowing, giving up their seats, or following men's orders; husbands dominating their wives; and belief systems considering women to be inferior to men. Several explanations positing various causes for these behaviors were tested, and strong support was found for two types of theories: materialist and psychodynamic. Significantly fewer displays of manliness, less wifely deference, less husband dominance, and less ideological female inferiority were evident in societies where men participated in child rearing and women controlled property. The associations with men's dominance were statistically significant even when controlling for a host of other potentially causal social, economic, and environmental factors.

The other extensive comparative study attempted to isolate tl of men's participation in child care on women's public status. The extent to which women participated in public decision making and whether they could hold leadership roles was evaluated with respect to a variety of potential causal factors (Coltrane, 1988). Father-child relationships were measured with reference to the frequency of father-child proximity, the amount of routine child care performed by men, and the likelihood of men expressing emotional warmth or support toward children. As in the other study, the association between close father-child relationships and women's public status was statistically robust, even when controlling for other factors. The results are consistent with Nancy Chodorow's (1978) theory that exclusive child rearing by mothers produces young men with psychological needs to differentiate from women and denigrate the feminine in themselves. Other interesting findings from this study concerned the importance of focusing on fraternal interest groups in analyzing women's access to public power and, following Sanday (1981), an association between men's child care and gender-balanced origin symbolism. Societies with distant fathers told myths about distant, sky-dwelling, all-powerful male gods like Zeus, whereas societies with nurturing fathers tended to tell stories about both male and female gods.

Extensive cross-cultural studies like these counter the essentialist claims of writers like Robert Bly. Although one cannot say much about specific causal paths from this sort of correlational analyses (much less "prove" causality or locate origins), one can at least rule out some improbable explanations and focus attention on theories that seem most plausible. These studies suggest that regardless of the ultimate reasons for fathers being involved with their children, when they are, it has important consequences for a social psychology of gender equality. In societies where men develop and maintain close relationships with young children, hypermasculine displays, competitive posturing, and all-male enclaves are rare. These societies allow both women and men to hold office and participate in public decisions, rarely require women to publicly pay homage to men, and tend to conceive of men and women as inherently equal.

Systematically comparing social structural patterns across diverse settings or historical periods allows one to consider the implications of a cultural emphasis on gender difference. By defining themselves as essentially different from women, men in some societies have excluded women from positions of power and dominated them in more intimate relationships. Belief in essential gender difference helps men maintain microstructures of inequality. Seen from this perspective, mythopoetic calls for reinstituting ancient male initiation rites carry regressive, not progressive, potential. The practices that accompany all-male initiation rites and everyday affirmations of masculine strength and fortitude typically work to the disadvantage of women and nondominant men. Although ritual gender segregation and celebration of difference may not theoretically or inherently imply male domination, in practice this is what tends to occur. Cross-cultural analysis suggests that the key to minimal gender dominance and deference is ongoing gender cooperation in child rearing and property control, not carving out separate domains for men and women.

Can "Masculinist" Methods Serve Feminist Goals?

The conventional sociological practices used in the previously mentioned studies, including comparing disparate societies, using large data sets, reducing social phenomena to numbers, and performing statistical tests, are sometimes criticized as "masculinist" or "colonialist." I am not alone in using such mainstream research methods to argue against sexist notions (Chafetz, 1984; Jayaratne, 1983; Sanday, 1981), but many researchers studying gender prefer qualitative, theoretical, oppositional, and standpoint methodologies (Reinharz, 1992). For instance, Dorothy Smith (1992) states that "when we employ standard sociological methods of work, we inadvertently realign the issues that concern us with those of the relations of ruling" (p. 96). At issue is whether one ought to use data that were collected without attention to limiting ethnocentric and androcentric biases; whether one can compare societies that are so different from one another; whether the use of variables and statistical associations can reveal anything of value; whether such methods manufacture false universals and promote evolutionary theorizing; whether such methods objectify, exploit, and alienate their "subjects"; and whether findings from such studies necessarily serve the dominant interests of men and colonial powers. These are not new concerns to anthropologists—who generally accept them—and they are concerns familiar to most feminist sociologists, though many conventional social scientists would reject these criticisms as too political or subjective.

For those who agree that past cross-cultural scholarship, and social science in general, has neglected women and perpetuated white Western men's understandings of the world, these criticisms are indeed quite serious. They have motivated numerous studies that place women's experiences in the foreground and provide richly detailed descriptions of the ways that women have exercised authority, struggled against patriarchy, and been active agents of change. These complex, multidimensional descriptive studies are theoretically rich and illuminating in their own right, but one ought to be able to generalize from them as well. In addition to conducting feminist ethnographies, case histories, and experiential studies, one can pursue an integrative and systematic understanding of social life that comes from explicitly comparative research designs with an emphasis on social structure. Feminist anthropologists, sociologists, and historians have illustrated that the meaning of womanhood or man-hood is historically and culturally unique. This does not mean that one should forsake attempts to compare across these unique viewpoints to formulate synthetic theories in an effort to understand the consistent and pervasive features of gender.

An emphasis on social structure is both illuminating and politically expedient. Such an approach does not require the claim that abstracted comparative knowledge is value free or inherently more objective than more interpretive or idiographic ways of knowing. Extensive comparative studies and other conventional social science techniques such as experi-ments and mathematical modeling allow one to generalize to larger populations, seek causal explanations, and formulate general principles of social organization. New studies using these techniques could be used against women and oppressed peoples, but this tendency is not inherent to the method. The danger stems, instead, from political causes, from the self-interested standpoints of those in power who use conventional meth-ods to invoke pseudo-objectivity and ignore issues of inequality and domination. This political threat is perhaps the most compelling reason that gender scholars should not abandon conventional methodologies to those who would maintain the status quo. Even if it should not be so, results of quantitative studies carry more weight in policy arenas than isolated personal accounts or even the best in-depth qualitative studies. Another compelling reason to use conventional social science methods to study gender is that when the right questions are asked, the knowledge generated helps to identify those issues and projects with the greatest potential for realizing social change.

Scientism and Postmodernism

Scientism is the prejudice that science objectively deals only with observable facts and that any investigation that does not employ natural science-like methods is "merely" subjective and therefore not explanatory (Lloyd, 1989). In the post-Kuhnian academy, one might hope that scientism would be dead, but it is still the dominant paradigm in many social science disciplines (Kuhn, 1970). In the interests of brevity, I will not restate why scientism, in its various forms, is intellectually false and politically dangerous. Instead, I turn to one of its main challengers, postmodernism.

Unifying a disparate number of feminist and nonfeminist scholars under the label "postmodernism" is itself misleading, but I do so to question some emergent idealist and particularist tendencies in gender studies. Postmodern approaches are enlightening because they attempt to deconstruct false dualisms of mind/body, culture/nature, man/woman, modern/ primitive, reason/emotion, subject/object, and so forth. Images of "fractured," "decentered," and "reflexive" selves that appear in postmodernist writing help to critically evaluate overly simple concepts and categories. In its more extreme forms, however, postmodernism's focus is solely on language and its role in the perception of reality. Discourse and cognition are important, but there is much more than this to social life. If one focuses too much on language as constructing reality, solutions to injustice tend to be clever word games, and the concrete bases of social inequality are slighted. Describing the social world as floating fields of symbols manipulated by reflexive agents probably captures a phenomenological "reality," but one needs to ground such analyses in patterns of material conditions (Coltrane & Hickman, 1992). By relying too heavily on deconstructionism, one too easily overlooks persistence and oppression in favor of historical, symbolic, and subjective particularity.

The postmodern tendency to ignore social structure undermines sociological attempts to understand gender inequality. It is now increasingly common to reject a sociology that seeks systematic regularities and patterns of causality. For example, most feminist researchers caricature role theory or set up structural-functionalism or structural-Marxism as rhetorical "straw persons." Although many feminist sociologists retain a revised concept of social structure, other gender scholars show disdain for even middle-level theoretical abstraction as they attempt to honor diversity and give voice to silenced women. My fear is that the heuristic value of social structure could be lost by failing to generalize across situations, even if those situations include diverse peoples living unique lives.

The postmodern emphasis on particularity and language also discourages one from seeking causal explanations. Without some concept of social causality, one can only describe a multitude of unique experiences and talk endlessly about talk. Kuhn and his successors were right in pointing out that science has no special claim to truth, but one still needs to look for causal patterns in the social world and ask why things happen as they do. Theories need to remain causal, even if most of the research methods cannot adequately prove causality (Lieberson, 1985). Perhaps one should reject both scientism and postmodernism while simultaneously relying on their contradictory root assumptions. In researching masculinities, one might look for both regularized similarity and particularistic difference. By using multiple methods and relying on diverse ways of knowing, one might move closer to some tentative conclusions about which theoretical explanations for gender inequality are most plausible.

Rejecting conventional social science methods and liberal philosophic traditions is provocative, but it carries some internal contradictions. Descartes, Bacon, Hobbes, Rousseau, and the others were "sexist" and "elitist," and their ideas are suspect because of it. Nevertheless, Western liberalism can be seen as providing the impetus for the civil rights movement as well as the women's movement. Similarly, science has emancipatory as well as destructive potential (Jansen, 1990; Olson, 1990). New false dichotomies are created by branding specific research techniques (i.e., quantitative sociology) as inherently "male" or "masculinist" (O'Brien, 1989; Seidler, 1989). Critiques of masculinist science as stemming from Western men's proclivity to objectify and dominate others (Easlea, 1981) provide insights into relationships between knowledge and power, but attributing some essential gendered nature to these specific research practices is misleading.

If one takes seriously recent calls to situate and historicize the sociological analyses of gender, then one should avoid the false dichotomy between "male" and "female" research. *Quantitative/empirical/deductive/ explanatory* research such as mathematical data analysis, random sample surveys, extensive cross-cultural comparisons, and experiments are not necessarily masculine. *Qualitative/intuitive/inductive/exploratory* research such as ethnography, interviewing, participant observation, oral histories, and intensive case studies are not necessarily feminine. Even if there are proportionately more men doing the former and proportionately more women doing the latter, one should remember that the association with gender is historically specific and socially constructed. For example, in the early part of the century, quantitative social science methods were first advocated by women, and for a time they were considered "feminine"

(Deegan, 1988). It was only later that surveys and mathematical modeling became associated with men and masculinity.

Research findings are also employed for political purposes. Study methods that produce easily understood conclusions about the causes and consequences of gender inequality become increasingly important as fundamentalist and backlash movements call for reinstating patriarchal privileges. Pseudoscientific studies carry especially high credibility with policy makers. To abandon conventional social science to those who would support existing patterns of gender stratification would be a grave political mistake. Similarly, to ignore the knowledge created by systematic empirical inquiry because others have made a fetish of science would be a profound intellectual error. How, then, might one retain some aspects of conventional social science in studying masculinities, while at the same time integrating recent feminist insights?

Standpoint Theories and Men's Studies

From what standpoint should men (or women) study masculinity? Women studying gender can begin from a feminist standpoint, from the "actualities of women's lives," the "concrete, relational, subjugated activities" of women (Smith, 1987). Feminist standpoint theorists argue that this perspective affords them a more encompassing and empowering grasp of social life than conventional social science that represents the views of dominant men (Harding, 1986; Hartsock, 1983; Smith, 1992). Standpoint theories favor process over static categorizing and treat the personal as both political and theoretically enlightening. What can standpoint theories tell about how to study men and masculinities?

The most basic insight from standpoint theories is that everyday life—the concrete activities people do—structure perception, attitudes, and ways of knowing. Where one stands shapes what one can see and how one can understand it. One way to use standpoint theories is to focus on how activities conventionally performed by women (e.g., child care) might structure the consciousness and behavior of mothers and fathers in similar fashion (Coltrane, 1989; Risman, 1987) or how couple dynamics might respond to similar power inequities regardless of gender or sexual preference (Blumstein & Schwartz, 1983). This type of analysis, by focusing on how gender and its related standpoints are socially constructed under specific microstructural conditions, can tell much about the creation and maintenance of gender difference and gender inequality.

If one focuses on the lived reality of most men's lives, however, one also runs the risk of reproducing patriarchal consciousness. Focusing on men's standpoints will typically produce a picture of men's felt powerlessness. One must be careful to acknowledge that these same men exercise considerable power in their lives, particularly over women, but also over other men. This contradictory coexistence of felt powerlessness and actual (if latent) power is quite common for men. For instance, family violence researchers are finding that men's subjective sense of lost or slipping control is often a precursor to wife beating. The "partial and perverse perspective" (Harding, 1986) that has come from men studying men in the past may be recreated by contemporary scholars if they adopt an uncritical stance that treats men as victims. In contrast, Messner (1990) identifies an emergent genre in the sociology of sports that integrates the personal experience of male victimization with the promise of masculine privilege. He notes that concrete examination of men's lives can reveal the social mechanisms through which men's power over women is constructed but also recognizes the political tension around emphasizing too much the costs, rather than the benefits, of masculinity. The "tricky balancing act" (Messner, 1990, p. 145) of profeminist men's studies is open to attack because men scholars share institutional power and privilege and because any emphasis on the victimization of men can be seen as detracting from the business of exposing women's oppression (Harding, 1986; Jardine & Smith, 1987). Messner advocates an inclusive profeminist approach that integrates analyses of masculinity with class, race, and sexual inequalities and, above all, highlights gender oppression. This follows Connell's (1987) call for a focus on history, process, and struggle surrounding hegemonic and subordinated masculinities.

In order to illuminate how gendered interaction and power are socially structured, I suggest that researchers attempt to integrate men's standpoints into gender studies in at least three ways: (a) by focusing on men's emotions, (b) by studying men in groups, and (c) by placing men's experiences in a structural context. First, one needs to get men talking about their emotional lives in some detail, even if, or perhaps especially because, they may lack a vocabulary for doing so. Researchers cannot afford to accept men's superficial characterizations of their internal states and need to push them for self-reflection. Many men are motivated by fears and insecurities that conventional sociological research strategies do not easily capture. For example, a man who runs court-referral groups for abusing men told me how he uses a "freeze-frame" technique to get men to talk about, and thus become aware of, their emotions. He stops the men while they are presenting accounts of battering instances and repeatedly demands that they tell him details about what they were feeling at certain key moments. The emotion he hears most, particularly the one men report having just before they hit women, is fear (see also Lisak, 1991). Researchers need to be able to specify the types of insecurities (and senses of self-importance) men report in various circumstances and begin to document their behavioral counterparts. By looking at how men experience, organize, and talk about their emotions, one might begin to build bridges between interactionist, psychodynamic, and power-based theories of gender.

I am not suggesting a simplistic acceptance of emotional or autobiographical material as epistemologically privileged discourse. Much writing in men's studies is autobiographical or confessional, but rarely gets past the insight that men are taught to be competitive and have trouble expressing their emotions. One should guard against the tendency in some scholarly writing to accept one's felt emotions or bodily sensations as somehow superior or more authentic than other ways of knowing, because emotions and bodily experiences are also socially constructed, often in the service of power and domination. I think researchers should focus on men's emotionality, not because it is epistemologically privileged, but because it may be an illuminating fault line for men between what is and what should be (Smith, 1987).

A second way to take men's unique standpoints into account is to focus on how men create difference, exclude women, and use privileged information. Feminist scholars have countered androcentric scholarship by bringing the women back in, focusing on their experiences and giving voice to their silenced concerns. One reason to focus on men's standpoints is to find out how and why they exclude women. Men are in a unique position to do research on groups of men and to identify processes through which men create rituals, reaffirm symbolic difference, establish internal hierarchy, and exclude, belittle, dominate, and stigmatize women and nonconforming men. Locker rooms, playing fields, board rooms, shop floors, the military, and fraternal organizations of all types provide access to the relations of ruling (Goode, 1982; Smith, 1992). Investigating men's standpoints allows the examination of privileged sources of information that, although incomplete and falsely universalizing, can contribute to the understanding of the exercise of men's power.

Men should not be the only ones to study masculinity, because women's standpoints are also necessary for a full understanding of gender relations. Thus, my third focus concerns the relational context of gender and brings me back to the need to highlight power and identify structural patterns. Individual actors and their experiences are obviously important, but researchers also need a focus on patterns of relationships between men and women, among men, and among women. One fruitful way to validate both difference and similarity and highlight both agency and structure is to identify the conditions under which gender becomes salient in everyday life. What types of settings and interactions are likely to call for participants to use gender in understanding or expressing their thoughts, feelings, and actions? Who brings up gender in social interaction and when is it subtly inferred? One should attempt to determine when gender is invoked as a prerogative-maintaining move by men, when and how gender is used by men in group settings, and what relationship the use of gender has to felt insecurity.

   If one can identify the typical purposes and costs of men's and women's use of gender as an interactional resource, one will better understand how it facilitates or inhibits social interaction and at whose expense those interactions occur. One might also focus on internal conversations about gendered feelings or behaviors. This relatively "micro" approach follows Goffman (1977) and West and Zimmerman (1987) by conceptualizing gender as an actively constructed accomplishment of ongoing interaction, but it also suggests a focus on contextual, structural, and psychodynamic correlates of such activities. Such an approach might render the "doing" of gender amenable to conventional sociological research practices because one could focus on identifying the common features of situations that called for gender to become salient. Researchers need to document and categorize the microstructures (Risman & Schwartz, 1989) under which men and women use gender in particular ways. Systematic studies are also needed of "gender strategies" (Hochschild, 1989) to assess the extent to which they are uniquely crafted and to identify broad patterns of regularity in their form and use across historical, cultural, geographic, economic, and institutional contexts. By using comparative sociological methods, focusing on the concept of social structure, and paying attention to gender as an interactional resource, one can better understand how gender is actively constructed by social actors. Documenting how power and material conditions are associated with women's and men's standpoints can counter essentialist claims, contribute to public debates about gender, and ultimately transform society. By not forsaking traditional social science practices, perhaps scholars can literally, not just figuratively, deconstruct gender inequality.

References

Bleier, R. (1984). *Science and gender.* New York: Pergamon.

Blumberg, R. L. (1984). A general theory of gender stratification. In R. Collins (Ed.), *Sociological theory* (pp. 23-101). San Francisco: Jossey-Bass.

Blumstein, P., & Schwartz, P. (1983). *American couples.* New York: William Morrow.

Bly, R. (1990). *Iron John: A book about men.* Reading, MA: Addison-Wesley.

Brod, H. (Ed.). (1987). *The making of masculinities.* Boston: Unwin Hyman.

Canaan, J., & Griffin, C. (1990). The new men's studies. In J. Hearn & D. Morgan (Eds.), *Men, masculinities and social theory* (pp. 206-214). London: Unwin Hyman.

Chafetz, J. S. (1984). *Sex and advantage.* Totowa, NJ: Rowman & Allanheld.

Chodorow, N. (1978). *The reproduction of mothering.* Berkeley: University of California Press.

Clary, M. (1982). *Daddy's home.* New York: Seaview.

Collins, R. (1988). The micro contribution to macro sociology. *Sociological Theory, 6,* 242-253.

Coltrane, S. (1988). Father-child relationships and the status of women. *American Journal of Sociology, 93,* 1060-1095.

Coltrane, S. (1989). Household labor and the routine production of gender. *Social Problems, 36,* 473-490.

Coltrane, S. (1992). The micropolitics of gender in nonindustrial societies. *Gender & Society, 6,* 86-107.

Coltrane, S., & Hickman, N. (1992). The rhetoric of rights and needs. *Social Problems, 39,* 401-421.

Connell, R. W. (1987). *Gender and power.* Cambridge: Polity.

Deegan, M. J. (1988). *Jane Addams and the men of the Chicago school, 1892-1918.* New Brunswick, NJ: Transaction Books.

Easlea, B. (1981). *Science and sexual oppression.* London: Weidenfeld & Nicolson.

Elshtain, J. B. (1981). *Public man, private woman.* Princeton, NJ: Princeton University Press.

Engels, F. (1978). The origin of the family, private property and the state. In R. Tucker (Ed.), *The Marx-Engels reader* (pp. 734-759). New York: Monthly Review Press. (Original work published 1891)

Farrell, W. (1986). *Why men are the way they are.* New York: McGraw-Hill.

Goffman, E. (1967). *Interaction ritual.* New York: Anchor.

Goffman, E. (1977). The arrangement between the sexes. *Theory and Society, 4,* 301-331.

Goffman, E. (1979). *Gender advertisements.* New York: Harper & Row.

Goldberg, H. (1976). *The hazards of being male.* Ithaca, NY: Cornell University Press.

Goode, W. J. (1982). Why men resist. In B. Thorne & M. Yalom (Eds.), *Rethinking the family* (pp. 131-150). New York: Longman.

Griffin, S. (1978). *Woman and nature.* New York: Harper Colophon.

Haraway, D. (1978). Animal sociology and a natural economy of the body politic. *Signs, 4,* 21-60.

Harding, S. (1986). *The science question in feminism.* Ithaca, NY: Cornell University Press.

Hartsock, N. (1983). The feminist standpoint. In S. Harding & M. Hintikka (Eds.), *Discovering reality* (pp. 283-310). Boston: Reidel.

Hearn, J., & Morgan, D. (Eds.). (1990). *Men, masculinities and social theory.* London: Unwin Hyman.

Hochschild, A. (1989). *The second shift.* Berkeley: University of California Press.

Irigaray, L. (1981). And the one doesn't stir without the other. *Signs, 7,* 56-79.

Jackson, D. (1990). *Unmasking masculinity.* London: Unwin Hyman.

Jansen, S. C. (1990). Is science a man? *Theory and Society, 19,* 235-246.

Jardine, A., & Smith, P. (1987). *Men in feminism.* New York: Metheun.

Jayaratne, T. E. (1983). The value of quantitative methodology for feminist research. In G. Bowles & R. D. Klein (Eds.), *Theories of women's studies* (pp. 140-161). London: Routledge & Kegan Paul.

Kandiyoti, D. (1991). Bargaining with patriarchy. *Gender & Society, 2,* 274-290.

Kaufman, M. (Ed.). (1987). *Beyond patriarchy.* Toronto: Oxford University Press.

Kaufman, M. (1993). *Cracking the armour: Power, pain, and the lives of men.* Toronto: Penguin/Viking.

Kimmel, M. (1990). After fifteen years. In J. Hearn & D. Morgan (Eds.), *Men, masculinities and social theory* (pp. 93-109). London: Unwin Hyman.

Kimmel, M., & Messner, M. (Eds.). (1989). *Men's lives.* New York: Macmillan.

Kohn, M. (Ed.). (1989). *Cross-national research in sociology.* Newbury Park, CA: Sage.

Kuhn, T. (1970). *The structure of scientific revolutions.* Chicago: University of Chicago Press.

Leacock, E. (1981). *Myths of male dominance.* New York: Monthly Review Press.

Lieberson, S. (1985). *Making it count.* Berkeley: University of California Press.

Lisak, D. (1991). Sexual aggression, masculinity, and fathers. *Signs, 16,* 238-262.

Lloyd, C. (1989). Realism, structurism, and history. *Theory and Society, 18,* 451-494.

Lorber, J. (1986). Dismantling Noah's ark. *Sex Roles, 14,* 567-580.

Marx, K. (1978a). The German ideology. In R. Tucker (Ed.), *The Marx-Engels reader* (pp. 146-200). New York: Monthly Review Press. (Original work published 1846)

Marx, K. (1978b). The eighteenth brumaire of Louis Bonaparte. In R. Tucker (Ed.), *The Marx-Engels reader* (pp. 594-617). New York: Monthly Review Press. (Original work published 1851)

Messner, M. (1990). Men studying masculinity. *Sociology of Sport Journal, 7,* 136-153.

Morgan, D. (1981). Men, masculinity and the process of sociological enquiry. In H. Roberts, *Doing feminist research* (pp. 83-113). London: Routledge & Kegan Paul.

Nichols, J. (1975). *Men's liberation.* New York: Penguin.

O'Brien, M. (Ed.). (1989). *Reproducing the world: Essays in feminist theory.* Boulder, CO: Westview.

Olson, R. (1990). Historical reflections on feminist critiques of science. *History of Science, 28,* 125-147.

Ortner, S., & Whitehead, H. (1981). *Sexual meanings.* Cambridge, UK: Cambridge University Press.

Osherson, S. (1986). *Finding our fathers.* New York: Free Press.

Pleck, J. (1981). Men's power with women, other men, and society. In R. A. Lewis (Ed.), *Men in difficult times* (pp. 234-244). Englewood Cliffs, NJ: Prentice Hall. (Original work published 1977)

Ragin, C. (1987). *The comparative method.* Berkeley: University of California Press.

Reinharz, S. (1992). *Feminist methods in social research.* New York: Oxford University Press.

Risman, B. J. (1987). Intimate relationships from a microstructural perspective. *Gender & Society, 1,* 6-32.

Risman, B., & Schwartz, P. (Eds.). (1989). *Gender in intimate relationships.* Belmont, CA: Wadsworth.

Rossi, A. (Ed.). (1985). *Gender and the lifecourse.* New York: Aldine.

Sanday, P. R. (1981). *Female power and male dominance.* Cambridge, UK: Cambridge University Press.

Sattel, J. (1976). Men, inexpressiveness, and power. *Social Problems, 23,* 469-477.

Seidler, V. (1989). *Rediscovering masculinity.* London: Routledge.

Smith, D. E. (1987). *The everyday world as problematic.* Boston: Northeastern University Press.

Smith, D. E. (1992). Sociology from women's experience. *Sociological Theory, 10,* 88-98.

Stacey, J. (1983). The new conservative feminism. *Feminist Studies, 9,* 559-583.

Tiger, L. (1969). *Men in groups.* New York: Vintage.

West, C., & Zimmerman, D. H. (1987). Doing gender. *Gender & Society, 1,* 125-151.

Wilson, E. O. (1975). *Sociobiology.* Cambridge, MA: Belknap.

4
Ethnographies and Masculinities

DON CONWAY-LONG

As analysis of the nature of difference has moved to center stage in current theoretical approaches to gender, anthropology has also returned to its earlier importance as a primary discipline in gender studies. The importance of anthropology in studying *difference* should be evident; explaining differences was one of the original raisons d'être for the emergence of the discipline in the 19th century. What was examined *between* cultures then has come to be just as important *within* cultures now, that is, an early and simplistic approach to cross-cultural analysis that set up an "us-them" framework for difference has blossomed into a recognition of the multi-faceted realities within any social or cultural grouping. This does not mean that seeking cross-cultural similarities is no longer useful; it certainly is. Such a search for shared structures of masculinities throughout the world made possible David Gilmore's recent work *Manhood in the Making* (1990). However, one of the failings of this particular study is the lack of recognition of the plurality of masculinities *within* any of the cultures he analyzed.

Gilmore's work is an important addition, though, to the slowly growing body of anthropological studies of men and masculinity. These studies, although indebted to studies of women by women, remain a few steps behind feminist anthropology in the application of theory. Feminism has moved beyond the initial idea of the universal nature of woman's second-class status to recognize diversities of types even within a particular localized ethnic group, let alone within a larger, more complex national group.[1] But the realization that the same thing is true of masculinities has managed to elude the grasp of many ethnographers, who seem to be still utilizing the Parsonian view of normative standard case. In the only other

61

approach, when a man just doesn't fit, deviance becomes the stock framework for analysis.

Gilmore, for example, approaches his subject with the apparent expectation that each culture he studies (the Mediterranean rim, the Truk, the Samburu, the Sambia, Tahitians) will have a single "masculinity" that cannot be explained sufficiently by conflict theory, biology, or strict Freudianism. He seeks his explanation in a social-environmental synthesis. Violent testing of masculinity, trials of strength and endurance in which men risk their lives, and dangerous rites of passage and initiations seem to pervade all systems of masculinity he examines, including the most gentle peoples such as the !Kung or the Fox. Variations among cultures seem concerned more with the *extent* to which the trials are taken than whether or not they are present. Explaining the seeming ephemerality of manhood is the basic puzzle. Why do so many forms of masculinity seem to view their "maleness" as so fragile, so much of an attainment, so often a goal sufficiently beyond an individual man's reach that it keeps him struggling on for a lifetime? Gilmore's answer lies in the social need to prevent men from "regressing" to the state of unity with mother, with the feminine. Manhood imagery, he says, is "a defense against the eternal child within, against puerility, against what is sometimes called the Peter Pan complex" (1990, p. 29). The reason such a masculine complex is socially acceptable is due, according to Gilmore, to the requirement that men be capable in reproduction, provisioning, and protection, all of which "demand assertiveness and resolve" as well as "a mobility of action, a personal autonomy" (pp. 48-49). With this argument, he approaches (though he fails to refer to) the psychoanalytic sociology argued by Nancy Chodorow (1978) and further developed by Rubin (1983), Ehrensaft (1987), Benjamin (1988), and Johnson (1988). Gilmore's book is a good start, in my view, in the attempt to elicit a summary of gendered behaviors that positions the male, instead of the female, as the primary enigma to be explained.

But there are problems with Gilmore's book. First, nothing in his analysis explains why women are not recognized for their contributions to reproduction and provisioning, or why they are often forbidden to protect the group at large. He never asks why it is that, whatever it is that a man does, his act is more important, more valued than a woman's comparable, even identical, activity. In other words, he does not demonstrate a theory of patriarchy, that is, a system of power relations of men over women. Second, he assumes in each case of exception to *the* manhood ideology that he posits, whether these exceptions are a single individual in Andalusia or all men in Tahiti, that the deviants have no "manhood ideology" of their own. This is a patently false assumption, because the men often (though not always) successfully carry out at least some of the basic local requirements in the performance of masculinity and seem to be far more than mere failures at the game of masculine performance. This is a clear reflection of the failure of sex role theory; if a man fails or a group of men fail to live up completely to the hegemonic rules of global and Western-defined masculinity, then and therefore he or they have no masculinity worth studying of his or their own, nor is it interesting even to wonder why and how he or they construct difference within the category male/ masculine. The recognition of difference *within* this gendered category called masculinity and an identification of the plurality of masculinities are the beginnings of the deconstruction of dominant masculine "doxa,"[2] because the struggle among men is equally important as the struggle for dominance over women and children. The simple recognition of the multiplicity of masculinities would have improved Gilmore's work immensely.

Honor, Shame, and the Mediterranean

Gilmore's work is the first wide-ranging global view of masculinity of which I am aware, but there have been numerous detailed studies of particular masculinities throughout the history of ethnography. For example, Peristiany's 1966 collection on honor and shame in the Mediterranean provided an initial model for many subsequent works on the circum-Mediterranean area. Honor and shame, to Peristiany, are the two poles of an evaluative process. "Honour is at the apex of the pyramid of temporal social values and it conditions their hierarchical order. Cutting across all other social classifications it divides social beings into two fundamental categories, those endowed with honour and those deprived of it" (p. 10).

As might be expected of works of 30 years ago, Peristiany's collection is written in a generic masculine style that does not pursue the implications of gender as fundamental categories that could provide an additional layer of meaning for the analysis. In asking what all the groups studied have in common, Peristiany (1966) finds the answer in the structure of small-scale society, in the personal relations of solidarity. Within such systems in which the individual reflects the group, this individual "is constantly forced to prove and assert *himself*" (p. 11, emphasis added). The words do not mean what one can read in them today. *He* may be "constantly 'on show,' " *he* may be "forever courting the public opinion of his 'equals,' " but the maleness of the actor is never clearly perceived as being central to the explanation. A superficial recognition that the honor in question is based partially on the protection of the sexual purity of women is certainly there, but the implications are not pursued. Nor does the Don Juanism studied by Baroja in this collection reflect an awareness that the seduction of women, given the protection of their "purity," is a competitive arrangement among men in which women are part of patrimony. The writers here actually approach the possibilities of analytical deconstruction of this gendered system of power relations as they detail the inconsistencies of linking honor to the testicles, sexual purity to the woman's maidenhead, tamed men to castration, and shamed women to a female's sexual behavior outside of marriage. But they do not make it explicit. When Pitt-Rivers notes that the "*natural* qualities of sexual potency or purity and the moral qualities associated with them provide the conceptual framework on which the system is constructed" (Peristiany, 1966, p. 45, emphasis added), one knows a theoretical blind spot has cloaked the very inconsistencies they had almost grasped. The "naturalness" of the sex/gender system is too often assumed in the work of this period. The problem of the elusiveness of masculinity and the question of exactly why it must be performed with such intense commitment is left for future ethnographers.

Brandes (1980), in his study of folklore and ritual in Andalusia, begins to ask this question. He places his understanding in men's memories of powerlessness as children, their discomfort at the structures of class domination and difference, and their adult fear of femininity and of women's power as it is expressed through sexuality. He perceives the object of his study, folklore, as a masculine-defined realm that expresses the relations of dominance and control so central to the psychology of masculinity. It is a decided improvement on the earlier volume.

A more recent work follows the principles laid out in Peristiany's work. Gilmore (1987) edits a collection that sets out to reexamine the basic framework of honor and shame. From the perspective of 20 years later, two criticisms are directed at the earlier model. First, Gilmore asks whether it is fair to impose a totalized, somewhat reductionist model on all these Mediterranean societies. (One might ask why he then imposed an equally reductionist model on global masculinities in his 1990 work.) Is it fair to portray the area as swirling in an "unrelenting masculine contentiousness"? Are these "manhood ideals" merely an *etic*[3] (that is, an external observer's) interpretation that, although consistent with practice, is "unlikely ever to be consciously thought or spoken by those who have created" this social practice? (Thanks to Scott, 1985, pp. 138-139, for this observation.) What about generosity, honesty, or hospitality as equally important descriptive systems, especially in the actual discourse of *emic* (that is, an insider, a "native") self-description? Is the recognition of diversity lost in the generalized honor-shame dichotomy? (Gilmore, 1987, pp. 5-6). This is a good beginning for the identification, celebration, and explanation of diversity that any contemporary model must include.

Second, Brandes, in the collection's concluding article, challenges the previously portrayed inextricability of honor with the male, shame with the female. A dishonored male is shamed (feminized); a masculinized female earns honor. It is an improvement on the analysis in the Peristiany collection discussed earlier to identify the association as a gendered one, not one based on a biological sex category so much as rooted in actual (and malleable) daily behavior (Brandes, 1987, p. 122). It is also more consistent with a practice-based approach that recognizes daily negotiation over the somewhat variable boundaries that cultures construct between genders.

The sophistication of the model has also been improved by the addition of insights from Chodorow's psychoanalytic sociology and Bourdieu's (1977) practice-based approach, as well as general feminist challenges to male-defined frameworks of analysis. Sexuality here "is perceived through a competitive idiom by which men jockey for control over women as objects to achieve narcissistic gratifications and dominance over other men. Sexuality is a form of social power" (p. 4). The struggle among men is identified as reflecting "shared male anxieties about feminization" (p. 11). Men fear being made passive, vulnerable, female—whether by the actions of men *or* women. But Gilmore (1987) does suggest the possibility, because masculinity is seen as so ephemeral, so much at peril, that a secret desire may underlie the bluster of masculine drama: "Androcentric sexual ideologies, for which machismo may stand as a convenient label, represent a reaction-formation or 'masculine protest' against unacceptable wishes not to have a penis, to be like a woman, to be dependent, to restore the early psychic merging with the mother" (p. 13).

It is in this context that Gilmore (1987) wonders about the absence of male rites of passage to adult manhood in the region. Such rites as do exist are "amorphous" or "tacit" at best. Because each boy must make a "hazardous spatial and behavioral transition from the female world to the homosocial world of men," thereby breaking the ties with mother and the feminine, it becomes necessary to take the main indication of difference and objectify it with great symbolic value (p. 15). The result is the "hypervaluation of the male genital and the almost priapic obsession with phallic assertion in the ethnomasculinities of Mediterranean societies" (p. 13).

This is a reasonable approach to take, one which is complemented by other work on the Mediterranean area. Tillion (1966/1983) argues, in a fascinating polemic on the "persistent debasement of the female condition" in this area, that the fears of loss of control to women contributed to what she calls the "republic of cousins." Countering Levi-Strauss's "elementary" exchange of women in exogamy, Tillion views the Mediterranean system as one of tribal endogamy among patrikin, keeping tribal property in the tribe and daughters in the family. She associates these aspects of tribal culture with pronatalist expansionism, with "virile brutality" for men complemented by virtue and "occultation" (both veiling and physical limitations in public space) for women. As a result of low levels of accepted authority, women still end up with great though unauthorized social power; fear of women's magic and witchcraft abounds. Whether or not one accepts the validity of her claim that Mediterranean endogamy approaches the "brink of incest (and sometimes beyond it)," the perspective does add an interesting layer of interpretation to the overall picture.

Alternative Sex-Gender Systems in the Pacific

Another world area that has produced numerous texts on gender is the South Pacific. Beginning with Margaret Mead and Malinowski, studies of the sexualities of native groups or the particular constructions of masculine/feminine have been plentiful; it is perhaps their geographic distinctiveness that has enabled Western ethnographers to make so much of these differently constructed sex/gender systems. Studying Samoan or Papuan peoples has permitted "other-making" in which the native is sufficiently different as to leave the Western observer safely distant in her or his "objective" interpretation. It was easier, for example, for Mead to use the Samoans as an example of sexual freedom than it would have been to wax poetic about similar behaviors in the United States; what was a norm in Samoa would have been deviance in the Americas. Whether or not Mead correctly interpreted her data is not the point; the use to which it was put—challenging child-rearing practices regardless of the material conditions that created them—is the issue. Brash importation of the practices of a different sociocultural system into a postindustrial nation will not produce the same results and should not be expected to do so. This mentality is a result of separating the social constraints on the individual (Durkheim) from the psychological, unconscious constraints (Freud) and once again from the constraints of material conditions (Marx). Culture may well be shreds and patches, yet each shred, each patch must be understood as thickly, as widely, as deeply, and in as many conceptual realms as possible.

This is part of the intellectual background for Herdt's work on the construction of masculinity in Papua New Guinea (1981, 1984). Herdt argues (1981) that the false antithesis between society and individual harmed anthropological theory building in the past and was an issue he wished to overcome in his work. It is an essential limitation to transcend particularly because he intended to study the construction of gender, which can easily be seen to involve symbolic (and ritual) constructions that have roots in social, psychological, and material categories. This necessitates, as Herdt notes (1981, pp. 8-9), overcoming the historical tension between anthropology and psychoanalysis. This is what he sets out to do.

The problem he wanted to explain was the existence of prescribed male-male fellatio in the development of boys into men, in which a daily consumption of semen is believed necessary to build a boy into a man. Obviously an extreme variation from the homophobic constructions in the circum-Mediterranean, this behavior has fascinated ethnographers, particularly because the behavior is smoothly incorporated into a masculine ideological and behavioral system that otherwise reflects similar concerns to those in Mediterranean societies.

Accompanying this prescribed fellatio is a ritual avoidance of women and a belief in the polluting effects (and even lethality) of menstrual blood. Curiously, this system of rearing boys into young men results in a reportedly exclusive heterosexual relationship with the wife by the time the young man becomes a father for the first time (though Herdt reports in 1981 an interim bisexual pattern for a period of time after marriage that other works [Godelier, 1986; Herdt, 1984] do not identify). This developmental process of early "homosexuality" transforming into a mature adult heterosexuality contradicts most of the attempts to theorize how homosexuality and heterosexuality are produced in Western culture. The clear cultural construction of a male-male sexuality has little to do with Western gay lifestyles or, for that matter, with currently popular Western theories of the possible genetic roots of homosexual behavior. The possibility that sexuality itself—homo, hetero, or bi—could be culturally constructed phenomena is still quite difficult for many in the West to grasp. The arbitrariness of the symbol becomes obfuscated by the powerful ideological process of naturalizing that symbol.

In addition, the secretiveness of the homosexual cult among men leads Herdt to accept the necessity of talking in terms of sexual subcultures of masculine and feminine. What emerges are separate rituals for men and for women that are central to the development of each as gendered identities. The rituals incorporate symbols that are interpreted individually yet result in collective beliefs and behaviors. As found in the arguments of Combs-Schilling (1989) concerning Morocco, public ritual performance is an essential process in the creation of gendered meanings. These gendered meanings, regardless of the culture involved, must be understood at the level of both the psychodynamics of individual erotic cathexis *and* the collective ritual behaviors that constitute tribal, ethnic, or national unity. As Herdt (1981) puts it, "our most urgent and significant questions about the anthropological phenomena of ritual symbolism involve the mind (subjective processes) and behavioral development" (p. 12).

It is of great interest in understanding gender symbology that girls are frequently thought to be born with all the necessary internal functions to become a biologically full-grown woman naturally. No intervention is necessary. Boys, on the other hand, require intervention to develop; it is such an idea on which the daily ingesting of semen in New Guinea is based. Among the Sambia, semen builds men; without it, boys remain feminized. In other places, war builds men. So does sexual conquest or the acquiring of riches. But *something* must be done to make a boy a man; some proof of masculinity, some achievement, is necessary.

The extent to which the denial of women's power to give birth to men is taken can be fascinating; it is from an act of male-male fellatio that the first woman was parthenogenetically created, says Sambia myth. As well, semen, when fed to premenarche Sambia girls, helps "sexualize" them, causing the onset of menstruation and the eventual production of breast milk. Men thereby believe they have some power over women's natural development. The Sambia also claim that it takes 40 to 50 ejaculations into the vagina to build a fetus; semen combines in some hazy fashion with women's blood to produce a child. Semen is mighty stuff in this symbolic system. (Data for this section is drawn from Herdt, 1981, 1984; Godelier, 1986.)

Yet at the same time men's power is limited; "men fear masculine atrophy" (Herdt, 1981, p. 250). Their semen is depletable and must be built up (secretly) by the ingestion of tree sap. There is also fear of the castrative power of the vagina, which can become so "hot" as to drain the man of all his "water"—semen. Fear of women's power is the subtext of much of belief system in this male subculture. In the early stages of male initiation, many rituals are performed to bleed (literally) the young boy of the poisons built up from his long association with the women's world. Myths of sexual difference and danger pervade the symbolic atmosphere.

> Each society becomes preoccupied with only a handful of myths. Men's and women's capacities to project their myths into cultural idiom, to nurture them, to deny their personal doubts about them or sanctify them imperiously in ritual, at whatever price (while sustaining the consequences of so doing), presage the quality of life and the eventual successes and failures of that society. (Herdt, 1981, p. 16)

The male idiom is described by Herdt in his conclusion as a way of utilizing the sexual divisions to gender the world, anthropomorphizing natural phenomena, and performing a process of "perceptual splitting" that polarizes the world into an antagonistic system (1981, pp. 299-300). As a result, "[c]ertain affects (at manifold levels of subjectivity) are thus split off from one's sense of self and become feared, denied, or adored as 'things' holding a dangerous power beyond oneself. Perceptual splitting is thus a symbolic mechanism having feedback effects in individual experience, cultural ideology, and social relationships" (p. 300).

This becomes all the more useful when compared to Benjamin's (1988) argument that gender splitting is the root of dominant-submissive relationships in the West. The resultant system of differential power in which, regardless of male fears of the feminine, what men do is more culturally valuable than what women do, all the way down to the biological basis of reproduction, grants men a very real cultural validation that, at least publicly, is denied to women. Although admittedly different in form, the context of power relations between these sex/gender categories is similar in content and subsequent effect to that in Western systems. As Foucault (1979, 1980) conceives of power and knowledge in a unitary interrelationship (power/knowledge), so can one conceive of gender and power; identity is gender is level of validation is access to power in society.

> [T]he differential access to the process of validation is a major determinant of the ways that individuals experience gender relationships: much of the significance of work and consumption in our society derives from their

importance as major contexts in which men and women can display, compare and evaluate their subjectivities. (Errington & Gewertz, 1987, p. 132)

But there is still more to the relations of power here than mere sexual antagonism (as Herdt & Poole, 1982, make clear). There remains the possibility that some form of envy of reproductive powers of women is involved, which produced ritual blood-letting among men (nose bleeding, circumcision itself). The amount of male energy put into sexual hostility, into constructing and performing masculine ritual, into endowing the male genital and its fluid emission with near-deific power seems so much to be built on basic insecurity, on perceived powerlessness rooted in the basic sexual (reproductive) division of labor. It is, after all, women who produce children from their bodies, who feed them from their breasts, who bleed in tandem with the changes of the moon. Then it is also women who are charged with the rearing and socializing of male children, thereby requiring (as long as the masculine is conceived as totally different from the feminine) the eventual reclamation of male children from the world of the female. This combination of biological reality and social organization may well turn out to constitute far more of cultural underpinnings than yet imagined. Men need to "do" something to become or be masculine; women, though, naturally embody their own femininities. What will it take to escape such dualism? Anthropology's contribution to answering this question is in the realm of ethnomethodological examination of the stuff of culture: practical daily behaviors, symbols and meanings, and structures of communication.

The Practice of Daily Lives

Practical taxonomies, which are a transformed, misrecognizable form of the real divisions of the social order, contribute to the reproduction of that order by producing objectively orchestrated practices adjusted to those divisions. (Bourdieu, 1977, p. 163)

Bourdieu's theory of practice is offered in a context of analyzing Kabyle Berber gender relations in Algeria. Berber male honor, he argues, is nothing but a "cultivated disposition," constituted through body practice and mental constructions, which produces a series of ritual exchanges in the daily practices of life. Such rituals are rules for manifesting identity, but the performers of these rules are less than fully conscious of them as jural behavior. The magic of these rules is that it is their nonconscious nature that makes them so powerful and that produces and maintains their dominance as doxa. This idea parallels Gramsci's (1971) views that the hegemony of ideology reduces the necessity of direct political coercion; what is accepted as natural behavior cannot be a realm of political struggle. "The rule's last trick is to cause it to be forgotten that agents have an interest in obeying the rule" (Bourdieu, 1977, p. 22).

Masculinity itself becomes a *performance* of dominance, following certain directions from an unseen (and often unrecognized) ritual director whose commands pervade language systems, physical kinesics and proxemics, psychoanalytic structures, and symbolic categories. The ways in which men speak, move, express desire, and construct symbols become dramatic performances that, due to the process of naturalization described by Bourdieu and feminist analysts of gender, are often outside the realm of social and political discourse. The struggles of sexual politics then become a process of negotiation over the boundaries between the universe of the undisputed and the public realms of sex/gender discourse. As Bourdieu (1977) points out:

> The dominated classes [which in *my* reading include women, lesbians, and gay men] have an interest in pushing back the limits of doxa and exposing the arbitrariness of the taken for granted; the dominant classes [read here men, or heterosexuals] have an interest in defending the integrity of doxa or, short of this, of establishing in its place the necessarily imperfect substitute, orthodoxy. (p. 169)

Gender Doxa: A Few Examples

French structuralism argued the universality of systems of oppositions, although the nature of the paired symbols remained arbitrary. In Bourdieu's discussion of Kabyle systems of opposition (male/dry/light/outside/hot/spiced versus female/wet/dark/inside/cold/bland [p. 142]), one finds some that do not correspond to European categories. Male/intellect/rational/cold and female/emotion/irrational/hot correspond more to the philosophies of European peoples. But in both European and African systems, "female" is left, while "male" is right. European languages add an additional layer of meaning that contributes to the disempowering of women. Why is left-handedness perceived as a social danger, as sinister (French *sinistre* = left)? Why does the right confer the meaning of correctness, soundness, and genuineness, as well as just claims based in morality (this is true in English, French (*droit*), and German (*recht/re-chte*). How many educated European people would be able to conceptualize, explain, and realize the impact on gender of these associations? I suspect that very few could do so. In any case, on the occasions when a linguistic issue *is* brought out of a *doxa* closet into the public realm (for example, the generic masculine usage in English), men and a fair share of women have typically responded by proclaiming its orthodoxy, its correctness, and, if you will, its *right*ness. The message is clear: Do not dispute the natural, the comfortable, the known.

Similarly, how many are conscious of the male use of greater space, whether in sitting or standing positions? How many women are quietly irritated at the male prerogative to take both armrests in crowded theaters and how many men are totally (and quite conveniently) unaware that they do so? How many men would consider changing their physical position so their head would be at a lower height than that of the women with whom they are talking or arguing? (And how many would even understand the point of it?) These are some of the *physical* embodiments of power that remain nonconscious in the majority of people (see Henley, 1977, for a feminist classic in nonverbal communication). But as Bourdieu noted, probably a larger percentage of men remain unaware of this form of power than women.

Systems of Reproduction

How are such systems reproduced? Recalling Rosaldo's (1980) comment that "the individuals who create social relationships are themselves social creations" (p. 416), it becomes necessary to conceive of a cyclical system of (re)production that could be rooted in the psychodynamic and cathectic processes of child development. Seeking just such an understanding led Nancy Chodorow (1978) to ask the question "Why do women mother?" Recognizing that a child's attainment of identity as self and as gendered being are closely connected, if not always coincident, and that such attainment takes place in a gendered environment where women are the primary caretakers in the earliest years, signifying to the child a basic division of labor; recognizing also that the attainment of masculinity is a different process from that of femininity because the male must break free from the nurturing power of the mother through the violence of a second birth into his masculinity, one finds a clear explication of the habitus[4] of gender—an embodiment of sex-based gender arrangements that remain hidden from the social eye (and the social "I") due to their close association with the biology of reproduction. Bourdieu (1977) argues, I think correctly, that the child learns a sexual identity and a division of labor simultaneously, "out of the same socially defined set of inseparably biological and social indices" (p. 93). I can think of nothing that is more naturalized than the gender arrangements (appropriate sexual behavior, gender behavior, division of labor) that have been constructed on the biological divisions of sex. These arrangements are considered to be objective, natural, and above human choice. As Bourdieu (1977) argues:

> [T]he habitus makes coherence and necessity out of accident and contingency: for example, the equivalences it establishes between positions in the division of labour and positions in the division between the sexes are doubtless not peculiar to societies in which the division of labour and the division between the sexes coincide perfectly. (p. 87)

Nor is perfect coincidence necessary for the perpetuation of the idea of the naturalness of the divisions. The axiomatic "exception that proves the rule" is a masterpiece of obfuscation. In such depoliticized systems of explanation, norm and deviance cloak the nature of power to impose its definition of the world. Practice-based theory, on the other hand, explicitly incorporates the dynamics of power and history, permitting one to reach the level of the doxa that underlies accepted discourse. Gramsci, for example, perceiving the interconnectedness of the sex/gender system and the structure of work processes, suggested that "the struggle of women to end their own oppression within a patriarchal society will activate new patterns of thought and behavior that could eventually penetrate bourgeois hegemony within the workplace" (as quoted in Boggs, 1972, pp. 99-100). To paraphrase Frederick Douglass, hegemonic power concedes nothing (neither doxa nor orthodoxy) without a demand from those who are willing to question the natural.

Ritual and the Ephemerality of Masculinity

> But it is in the dialectical relationship between the body and a space structured according to the mythico-ritual oppositions that one finds the form par excellence of the structural apprenticeship which leads to the embodying of the structures of the world, that is, the appropriating by the world of a body thus enabled to appropriate the world. (Bourdieu, 1977, p. 89)

Bourdieu's argument corresponds to that of Chodorow, in its claim that it is in the emotional-physical relationships between children and their parents that one can find the embodiment of the reproduced structures of gender inequality. In addition, it parallels the argument of Combs-Schilling (1989) on the constitutive nature of ritual in Morocco. In the daily (and life cycle) rituals of human experience are found the roots of the socially constructed person, what Bourdieu calls the "socially informed body" (1977, p. 124), which when properly scrutinized can yield the deconstruction of the relations of power that are hidden in "normal" behaviors. For example, as noted earlier, the male sense of honor has been made much of in the Mediterranean area (Bourdieu, 1979; Gilmore, 1987; Peristiany, 1966). Bourdieu argues that the interests of men are linked to the material and symbolic interests of their family, a major representation of which is the symbolism of honor maintained by the protection of women's chastity. The fact that this becomes hegemonic, framing both men's and women's sexual discourse (p. 92), should not disguise its roots in male insecurities about their abilities to control women, who are, due to child-rearing arrangements, totally in control of male children in their early years. A man's socially constructed need to know who his children are (so as to pass on patrimony *and* to know his virility is unquestioned) is deeply incriminated in the uncertainty of "maleness" and the concomitant need to prove masculinity repeatedly in daily ritual (see Brandes, 1980, for an excellent view of the Andalusian form of this practice). As argued in Gilmore's introduction to a 1987 collection on Mediterranean honor, erotic and economic power become conflated in a competitive struggle for "performance" among men (pp. 4-5). It takes constant male vigilance to prevent the destruction of family honor by women; female power, through sexual behavior, is a constant concern, a behavioral antifetish, a fixation.

Such rituals are constructed with the building blocks of taxonomies and beliefs that are nonconscious and unconscious. The relations of power between men and women are rarely what they seem; in fact, the bluster of male control, physical violence, and sexual dominance are often a reaction to the underlying psychological reality of the child's experience of overwhelming female power. Male dominance is real, with very real effect, yet it is built on insecurity and fear of loss of masculinity through the (subversive) action of women or other men. Women's (and men's) humor often reflects a knowledge of this fact (see Dwyer, 1978, for folktales from Morocco that give testimony to this). But the participants are rarely able to theorize the nature of the underpinnings of their relationships. As Bourdieu

(1977) points out, "Every established order tends to produce . . . the naturalization of its own arbitrariness" (p. 164). That is the barrier to self-awareness. One naturalizes male dominance in social practice and discourse, claiming orthodoxy for its known rules, and rarely if ever reaches the underlying doxa of male insecurity and fear of returning to the original embrace of the mother and the feminine.

Negotiation, Structures, and Psychodynamics

As an example of the naturalizing process by which gender is obfuscated in ethnography, I offer a critique of Lawrence Rosen's 1984 book *Bargaining for Reality*. Rosen focuses on the idea of negotiating one's daily reality, an idea which has its roots in the ethnomethodological approaches of sociologists Garfinkel (1967/1984) and Goffman (1977). Their focus on the microlevel of individuals in interaction yields the basic idea that life is dramaturgy, performance, a daily construction and reconstruction of role and identity. With different people in different circumstances each person presents different personalities; the way you are with your mother is not the way you are with your employer, your best friend, your child. Each circumstance, in this view, presents the opportunity for self-construction. This sociology of the social actor sets the scene for Rosen's (1984) approach: "Everywhere I looked I was struck by the extent to which social life and ideas that informed it possessed an open, malleable quality that took shape only as these concepts and relationships became attached to and identified with the lives of individual men and women" (p. 1). He found it very difficult to approach Moroccan society with the idea of a structure that constrained and shaped people's lives. Instead, the malleability of meaning constructed in particular interactions seemed to inform at a level higher than of any other single analytic system.

> [I]t began to seem mistaken, in the realm of Sefrou [Morocco] social life, to try and capture from a single perspective the *ongoing creation of social relations* [emphasis added] and the patterns that could be observed at any given moment. What was needed, rather, was an orientation and a chosen set of cultural attributes that would allow me to move back and forth between form and process, concept and enactment, individual effort and collective attachment in such a way as to capture the living quality of my subject. (Rosen, 1984, p. 2)

Rosen writes of "form and process, concept and enactment, [and] individual effort and collective attachment" in the previous quote. Although these are a good set of processual dualities, "form" here becomes primarily conceived as a linguistic and conceptual structure, power and domination are insufficiently explored, and history is put on a back burner, referred to primarily in the context of the Islamic theoretical past. "The cultural stress and repercussions of individual action—the free play of personality—*determine*, to an extraordinary degree, the shape and operation of everyday social life" (Rosen, 1979, p. 20; emphasis added). Clearly, this determinism has gone too far in one area and not far enough in others. The structuring and shaping of individual consciousness and choice that takes place in, for example, gender, is erased from the picture entirely. For it is abundantly clear to the visitor that Moroccans have a powerful set of gendered meanings that shape their lives.

Yet, in what is perhaps a too literal response to the poststructural creed, Rosen stresses but one of the Gerson and Peiss (1985) trio of themes: By focusing on negotiation, he leaves the bargaining process without material context or an awareness of the structuring constraints of individual consciousness (and unconsciousness, for that matter). But granting the limitations of the analysis, he does have it right on one count; the idea of negotiation of daily relationships is an extremely useful approach to the real dynamism of people's (and not only Moroccans') lives. The problem is in what the theory overlooks, not in what it offers. Although negotiation or bargaining is a part of social interaction, Rosen forgets that one negotiates from a position; the prior structuring he was so loath to identify must be brought back into the picture. Individuals perform their (gendered) identities with a combination of variable response and fixed foundation. What Rosen overlooks is the naturalized symbol that one takes for granted culturally.

It is evident, then, that Bourdieu's combination of the naturalizing of the arbitrary symbol with the daily acting out of realities is a potent and practical method for making sense of daily (gendered) life. The approach is easily tied in with the psychodynamics of sex/gender systems and family life, as well as with the structuring capacities of economic systems and historical facts. In the end, gender can be clearly perceived in its complexities only through the structuring of symbols, psychodynamics, and political economy, and the agency of the individual acting to make sense of daily events and struggles.

Conclusion

I set out in this paper to review some theoretical approaches to masculinity in anthropology and their applications in ethnographic work. In conclusion I wish to review some of the arguments I believe have been most important in this review and make a few final points. First, the study of men and masculinity is a long overdue attempt to take the focus off women as the (one and only) problem to be explained. I believe that the realm of men and masculinity encompasses some extremely serious social problems that should militate against the (male) tradition of leaving the realm of gender solely in the world of women—whether as gendered actors or as ethnographers. None of this is intended to suggest that the work done with women is less important, less necessary. In fact, as the historical record makes clear, reasonably good work on men and masculinities can be done only in a context in which women are arguing their own realities, their own perspectives on the problems humans all face. The point is more that researchers all need to overcome the ghettoization of questions dealing with sex and gender to the realm of women. This point is made by Dwyer (1982, p. 266) who notices the sexual division of labor even within anthropology; the work men do has tended to differ from the work women do, and be taken (per usual) as more important. Women have been challenging that oversight by doing some of the types of work men have traditionally done; it is men's turn now to listen to women and begin asking the questions traditionally asked about women and femininity about (the male) sex and (various masculine) gender constructions.[5]

Second, it is essential to attempt to move beyond falsely conceived theoretical dichotomies, whether they be objective/subjective, emic/etic, or materialist/symbolic. Such dualisms are the doxa of academia, providing the means of lengthening careers and carving out places in disciplinary histories. An interesting example of one ethnographer who admits the insufficient nature of his (seemingly) universalist theoretical framework is Maurice Godelier, who, in his fieldwork among the Baruya, came to recognize that he could no longer ignore questions of male domination. As he confesses:

> Like many others, I long believed that it was first necessary to fight for the abolition of class relations, and that all the rest—oppression between the sexes, races, nations—would unravel or be resolved once these class relations

had been abolished. It was a scientifically false vision of classes, races, and the sexes, a politically conservative vision which, in the name of revolution, justified us turning a blind eye to and doing nothing about all these other forms of domination and oppression. . . . (1986, p. xii)

Needed is more self-examination of this nature about the limits of theoretical perspectives. Perhaps I should note here that I often appear to be arguing that sex/gender analysis can explain everything; that is incorrect. My point is that it may prove to be more enlightening than ever suspected about problems that at first glance appear to have nothing to do with sex or gender. As Gilmore (1987) notes, in his suggestion of the power of gender in explaining dualist symbolic systems, the "study of gender, of sexuality, and of other variable concepts of male and female . . . may be the lost key to a deeper understanding of culture" (p. 17). But there is still plenty left to be done to fully explore his suggestion.

Third and last is a challenge that researchers have hardly begun to face in the field of gender studies, let alone within the discipline of anthropology. The assumption has been nearly universal that "the biological difference in the functions of females and males in human reproduction lies at the core of the cultural organization of women's and men's relations" (Yanagisako & Collier, 1990, p. 141). But how was the assumption made that sex itself is more a biological than a social construction? "[H]ow has our culture come to focus on coitus and parturition as the moments that above all others constitute maleness, femaleness, and human reproduction?" (p. 141). Such assumptions about the naturalness of sex and sexedness have been underpinnings of so much of the discourse about gender; people have been blinded by the obvious biological connections of sexedness in the same way that people of earlier generations were blinded by what they considered to be the obvious associations of gender—through sex—to that biological base. Can people move beyond this?

> Our realization that the model of sexual reproduction and sexual difference so widely used is a particular mode of thinking about relations between people enables us to question the "biological facts" about sex. In dismantling the notion that sex is to gender as biology is to culture, we enlarge the analytical project to encompass the symbolic and social processes by which sex as a system of difference is itself culturally constituted. (Yanagisako & Collier, 1990, p. 141)

This, in my reading, is what Gayle Rubin (1975) was referring to in her article that was my introduction to the world of anthropology. Her argument for a unitary treatment of the interconnected sex/gender system is still the theoretical approach that moves me the most. It is my view then that it is still the work of anthropology to follow such a road.

Notes

1. See, for example, Sanday and Goodenough (1990) for a collection explicitly designed to demonstrate how contemporary anthropology is moving beyond earlier paradigms.

2. This is Bourdieu's (1977) term for the unstated yet fundamental and thereby "naturalized" beliefs by which a culture maintains systems of dominance and order.

3. These two terms—*etic* and *emic*—are derived from linguistics. What is phon*etic* is the range of possible sound in a language; what is phon*emic* is the range of sound that has meaning to the speakers of a language. The shortened forms have come to be codes in anthropological circles for the perspectives of an outsider and an insider relative to the culture (or language) being studied. The implication that what is *etic* is somehow objective and what is *emic* is subjective has been criticized as a false dualism.

4. *Habitus* is Bourdieu's term for the environmental structuring in a culture that (re)produces certain understandings. Habitus could include, for example, spatial separations (outside and inside the home) that shape a particular people's gendered patterns of behavior.

5. For example, in my own geographical specialization, Morocco, some very good work has been written on—and by—women (see, for example, Davis, 1983; Dwyer, 1978; Geertz, 1979; Mernissi, 1987; Rassam, 1980), but nothing really has examined men as men, even when men were the explicit focus of the work. For example, Rabinow's classic *Reflections on Fieldwork in Morocco* (1977) is essentially a series of encounters between (male) ethnographer and (male) others, examining the meaning of their encounters through the eyeglass of the then current desire for reflexivity. Yet their masculinity never enters the analysis as a factor, though it could have had, in my reading, strong significance and great explanatory value.

References

Benjamin, J. (1988). *The bonds of love: Psychoanalysis, feminism and the problem of domination.* New York: Pantheon.

Boggs, C. (1972, September-October). Gramsci's *Prison Notebooks. Socialist Revolution, Number 1, 2*(5), 79-118.

Bourdieu, P. (1977). *Outline of a theory of practice.* Cambridge, UK: Cambridge University Press.

Bourdieu, P. (1979). *The sense of honour in Algeria: 1960* (R. Nice, trans.). Cambridge, UK: Cambridge University Press.

Brandes, S. (1980). *Metaphors of masculinity: Sex and status in Andalusian folklore.* Philadelphia: University of Pennsylvania.

Brandes, S. (1987). Reflections on honor and shame in the Mediterranean. In D. Gilmore (Ed.), *Honor and shame and the unity of the Mediterranean* (Pub. 22, pp. 121-134). Washington, DC: American Anthropological Association.

Chodorow, N. (1978). *The reproduction of mothering: Psychoanalysis and the sociology of gender.* Berkeley: University of California Press.

Combs-Schilling, M. E. (1989). *Sacred performances: Islam, sexuality and sacrifice.* New York: Columbia University Press.

Davis, S. S. (1983). *Patience and power: Women's lives in a Moroccan village.* New York: Schenkman.

Dwyer, D. (1978). *Images and self-images: Male and female in Morocco.* New York: Columbia University Press.

Dwyer, K. (1982). *Moroccan dialogues: Anthropology in question.* Prospect Heights, IL: Waveland Press.

Ehrensaft, D. (1987). *Parenting together: Men and women sharing the care of their children.* New York: Free Press.

Errington, F., & Gewertz, D. (1987). *Cultural alternatives and a feminist anthropology: An analysis of culturally constructed gender interests in Papua New Guinea.* Cambridge, UK: Cambridge University Press.

Foucault, M. (1979). *Discipline and punish: The birth of the prison.* Harmondsworth, UK: Penguin.

Foucault, M. (1980). *Power/knowledge: Selected interviews and other writings 1972-1977* (C. Gordon, ed.). Brighton, UK: Harvester Press.

Garfinkel, H. (1984). Passing and the managed achievement of sex status in an intersexed person. In H. Garfinkel (Ed.), *Studies in ethnomethodology* (pp. 116-185). Cambridge, UK: Polity. (Original work published 1967)

Geertz, H. (1979). The meaning of family ties. In C. Geertz, H. Geertz, & L. Rosen (Eds.), *Meaning and order in Moroccan society: Three essays in cultural analysis* (pp. 315-391). Cambridge, UK: Cambridge University Press.

Gerson, J. M., & Peiss, K. (1985). Boundaries, negotiation, consciousness: Reconceptualizing gender relations. *Social Problems, 32,* 317-331.

Gilmore, D. (Ed.). (1987). *Honor and shame and the unity of the Mediterranean* (Pub. 22). Washington, DC: American Anthropological Association.

Gilmore, D. (1990). *Manhood in the making: Cultural concepts of masculinity.* New Haven, CT: Yale University Press.

Godelier, M. (1986). *The making of great men: Male domination and power among the New Guinea Baruya.* Cambridge, UK: Cambridge University Press.

Goffman, E. (1977). The arrangement between the sexes. *Theory and Society, 4,* 301-331.

Gramsci, A. (1971). *Selections from the prison notebooks* (Q. Hoare & G. N. Smith, Eds. & Trans.). New York: International Publishers.

Henley, N. (1977). *Body politics: Power, sex and nonverbal communication.* Englewood Cliffs, NJ: Prentice Hall.

Herdt, G. (1981). *Guardians of the flutes: Idioms of masculinity.* New York: McGraw-Hill.

Herdt, G. (Ed.). (1984). *Ritualized homosexuality in Melanesia.* Berkeley: University of California Press.

Herdt, G., & Poole, F. P. (1982). Sexual antagonism: The intellectual history of a concept. *Social Analysis, 12,* 3-28.

Johnson, M. M. (1988). *Strong mothers, weak wives: The search for gender equality.* Berkeley: University of California Press.

Mernissi, F. (1987). *Beyond the veil: Male female dynamics in a Muslim society.* Bloomington: Indiana University Press.

Peristiany, J. G. (Ed.). (1966). *Honour and shame: The values of Mediterranean society.* London: Weidenfeld & Nicolson.

Rabinow, P. (1977). *Reflections on fieldwork in Morocco.* Berkeley: University of California Press.

Rassam, A. (1980). Women and domestic power in Morocco. *International Journal of Middle East Studies, 12,* 171-179.

Rosaldo, M. Z. (1980). The use and abuse of anthropology: Reflections on feminism and cross-cultural understanding. *Signs, 5,* 389-417.

Rosen, L. (1979). Social identity and points of attachment: Approaches to social organization. In C. Geertz, H. Geertz, & L. Rosen (Eds.), *Meaning and order in Moroccan society: Three essays in cultural analysis* (pp. 19-122). Cambridge, UK: Cambridge University Press.

Rosen, L. (1984). *Bargaining for reality: The construction of social relations in a Muslim community.* Chicago: University of Chicago Press.

Rubin, G. (1975). The traffic in women: Notes on a political economy of sex. In R. R. Reiter (Ed.), *Toward an anthropology of women* (pp. 157-210). New York: Monthly Review Press.

Rubin, L. (1983). *Intimate strangers: Men and women together.* New York: Harper & Row.

Sanday, P. R., & Goodenough, R. G. (Eds.). (1990). *Beyond the second sex: New directions in the anthropology of gender.* Philadelphia: University of Pennsylvania Press.

Scott, J. (1985). *The weapons of the weak: Everyday forms of peasant resistance.* New Haven, CT: Yale University Press.

Tillion, G. (1983). *Republic of cousins: Women's oppression in Mediterranean society.* Atlantic Highlands, NJ: Humanities Press. (Original work published 1966)

Yanagisako, S. J., & Collier, J. (1990). The mode of reproduction in anthropology. In D. Rhode (Ed.), *Theoretical perspectives on sexual difference* (pp. 131-141). New Haven, CT: Yale University Press.

5

Some Thoughts on Some Histories of Some Masculinities

Jews and Other Others[1]

HARRY BROD

What is one studying when one studies men and masculinities? What are the relationships between studies of men and studies of women? What are the relationships between studies of *some* men and studies of others—in particular, what are the relationships between studies of dominant or hegemonic groups of men and studies of marginalized or nonhegemonic groups of men? In this chapter, I shall take up these questions. I shall do so by first undertaking a critical analysis of the development of current conceptualizations of these issues, taking as the guiding thread of my investigations the genesis of the concept "masculinities" in its present usage. I shall then apply the results of these inquiries to outline a method of analysis of nonhegemonic masculinities, using the situation of Jewish men as a case in point.

The concept of masculinities has become very popular very quickly. As far as I can determine, Jeffrey Weeks was the first to deploy it in anything like its current historical/sociological usage in a 1984 article subsequently incorporated into his 1985 book, *Sexuality and Its Discontents* (Weeks, 1985).[2] I pass over an earlier psychological rather than historical or sociological sense of the term in which it refers not to diverse social structures, in the senses that I shall specify shortly, but rather simply to the existence of multiple male archetypes in a sense derived from Jungian psychology (Gerzon, 1982).

The term then follows the pattern of a number of important conceptual innovations in that having first emerged in gay studies, it quickly migrates into men's studies, appearing late in 1985 in an article published in *Theory and Society* by Tim Carrigan, Bob Connell, and John Lee titled "Toward a New Sociology of Masculinity" (Carrigan, Connell, & Lee, 1985, reprinted in Brod, 1987, pp. 63-100, and Kaufman, 1987, pp. 139-192. See also Connell, 1987). There, it is linked to the concept of "hegemonic masculinity," about which I shall have more to say later on.

"Masculinities" was helped into the spotlight by my use of it in the title of a collection I edited, published in 1987: *The Making of Masculinities: The New Men's Studies* (Brod, 1987). By early 1989, Jeff Hearn, now editor of a book series published by Routledge, Chapman, and Hall on "Critical Studies on Men and Masculinities," began an article by talking about "these issues of men and masculinity, or masculinities, as has now become the radical convention, if that is not a contradiction in terms" (Hearn, 1989, p. 1). From initial coinage to convention within 5 years seems to me remarkably quick. This is clearly a word whose time has come, as its frequent usage in this volume demonstrates.

In the spirit of this volume, I would like to reexamine the concept of masculinities. I shall do so by contrasting it with an earlier formulation. It seems to me that much of the discussion carried on today about directions for the future of the study of masculinities would previously have been carried out, and indeed was carried out, as a conversation about directions for "men's studies."

Men's studies always assumed a certain relationship to women's studies. The dominant conception of both fields, and of their interrelationship, was deeply embedded in the discourse of "sex roles." This discourse, in turn, carried with it the heritage of the traditional "separate spheres" model of separate gendered domains. Although both women's and men's studies studied relations *between* the genders, each also took as its unique province relations between members of the same gender. An early and influential formulation of the proper object of the history of masculinity made this explicit:

> Women's and men's history take the same and different routes to the common destination of a history of gender. Each studies same-sex and cross-sex relationships; each identifies a relation unique unto itself, that among members of one sex—all-male relationships in men's history, all-female relationships in women's history. (Pleck & Pleck, 1980, p. 4)

If women's studies had its separate sphere of relations between women, whether named as a "female world of love and ritual," as in Carroll Smith-Rosenberg's pioneering lead article in the inaugural issue of *Signs* (Smith-Rosenberg, 1975), or as "women's culture," or by some other appellation, then so too did men's. Another important conceptual innovation originating first in gay studies and then adopted by men's studies was the use of the concept "homosociality" to designate aspects of this sphere, following the argument of Eve Kosofsky Sedgwick's *Between Men: English Literature and Male Homosocial Desire* (Sedgwick, 1985). Men's and women's studies, then, would each tend to their own particular gardens and conjointly harvest the fruits of their intersection. Hence, a crucial task of men's studies was to be an investigation of interactions between men, with particular emphasis on how men experienced these interactions *as men,* and not simply as generic human beings, the way in which patriarchal scholarship had viewed men. The privileging in these investigations of personal *experience* over social structure derived from a particular conception of the role of men's subjectivity in men's studies. As I put it in the introduction to *The Making of Masculinities* (Brod, 1987):

> In inverse fashion to the struggle in women's studies to establish the *objectivity* of women's experiences and thereby validate the legitimacy of women's experiences *as women,* much of men's studies struggles to establish the *subjectivity* of men's experiences and thereby validate the legitimacy of men's experiences *as men.* (p. 6)

Because men's subjectivity had been construed as constituting objective knowledge, while women's activities had been privatized and written out of history, emphasizing the subjectivity of masculinity was seen as a way of unmasking and depowering men's pretensions to objectivity, one of the important elements in anchoring patriarchal privilege. The idea was to particularize men's knowledge claims and thereby discredit their pretensions to universality (Hearn, 1989, pp. 39-43). Again, women's and men's studies are here conceived of as having complementary tasks.

The appearance of complementarity between the spheres painted by this picture was, however, deceiving. For the bringing to light of a previously ignored "women's culture" was *inherently* tied to a thesis about the politics of knowledge in a way that elucidating "men's culture" was not, though it certainly *could* be, too, when done in the right way. That is, the suppression of knowledge about women's world was part and parcel of the oppression of women. Hence, producing knowledge about women was part and parcel of antipatriarchal politics. Though analogous claims were made about the new knowledge about men produced by men's studies, and it was clear that this was where the sympathies and intentions of many of its practitioners were, it was not at all clear to many that it actually did or would play a similarly feminist role.

The difference has to do with the relations between knowledge and power. Foregrounding female-female relationships poses an inherent challenge to male power by breaking the male-imposed silencing of women's voices in any situation in which those voices are not reading male scripts. It was not as immediately obvious which power relations were being challenged by foregrounding male-male relationships. Indeed, in the concrete politics of academia it became necessary for proponents of men's studies to stress that they were not trying to strengthen men's power by diverting resources from women's studies, but rather that they advocated that the priority of support for women's studies had to be preserved (Brod, 1990, reprinted in Kimmel & Mosmiller, 1992, pp. 396-398).

Here, then, is the quandary. In focusing on relationships between men, men's studies *seemed* to be playing the role assigned to it by women's studies. Male scholars were hereby not trying to colonize or reterritorialize women's space, or telling women how to study women or gender, but were self-reflectively studying their own kind and tending their own gardens, as they had been told to do. (One must of course note that not all scholars working in men's studies are male. Yet the vast majority are, and discussions about the field are generally carried on, at least in feminist circles, as discussions about "What are the boys up to now?" [Bradshaw, 1982]). Or so they at least thought. Yet in doing so they seemed to be ignoring male-female relations and hence ignoring the question of male power over women, thereby reinforcing male privilege, precisely the opposite of what they were trying to do.

In the beginnings of a conceptual shift to which I wish to draw attention, the object of study of men's studies began to be conceptualized in a way intended to break down the gendered dichotomy between objectivity and subjectivity and between separate male and female domains, as well as to destabilize other dichotomies that structure traditional theories. Although early formulations, such as that of the Plecks cited previously, often implicitly invoked a separate spheres sex role model for the study of gender, by the mid-1980s this rhetoric stood side by side with more interactive, dynamic formulations. The terrain being explored here began to be situated, to adopt more sociological terminology, *between* structure and agency, public and private, institutions and experiences, "patriarchy" and individual "men" (Giddens, 1982). As I shall argue shortly, although men's studies scholarship *intended* to overcome these dichotomies, slippage occurred such that it became possible to sometimes speak of the experiences of men without paying sufficient attention to the institutional embodiments of patriarchy.[3]

Into this breach stepped the concept of masculinities, or rather, into the breach stepped the concept of masculinities in its intrinsic relation to the concept of hegemonic masculinity, as both appeared in the Carrigan, Connell, and Lee article cited earlier. Using gay masculinity as their prime example, but also taking note of issues of class and race, they deployed these terms to theorize gender relations in a way that emphasized the intrinsic interconnections between hierarchies among men and hierarchies between women and men. By simultaneously taking up the question of power as embedded in contested relationships *between* the genders and *within* male gender relations, this theoretical constellation would rectify the situation. Or so Carrigan, Connell, and Lee seemed to intend.

But as it became popularized in the hands of others, masculinities sometimes seemed to lose the dimension of power and simply signify plurality or diversity. It lost some of the Gramscian Marxist emphasis on cultural domination and the radical social constructionism embedded in it in its initial formulation. Perhaps the simplest way to make the point is to say that too much of what was written on masculinities did not sufficiently emphasize, if it noted at all, that masculinities are also patriarchies.

It may be instructive to at this point call attention to two particular points. First, it is interesting and ironic to note that Carrigan, Connell, and Lee manage to keep women in the picture even when their primary example of a nonhegemonic masculinity is gay masculinity, an arena in which those unfamiliar with gay life and culture often assume women do not play a significant role. Where women started to fade out of view was in analyses of groups of men where the norm was heterosexual. This may be taken as confirmation of (a) the argument the authors make in the article that gay studies has to date developed a much more sophisticated understanding of gendered power than men's studies and (b) the radical feminist thesis that heterosexual love and romance mask male dominance. Second, because I once heard a historian defend the lack of attention to women in particular analyses of masculinities on the grounds that this was simply what the sources showed, I think it essential to note that the role of women in the analysis is not entirely or even primarily an empirical question, but is at least in part a theoretical, conceptual issue. That is to say, the salience of any category in the analysis cannot be dictated solely by its salience in the sources. The absence of any category as well as its presence in any source can itself be problematized and made the subject of analysis (I shall return to this point in my closing comments). Numerous analyses coming out of women's studies have made the absence of any explicit mention of women in various texts their primary focus, and men's studies could well do the same.

I would like to note here one particularly striking way in which this issue of the presence of women in analyses produced in men's studies has recently emerged in critical discussions. About a year after I had written the first draft of this chapter, in which I had already made the points above, I came across two reviews, both published in March 1991, each of which reviewed two different recent books on men's history. I quote first from Michael S. Kimmel's review of *Making a Man of Him: Parents and the Sons' Education at an English Public School, 1929-1950* by Christine Heward (London: Routledge, 1988) and *Manliness and Morality: Middle Class Masculinity in Britain and America, 1800-1940,* edited by J. A. Morgan and James Walvin (New York: St. Martin's Press, 1987), from *Gender & Society* (5:1, 1991, pp. 118-121), and then I quote the concluding lines from J. William Gibson's review of *Secret Ritual and Manhood in Victorian America* by Mark C. Carnes (New Haven, CT: Yale University Press, 1990) and *Manhood in the Making* by David D. Gilmore (New Haven, CT: Yale University Press, 1990) from *American Quarterly* (43:1, 1991, pp. 128-133):

> As histories, both volumes add to our understanding of the emergence in the nineteenth century of middle-class masculinity as hegemonic in England and the United States. . . . As social science, however, each is significantly limited as an analytical tool by the systematic omission of one word: women. . . . Can we imagine a history of masculinity that does not place the relations between women and men as the central analytical process? To do so would write women back into historical invisibility, and this time in the guise of exploring gender. Certainly women and men, as gendered actors, deserve more than that. (Kimmel, 1991, pp. 120-121)

> To move the study of gender forward, the new masculinist scholars need to engage in a more direct dialogue with their feminist predecessors and contemporaries. Otherwise, the real danger of fragmentation and stagnation will hurt everyone's work. (Gibson, 1991, p. 133)

To Kimmel's and Gibson's critiques of these four works, with which I concur, I would add my own critique in the same vein of a fifth contemporaneous volume dealing with similar subject matter, *Meanings for Manhood: Constructions of Masculinity in Victorian America,* edited by Mark C. Carnes and Clyde Griffen (Carnes & Griffen, 1990). This volume is particularly instructive because it contains as a concluding chapter an overview of the chapters in the volume by Nancy Cott, in which she presents an analysis of a problem she identifies analogous to that which I have presented here and offers a useful solution:

> The tendency of essays in this collection to describe the "man's sphere" and the "woman's sphere" as though these were distinct physical sites—rather than ideological constructions about propriety—can probably be pinned on the earlier historiography in women's history. Women's historians are leaving behind this peculiar reification. The understanding of "spheres" as geographical more than ideological—as though life was physically divided into two arenas—was a reductive move, further exaggerated by equating the man's sphere with the "public," the woman's sphere with the "private." . . . Historians of women have lately been trying to distinguish between "woman's sphere" and women's culture—the latter something more portable or pervasive than geographical. Perhaps men's historians ought to do the same. (Cott, 1990, pp. 206-207)

I deem it very important that men's studies not come to denote a kind of separatist scholarship, which focuses only on male-male relations and leaves women out of the picture. Aside from the obvious sexism of such a practice, and its falsification of the historical record, this would be particularly troubling in the present period for at least the following two additional reasons. One, it would be distressingly ironic if men's studies scholarship went in such a regressive direction at precisely the moment when scholarship in general is taking a strong interactionist, deconstructive turn aimed at breaking down dichotomies of gender, race, sexual orientation, and other categories. I think it's been for some time now becoming increasingly clear that researchers are studying the social construction of gender and sexualities in a manner that makes it no longer possible to neatly parse out the construction of gender into men's versus women's studies, or lesbian and gay versus straight studies, for that matter.

Second, thinking about men in the popular mind has now been captured by the extravagances of what is called the "mythopoetic" men's movement (see Bly, 1990; Harding, 1992). This movement contains a kind of separatism that I and many others find deeply troubling, and I believe scholars should do as much as possible to distance ourselves from and critique the problematic aspects of this tendency (Brod, 1992).

Though the tendency to analyze masculinities as solely constructed along axes of relationships and power vis-à-vis men can once again render women invisible, as I have been arguing, I hasten to add that it need not inevitably do so. That is, an analysis may well show how men construct masculinities in their interactions with each other *if* this constructing is itself problematized and the construction of masculinities on intramale lines is itself shown to be an aspect of male privilege.

Having up to this point discussed the necessity for including women in analyses of masculinities, I now turn my attention more directly to the question of theorizing nonhegemonic masculinities. What I propose is that nonhegemonic masculinities must always be simultaneously theorized along two axes, the male-female axis of men's power over women within the marginalized grouping, and the male-male axis of nonhegemonic men's relative lack of power vis-à-vis hegemonic men. Further, the analysis must show the interrelationships between these two axes—the tensions, trade-offs, and contradictions experienced by nonhegemonic men as they try to position themselves in this terrain (Alcoff, 1989). Men of nonhegemonic groups are torn between the different and conflicting norms and standards of masculinity and patriarchy of their own and the hegemonic culture. Finally, women must be portrayed in this process as active participants who respond in various ways to men's positioning themselves in and at various sites, in varying degrees of resistance and accommodation, and as initiators of their own gender strategies.

The relational nature of gender as site and result of interactive negotiations amid structures of domination rather than as a set of static sex roles must be preserved in such analyses (Gerson & Peiss, 1985; Kimmel, 1986; Lopate & Thorne, 1978). The static, ahistorical overtones the sex roles framework inherits from its separate spheres heritage must be overcome in favor of a more radically dynamic and interactive social constructionist conception of gender. An influential formulation of the criticism of the concept of sex roles on which I am relying here was offered by Judith Stacey and Barrie Thorne in their 1985 article "The Missing Feminist Revolution in Sociology" (Stacey & Thorne, 1985):

Much of feminist sociology is cast in the language of roles ("sex roles," "the male role," "the female role") and emphasizes the process of "sex role socialization." This approach to the analysis of gender retains its functionalist roots, emphasizing consensus, stability, and continuity. . . . The notion of "role" focuses attention more on individuals than on social structures, and implies that "the female role" and "the male role" are complementary (i.e., separate or different but equal). The terms are depoliticizing; they strip experience from its historical and political context and neglect questions of power and conflict. It is significant that sociologists do not speak of "class roles" or "race roles." (p. 307)

In the remainder of this paper I turn to the case of Jewish masculinity to illustrate this theoretical frame as a case in point. Because I cannot here attempt even the beginnings of any kind of systematic, comprehensive analysis of Jewish masculinity, I shall begin by drawing on one argument from a work that is an example of the kind of analysis of which I am arguing there should be much more. In "Lifting Up the Shadow of Anti-Semitism: Jewish Masculinity in a New Light," Barbara Breitman (1988) analyzes what she, following Jacob Neusner, calls the "affective program" of the rabbis. The rabbinic tradition being referred to is that which emerges out of the tradition of medieval Jewish commentary and scholarship. Here is the rabbinic tradition's construction of the properly virtuous personality structure and set of emotional traits for Jewish men (quoting Jacob Neusner, "Emotion in the Talmud," *Tikkun,* 1:1, 1986, pp. 74-80):

> A simple catalogue of permissible feelings comprises humility, generosity, self-abnegation, love, a spirit of conciliation to the other, and eagerness to please. A list of impermissible emotions is made up of envy, ambition, jealousy, arrogance, sticking to one's opinion, self-centeredness, a grudging spirit, vengefulness. . . . aiming at the cultivation of the humble and malleable person, one who accepts everything and resents nothing . . . Temper marks the ignorant person, restraint and serenity, the learned one. . . . A mark of humility is the humble acceptance of suffering. . . . Submit, accept, conciliate, stay cool in emotion as much as in attitude, inside and outside. (Breitman, 1988, p. 106; elisions in original)

Breitman then uses psychoanalytic categories to argue that the self-abnegation called for by a people suffering under oppression for generations requires some psychic compensation. She argues that the rabbis found such compensation in two turns made in Jewish theology and culture: the rabbis' elevation of their own wisdom to near-divine status and a projection of their rage on to Jewish women. Thus Jewish sexism emerges as a simultaneous deflection and internalization by Jewish men of the dominant Gentile culture's anti-Semitism. This counterproductive strategy, counterproductive because it turns Jewish men and women against each other and thereby disempowers them from facing their true enemy, the hegemonic culture, appeals to Jewish men because it advances their own interests within Jewish culture if those interests are considered apart from their interests vis-à-vis the hegemonic culture. Hence, Jewish male sexism is imposed on Jewish culture by the hegemonic culture and also arises from within Jewish culture. Although it gives men more power from the standpoint of the internal dynamics of Jewish culture, it ultimately disempowers them relative to the hegemonic culture, because its sexism is a principal means by which Jewish culture internalizes hegemonic anti-Semitism and turns it against itself.

The particular forms Jewish masculinities take vary in changing historical circumstances as the community negotiates its identity within this matrix. Both women and men are participants in the articulations of gendered Jewishness. For example, the contemporary American stereotypes of the "Jewish Mother" and "Jewish American Princess" mark collisions between central European and United States norms and use Jewish women as scapegoats for anti-Semitic criticisms of Jewish culture for honoring strong independent women who took care of their families and for striving for economic successs, just as the stereotype of the Jewish man as a sexually impotent or incompetent bookworm (à la the early Woody Allen) marks an American anti-intellectualism and xenophobia. The latter also marks the connection between power and potency, as lack of patriarchal power appears as sexual emasculation (Lefkovitz, 1988).

Forced to affirm the value of the life of the mind, which is indeed traditionally valued in Jewish culture, against anti-Semitic attacks on it, many Jewish men have been forced into an overly rigid identification with this ideal to the extent that they perpetrate an overly zealous denial of the complementary life of the body, to their own great loss. The ideal of the intellectual Jewish male is held to so strongly because it emerges *both* from within the intellectual traditions of Jewish culture *and* as a defense mechanism against attacks on Jewish men for not conforming to dominant, more brawny standards of masculinity. It functions within Jewish culture as a mechanism of resistance by the culture as a whole against foreign gender norms imposed by the hegemonic culture but at the same time also as a means of perpetuating specifically Jewish patriarchal norms within a culture that valorizes intellectual over physical prowess. This sort of double bind is precisely characteristic of gender norms in non-hegemonic cultures.

Pressures on Jewish men to be "one of the boys" on the terms of the hegemonic culture lead them to deny their own cultural traditions and seek power vis-à-vis other men and vis-à-vis "their" women by seeking to conform to dominant norms. On the other hand, as a nonhegemonic "culture of resistance" to hegemonic norms, Jewish culture has an interest in fostering cross-gender alliances within the culture against the dominant culture. There are indeed strong egalitarian strains in Jewish traditions, in addition to its strong patriarchal strains.[4] Thus Jewish men face conflicting pressures for and against egalitarian relations with Jewish women and for and against Jewish as opposed to dominant non-Jewish forms of masculinity. Any account of Jewish masculinity must be sensitive to these complex and conflicting tendencies and pressures and sensitively attribute agency in the context of overarching structures all around.

Though I have used only the Jewish case as an example here, and even that only through one set of examples in the barest outline, I venture to hope that this has been sufficient to briefly demonstrate the type of questions to ask and the type of dynamics to account for in the many analyses of nonhegemonic masculinities that I think scholars need to undertake. Different particular issues will of course become salient in different nonhegemonic cultures. For example, as against the sexual emasculation of American Jewish men, many Third World men are "supersexualized," as were Jewish men in Nazi ideology (Dworkin, 1988; Staples, 1982). One must also be sensitive to inappropriate expropriations of concepts from nonhegemonic cultures by the hegemonic culture. For example, the use of the term macho as a synonym for sexist ignores the positive connotations of this term within Hispanic cultures, and its popularization in the United States is a case of Anglo men using their white skin privilege to deflect the critique of their male privilege, just as the use of working-class male images to denote traditional sexism renders the sexism of middle- and upper-class men less visible and therefore less challenged (Brod, 1989a, 1989b; Mirandé). Though the answers will differ, I think the types of questions one needs to ask will be very much the same.

I close with a comment on why I chose the Jewish case to illustrate my broader thesis about masculinities. The first and foremost reason is simply that this is who I am and what I know best. But there is another reason as well. The current tendency to pluralize masculinities and deconstruct gender is heavily influenced by the postmodern philosophical currents that arose after World War II, as well as by critiques by women of color of monolithic white Western feminism.[5] Postmodernism was born, however, not just out of a particular time but out of a particular place as well.

That place was Auschwitz. It was there that modernity and humanism, figuratively and literally, went up in smoke.

But the currently fashionable counterhegemonic trivium of "gender, race, and class," sometimes expanded to a counterquadrivium of "gender, race, class, and sexual orientation," does not accord anti-Semitism entry into the pantheon of notable oppressions integrated into contemporary analyses. This is despite anti-Semitism's absolute centrality in the social forces determining the historical events to which postmodernism responds. Just as one is prepared to castigate as sexist any analysis that ignores sexism, so I am prepared to castigate as anti-Semitic any analysis that ignores anti-Semitism. Most analyses of the social construction of gender, indeed most of postmodernism, fall into this camp.

If the accusation of anti-Semitism hurled against so much of current scholarship seems too harsh, let me then say just one more word about contemporary sensitivity, or lack thereof, to anti-Semitism. A certain sensitivity has by now been reached, at least in oppositional, counterhegemonic circles, to charges of sexism, racism, or heterosexism. That is to say, many people, if faced with such charges, have learned not to react defensively and are willing to reexamine what they have said or done to probe the validity of the charges, to see if they have been subtly and unintentionally oppressive or offensive. They do not react as if they are being charged with being rapists, members of the Ku Klux Klan, or queer-bashers. But people accused of anti-Semitism still tend to react as if they were being called Nazis. This is one of the lingering effects of the Holocaust. It has made rational discussion of subtle anti-Semitism virtually impossible. The Holocaust has scarred the political imagination of the late 20th century. The flames of the Holocaust have singed us all—flames do leave scars, and scar tissue is not flexible. The dark clouds generated by the smokestacks of the Auschwitz crematoria have so overshadowed all other aspects of anti-Semitism short of genocide that anti-Semitism still stands as a category apart, unintegrated into current thinking on gender and masculinities, even where one would think its relevance would be most obvious.

For example, the index to Klaus Theweleit's two-volume work on *Male Fantasies,* an examination of "the emotional core of fascism as it was revealed in the novels and memoirs of the Freikorps," German mercenary bands that evolved after World War I and became the basis for the Nazi militia and army, reveals mention of Jews on only 15 out of 1000 pages (Theweleit, 1987 & 1989). What does it mean that the primary German men's studies work to be translated into English, one that has received high praise both in Germany and the United States, and indeed contains much that warrants such praise, has such a glaring omission? If anti-Semitism can be so ignored here of all places, in an analysis of the origins of fascism, then it is no wonder that subtler issues of subordinated Jewishness and hegemonic Christianity have not received the attention they deserve in analyses of masculinities. To give but one other more distant example, do we fully understand the extent to which Victorianism in the United States in the latter 19th century was deployed to solidify "white" Anglo-Saxon gender norms against waves of "darker" immigrants and how this impacted on Jewish and other immigrant communities?

I hope that this chapter will help to engender, in both senses, further discussions of Jewishness and gender and of masculinities and femininities.

Notes

1. Earlier versions of this chapter were originally presented under the title "Emasculated Masculinities: Jews and Other Others" at the Canadian Political Science Association Convention, Victoria, British Columbia, May 27-29, 1990; "Crossing the Disciplines: Cultural Studies in the 1990s," a conference sponsored by the Oklahoma Project for Discourse and Theory and held in conjunction with the 15th Annual Meeting of the Semiotic Society of America, The University of Oklahoma, October 19-21, 1990; and at the Third Interdisciplinary Men's Studies Conference in Tucson, Arizona, June 6, 1991, sponsored by the National Organization for Men Against Sexism; and published in the 1993 *Working Papers* series of the Institute for the Study of Women and Men at the University of Southern California, Los Angeles.

2. I am indebted to Michael Kimmel for this reference, as well as for the observation that this follows a pattern of conceptual migration from gay to men's studies.

3. This critique has been raised by several reviews of men's studies books. See Lois Banner's Review Essay in *Signs, 14*(3), Spring 1989, pp. 703-708, and Anthony McMahon's review of Brod in *Thesis Eleven* #24, 1989, pp. 166-170. (I cannot resist noting here that the most extensive review of this book in the literature of the profeminist men's movement itself criticized it for harping *too much* on patriarchy and men's power. See the review by David Leverenz in *Changing Men, 19,* Winter-Spring 1990, pp. 19-20.)

4. On Jewish feminism see, for example, Susannah Heschel, *On Being a Jewish Feminist: A Reader* (New York: Schocken, 1983); Susan Weidman Schneider, *Jewish and Female: Choices and Changes in Our Lives Today* (New York: Simon & Schuster, 1984); Melanie Kaye Kantrowitz and Irena Klepfisz, eds., *The Tribe of Dina: A Jewish Women's Anthology,* rev. ed. (Boston: Beacon, 1989); Evelyn Torton Beck, ed., *Nice Jewish Girls: A Lesbian Anthology* (Trumansburg, NY: The Crossing Press, 1982); and the journals *Lilith* and *Bridges.*

5. I am indebted to Barrie Thorne for emphasizing the latter to me.

References

Alcoff, L. (1989). Cultural feminism versus post-structuralism: The identity crisis in feminist theory. In M. R. Malson, J. F. O'Barr, S. Westphal-Wihl, & M. Wyer (Eds.), *Feminist theory in practice and process* (pp. 295-326). Chicago: University of Chicago Press.

Bly, R. (1990). *Iron John: A book about men.* Reading, MA: Addison-Wesley.

Bradshaw, J. (1982). Now what are they up to? Men in the "men's movement." In S. Friedman & E. Sarah (Eds.), *On the problem of men: Two feminist conferences* (pp. 174-189). London: The Women's Press.

Breitman, B. (1988). Lifting up the shadow of anti-Semitism: Jewish masculinity in a new light. In H. Brod (Ed.), *A mensch among men: Explorations in Jewish masculinity* (pp. 101-117). Freedom, CA: The Crossing Press.

Brod, H. (Ed.). (1987). *The making of masculinities: The new men's studies.* Boston: Unwin Hyman.

Brod, H. (1989a). Fraternity, equality, liberty. In M. S. Kimmel & M. A. Messner (Eds.), *Men's lives* (pp. 276-287). New York: Macmillan.

Brod, H. (1989b). Work clothes and leisure suits: The class basis and bias of the men's movement. In M. S. Kimmel & M. A. Messner (Eds.), *Men's lives* (pp. 598-605). New York: Macmillan.

Brod, H. (1990, March 21). Scholarly studies of men: The field is an essential complement to women's studies. *Chronicle of Higher Education,* pp. B2-3.

Brod, H. (1992). The mythopoetic men's movement: A political critique. In C. Harding (Ed.), *Wingspan: Inside the men's movement* (pp. 232-236). New York: St. Martin's.

Carnes, M. C., & Griffen, C. (1990). (Eds.). *Meanings for manhood: Constructions of masculinity in Victorian America.* Chicago: University of Chicago Press.

Carrigan, T., Connell, R. W., & Lee, J. (1985). Toward a new sociology of masculinity. *Theory and Society, 14*(5), 551-603.

Connell, R. W. (1987). *Gender and power: Society, the person, and sexual politics.* Stanford, CA: Stanford University Press.

Cott, N. (1990). On men's history and women's history. In M. C. Carnes & C. Griffen (Eds.), *Meanings for manhood: Constructions of masculinity in Victorian America* (pp. 205-211). Chicago: University of Chicago Press.

Dworkin, A. (1988). The sexual mythology of anti-Semitism. In H. Brod (Ed.), *A mensch among men: Explorations in Jewish masculinity* (pp. 118-123). Freedom, CA: The Crossing Press.

Gerson, J. M., & Peiss, K. (1985). Boundaries, negotiation, consciousness: Reconceptualizing gender relations. *Social Problems, 32*(4), 317-331.

Gerzon, M. (1982). *A choice of heroes: The changing faces of American manhood.* Boston: Houghton Mifflin.

Gibson, W. J. (1991). Feminist ideas about masculinity. *American Quarterly, 43*(1), 128-133.

Giddens, A. (1982). *A contemporary critique of historical materialism.* New York: Macmillan.

Harding, C. (1992). (Ed.). *Wingspan: Inside the men's movement.* New York: St. Martin's.

Hearn, J. (1989). *Some sociological issues in researching men and masculinities* (Hallsworth Research Fellowship Working Paper No. 2). Manchester, UK: University of Manchester.

Kaufman, M. (Ed.). (1987). *Beyond patriarchy: Essays by men on pleasure, power, and change.* Toronto: Oxford University Press.

Kimmel, M. S. (1986). Introduction: Toward men's studies. *American Behavioral Scientist, 29*(5), 517-529.

Kimmel, M. S. (1991). Book Reviews. *Gender & Society, 5*(1), 120-121.

Kimmel, M. S., & Mosmiller, T. E. (1992). *Against the tide: Pro-feminist men in the United States, 1776-1990. A documentary history.* Boston: Beacon.

Lefkovitz, L. (1988). Coats and tales: Joseph stories and myths of Jewish masculinity. In H. Brod (Ed.), *A mensch among men: Explorations in Jewish masculinity* (pp. 19-29). Freedom, CA: The Crossing Press.

Lopate, H., & Thorne, B. (1978). On the term "sex roles." *Signs, 3,* 718-721.

Mirandé, A. Que gacho es ser macho: It's a drag to be a macho man. *Aztlan, 17*(2), 63-89.

Pleck, E. H., & Pleck, J. H. (Eds.). (1980). *The American man.* Englewood Cliffs, NJ: Prentice Hall.

Sedgwick, E. K. (1985). *Between men: English literature and male homosocial desire.* New York: Columbia University Press.

Smith-Rosenberg, C. (1975). The female world of love and ritual. *Signs, 1,* 1-29.

Stacey, J., & Thorne, B. (1985). The missing feminist revolution in sociology. *Social Problems, 32*(4), 301-316.

Staples, R. (1982). *Black masculinity: The black male's role in American society.* San Francisco: The Black Scholar's Press.

Theweleit, K. (1987 & 1989). *Male fantasies* (Vol. 1, S. Conway, Trans.; Vol. 2, E. Carter & C. Turner, Trans.). Minneapolis: University of Minnesota Press.

Weeks, J. (1985). *Sexuality and its discontents: Meanings, myths and modern sexualities.* London: Routledge & Kegan Paul.

6

Theorizing Unities and Differences Between Men and Between Masculinities

JEFF HEARN
DAVID L. COLLINSON

In sociology, as in most of the social sciences, "men" and "masculinity" are usually *implicit* but *central/centered:* They are at the center of discourses. Similarly, in much, though significantly not all, everyday social life "men" and "masculinity" are the One to the (many) Other(s). In contrast "women" have often been the object of discourses and/or at the margins of discourses objectified in relation to some supposedly neutral center of men. "Men" and "masculinity" are constantly known, referred to, implicated, assumed as the subject of discourse.

Indeed references to "masculinity" (singular) usually affirm this unitary voice of discourse. "Men" are talked of and about by "men," as well as by others, including "women," "girls," and "boys," and simultaneously "men" are relatively rarely talked on. They are shown but not said, visible but not questioned. Not talking of men is a major and structured way of not beginning to talk of and question men's power in relation to women, children, young people, and indeed other men, or perhaps more precisely men's relations within power.

In talking of "men," "masculinity," and "masculinities," it is particularly important to continually contextualize the discussion in power and power relations. We shall from here onward generally not be placing quotation marks around the words *men* and *masculinities,* but we will be using them only in that sense, which denaturalizes and problematizes them. As several commentators have recently pointed out, there is a danger in focusing on men and masculinities, even within critical work, in a way that *reexcludes* women and "femininities" (Brod, 1990). One way of avoiding this possibility is to consistently locate men and masculinities as power relations, including power relations with women, children, young people, and other men.

Current critical studies on men and masculinity, whether theoretical or empirical, face a particular and acute contradiction: to *name* men and masculinity; to make those categories visible and to recognize their power; and to *deconstruct* them, to undermine, subvert, and dismantle them. In this chapter we will make men and masculinity *explicit* and thus simultaneously, and somewhat paradoxically, assist in the *decentering* of men and masculinity in discourse. This involves making problematic the ways in which men and masculinity may be conventionally and unproblematically at the center of discourse, often as explicit or implicit, transcendent subjects, explanations, or foundations. Thus in this chapter we attempt to contribute to the more explicit, yet deconstructive, theorizing of men and masculinities, in a way that avoids recentering men at the center of discourse. This is an urgent and necessary task for understanding/changing men in both the general and the particular, both historical and contemporary analysis, and both theory and practice.

We shall attempt to do this in the following sections: first, the exploration of some of the different uses of the terms both within and outside sociology; second, a brief discussion of some of the major challenges to implicit and often nongendered uses; third, a consideration of some possible ways of relating men and masculinities; and fourth, spelling out some of the many, diverse ways in which men and masculinities may be both social unities and social differences (or subject to social differences), and may both be social divisions and relate to other social divisions. This is followed by a discussion of some specific examples of types of men and masculinities and a critique of the types of approaches to men and masculinities. In conclusion, we briefly consider the significance of this analysis of categories in the context of historical change.

The Social and the Sociological

The categories of men and masculinity are taken for granted in the social sciences, in sociology, and indeed in everyday social life. Within most sociological inquiry, the categories usually remain implicit and untheorized. This may even apply to some social scientific analyses that are broadly sensitive to gender or to the theorizing of the category of women. Yet sociology, like everyday social life, is continually involved in the production and reproduction of categories of men and masculinity. This is so in terms of the use of categories that are produced by men (and masculinities), both as everyday social actors and as sociologists (with their own everyday social life, of course), and the use of categories that themselves refer to types of men and masculinity.

Although our major interest here is with the case of sociology, much of what we are saying applies to the other social sciences. Indeed, the implicitness of the categories of men and masculinity applies all the more so in economics, political science, and management theory, at least in their dominant malestream traditions (O'Brien, 1981). The cases of anthropology, psychology, psychoanalysis, and social psychology are somewhat distinct. These have their own strong malestream traditions in which culturally specific gendered notions of males and females have figured. However, in these cases, albeit for different reasons, the categories of males and females have often been used in a naturalistic manner—in one case, within a discourse of Nature/Culture and Race/Culture, and in the other within a discourse of Body/Mind and Biology/Personality. Thus within the broad context of the social sciences, sociology could be said to be relatively more open to the deconstruction of gender than those social sciences with rather stronger naturalistic or culturalistic traditions.

Implicit Men, Implicit Masculinity

Sociology is full of analyses that take men for granted as the dominant gender. A classic example of this kind of recasting of men and masculinity can be drawn from Max Weber's (1967) *Protestant Ethic and the Spirit of Capitalism* (also see Bologh, 1990; Morgan, 1992). Weber appears to draw his own examples of both the Protestant ethic and the spirit of capitalism from social and historical accounts about men, both as individuals (Martin Luther, Benjamin Franklin) and as collectivities (Calvinists, Baptists). The possible Protestant ethic of women or the "spirit of women capitalists" is not explored—presumably they were at home or on the shop floor of the chocolate factory, not in the counting house or the board room. In the light of these complications, we may ask to what extent Weber was bringing his own masculinity to bear on the construction of the ethic and the spirit.

Somewhat similarly, neither Marx nor Durkheim presented a critical appraisal of men or masculinity within economic class and exploitation (see O'Brien, 1979; Hearn, 1987), and ritual and anomie, respectively. Marx's analyses of exploitative class relations and Durkheim's analyses of ritual and anomie are usually analyses of men and specific forms of masculinity. In other sociological texts words specifically describing collectivities have often been used to mean men. "Society," "working class," and "organization" may all be used to mean men or particular types of men, such as working-class men or men managers. These have often been ways for men to talk about men without saying so.

The second and inverse case is when the term *men* is used to refer to people, humans, or adults, that is, excluding young people in the last case. Men may in this case become society, rather than vice versa.

A third and more complex case is for gender to be invoked, but only (or overwhelmingly) in relation to women and femininity. In contrast, apparently nongendered concepts and constructs may be invoked in relation to men and masculinity. An interesting example of this is to be found in recent debates on class and gender in sociology. The main terms of the debate have been set between economic approaches to class and stratification, based on employment, on the one hand, and *women's* relationship to these approaches, and specifically husband's employment, on the other. The former approaches are presumed to be nongendered, the latter approaches gendered. However, these former approaches are, of course, just as gendered (even though they are gendered implicitly) as the latter. The difference is that the former are gendered around the implicit assumption of men as simultaneous employees and heads of economic household units. This problem is approached in rather different ways by, among others, Sylvia Walby (1986), in terms of husbands as a class, and Christine Delphy and Diana Leonard (1986), in terms of the hereditary transmission of the constitution of classes. What is rare is an explicit attempt to develop a gendered analysis of men and their economic class position.

Explicit Men, Explicit Masculinities

Following these usages, there are a number of ways in which the categories of men and masculinity are used explicitly. In some cases, the term *men* may be used to mean males. In their sociological usage a contrast is sometimes drawn between males as sex, and men as gender; even so, the terms *males* and *male* are frequently used to refer to people who are men and who are unlikely to be sexed as males. Men are not (necessarily) males, and vice versa. There are a number of reasons for this, including cultural specificities in men and males; distinctions between boys, men, young males, and males; the 15 forms of intersexuality (that do not conform to XX or XY chromosomal patterns); the various physiological and cultural forms of gender change, whether temporary or permanent; and the differential relation of men and males to history and trans-history respectively. Men certainly exist in relation to the category of male(s). Indeed we find it helpful to see men as "a gender that exists or is presumed to exist *in most direct relation* to the *generalized male sex,* that being the sex that is not female, or not the sex related to the gender of women" (Hearn, 1989c, p. 11; emphases in original).

These (sociological) distinctions are, of course, not necessarily in keeping with other societal usages of the terms *men* and *males*—as, for example, in government and other official statistics. In the British case, births, deaths, and much other demographic information are unambiguously classified for males and females, although much, though not all, information on economic activity is classified by men and women (OPCS, 1984a, 1984b).

Another form of explicit use of *men* and *masculinity* is when the terms are invoked in an explicitly gendered form, but without consideration of their social constitution and social problematization. Of particular interest here are those texts focusing on organizational or managerial material that use the term *man* or *Man*. For example, Walker and Guest's (1952) *Man on the Assembly Line* actively deals with men, but does not explore either the social construction of men or the specific implications of being on the assembly line for the construction of masculinity. The initial focus on men is soon displaced by analysis in terms of workers. The two categories soon become interchangeable in the analysis. Having said that, there is a mass of information in this and similar texts that can be reformulated in terms of the construction of forms of masculinities. This issue is handled rather differently in Whyte's (1956) *Organization Man,* where we do find a more explicit discussion of masculinity—perhaps prompted by his consideration of the relationship of home and work.

Finally, in this section, we need to note those usages of *men* and *masculinity* that (a) are explicit, (b) refer to gender, and (c) base their use in the acknowledgment of social constitution and social problematization. It is rare in mainstream/malestream sociology for all three criteria to be satisfied. An example of a recent study that goes some way in this direction is that by Keith Grint (1988) on the historical development of equal (or unequal) pay in the Post Office from 1870 to 1961. In this case *men* is used to refer to aggregation of certain individual men and to the interactions of those men. *Men* can also be used as a collective term over and above aggregation of particular men.

At this point it may be useful to note an important methodological issue—namely, that the (explicit) invoking of formerly implicit social categories brings a double challenge to the analyst: On one hand, there is the possibility of objectifying and fixing those categories, so obscuring the analysis of lived experiences; on the other, there is the possibility of deconstructing those categories, thus transcending them, historically and conceptually, and obscuring lived experiences in a different way. This double challenge is a general methodological issue that may apply in the analysis of most social categories, perhaps most social phenomena. It also has a resonance with the political dilemmas around the historically temporary adoption of categories by those who are so categorized *by others,* as a paradoxical basis for *their own* political organization, action, and change. This usually involves the redefinition of the meaning of particular identities in a more valued and positive light. An example of this is the use of the category of homosexual, initially given in medical and other professional discourses, as a basis for subsequent political organization, action, and change by people identifying with same-gender sexualities. Such political action may in turn be constrained by those particular identities.

Challenges to Nongendered Categories of Men and Masculinity

Many perspectives and standpoints have challenged some of the practices described in the previous section. Most obvious, and probably most influential, among these critiques are feminist theory and practice and the feminist naming of men as men (Hanmer, 1990). Although feminist theory and practice have addressed the problem of men throughout its development, the major emphasis relevant to our discussion has been, perhaps not surprisingly, on the analysis of women's experiences of the consequences of men's domination rather than the focused theorization of men and masculinity. However, in different ways other challenges have also named men as gendered. For example, gay scholarship, by virtue of its reference to same-gender sexuality, necessarily names people in terms of gender. Having said that, gay (men's) scholarship does not necessarily address wider issues of men and masculinity explicitly, nor indeed is it always sympathetic to feminism (Stanley, 1984). A further challenge has come from the variety of writing by men that explicitly focuses on men. Some of this has been presented under the self-given title of "men's studies"; some do are not adhere to that framing. Some are explicitly antisexist, antipatriarchal; some are not so (Hearn 1989b, 1992; Hearn & Morgan, 1990).

Different kinds of challenge have come, though usually less directly, from poststructuralism and the deconstruction of structures and from postmodernism, both as the sociology of postmodernism and postmodern sociology. Often these particular theoretical perspectives have been produced with little reference to gender, another way for men to talk about men without saying so. Poststructuralism and postmodernism can be seen as a general criticism of fixed categories and categoricalism in theorizing gender (Connell, 1985); they have also interacted with feminist (e.g., Morris, 1988), gay (e.g., Weeks, 1985), and men's antisexist scholarship (e.g., Brittan, 1989).

The last few years have seen a shift toward a growing emphasis on cultural theory, semiology, and poststructuralism in the critical study of men and masculinities. This is to be found in different ways in texts such as *Male Order* (Chapman & Rutherford, 1988) and *Masculinity and Power* (Brittan, 1989). Another example is Middleton's (1989) arguing for the philosophical superiority of difference over oppression as a basis for theorizing men, and thus gender. To be more precise, each of these three texts can be located in that tension between categoricalism and practice-based politics (cf. Connell, 1985). Rather similar issues have been highlighted in various empirical studies, such as those by Cockburn (1983) on men in the newspaper industry and by Willis (1977) on young working-class men. Both of these consider both the unities and differences between men, and some of the interrelationships of these unities and differences.

The above challenges, and indeed their relationships with each other, seem to represent the most hopeful possibilities for the explicit analysis of men and masculinity. Before considering some of the unities and differences between men and masculinity in the light of those challenges, it is necessary to say a little about the relationship of men and masculinity.

The Relationship of Men and Masculinity

It will already be apparent that men and masculinity are not two fixed concepts: They have different meanings and significances within different discourses. Thus there is not one given relationship of men and masculinity. It is probably fair to say that the dominant way of relating men and masculinity within the social sciences has been the sex (gender) role perspective. This has been extensively criticized in recent years, for example in terms of the neglect of historical change and an adequate theorization of the individual and society (Connell, 1985, 1987; Eichler, 1980). We broadly accept these critiques and thus we are concerned here with formulations that explicitly recognize the importance of power relations and practice. As noted, these critiques have also led to the recognition of the importance of speaking of masculinities (plural) rather than just masculinity (singular) (Carrigan, Connell, & Lee, 1985).

So how does one relate men to masculinities, and vice versa? One powerful way is to see men as existing and persisting in the material bases of society, in relation to particular social relations of production and reproduction; in comparison, masculinities exist and persist as ideology, often in their surface form in terms of elements of production and reproduction (Hearn, 1987, p. 98). Particular masculinities are not fixed formulas but rather they are combinations of actions and signs, part powerful, part arbitrary, performed in reaction and relation to complex material relations and emotional demands; these signify that this is man. Masculinities are thus ideological signs of particular men of the gender class of men, particularly in relation to reproduction broadly defined. For example, "being macho" (itself a racist turn of phrase) involves a variety of ideological signs of particular men of the gender class of men. This ideological and significatory emphasis may be supplemented by the agency and strategy of what men do to reproduce ourselves/themselves as men or our/their sense of self as men.

Masculinities thus provide sources of and resources for the development and retention of gender identity. These emphases on ideology, signification, and agency should not divert attention from also seeing masculinities in terms of the ordering of institutional practices. A useful example of seeing masculinity as the ordering of institutional practices is Christine Heward's (1988) *Making a Man of Him*. In this text, she argues that "(i)t was through their sons that parents sought to ensure the family's future social position. Bringing up sons was about masculinity but it was much more importantly about social class. . . . Becoming a man was about having a suitable occupation, income and social position, able to support a dependent wife and accompanying household" (p. 197). Further approaches to masculinity include the institutional ordering of personality, the development of life histories, and the relation between the two of them.

These brief attempts to relate men and masculinities are all very well, but they do not resolve the need for a relational or dialectical approach to gender. Or to put this another way, they do not address the complexities of the many ways in which men and masculinities, and their relationships, are themselves located within socially variable forms of gender relations. Thus in referring to gender classes, material bases, ideologies, signs, practices, and so on, it is necessary to understand these in a relational and therefore fluid way and not in any fixed sense.

Men, Masculinities, and Social Divisions

Having focused on some of the possible relations of men and masculinities, we now turn more directly to the relationship of men and masculinities to social divisions. We shall consider these relationships in terms of both the unities that exist between men and between masculinities and the differences that exist between men and between masculinities. These unities and differences are inextricably interrelated: They are a condition and consequence of each other. Just as control and resistance reproduce each other, so do unities and differences of men and masculinities. In several senses social divisions, such as those of age, ethnicity, economic class, and so on, may produce and be produced by men and masculinities as categories. The social unities and the social differences between different men and masculinities are themselves produced by men, and indeed by masculinities. Social categories, such as men, and also women, as well as other categories that may be socially defined as nongendered, for example, the working classes, may themselves be dominantly produced and reproduced by men. Thus the relationships of men and masculinities to social divisions must take into account:

1. Men and masculinities being social divisions
2. Men and masculinities being formed in/by social divisions
3. Men and masculinities forming other social divisions
4. Men and masculinities also forming unities and differences that reflect and reinforce other social divisions

All the above analysis and examples also have to acknowledge cultural variability. What might be meant by men, masculinities, social divisions, and their various relationships varies between and within societies and cultures.

Unities and Commonalities

First, let us consider the unities, or commonalities between men, that is, men as a class or a gender class. Here we are concerned with social divisions of men, as distinct from those who are not men, most obviously women, children, and boys, as well as others of different genders (and/or sexes). This perspective is implicit and sometimes explicit in feminist, especially radical feminist, analyses: Women may be seen as a class, with the implication that men, too, are a class. So men are "not women" who oppress women (see Braidotti, 1987). Then we are obliged to ask what is the nature or basis of that gender class relationship and its comparability or otherwise to economic class relations. There are a number of variants on this gender class approach: Gender class as a general political statement, gender as a given biological essence, and gender as sexuality (MacKinnon, 1982) and those more specific feminist formulations—men as the "main enemy," as that class that benefits from the family mode of production—*in the home* (Delphy, 1977), and men as the class concerned with appropriating the means of reproduction (O'Brien, 1981). A major point about these latter two formulations is the notion that all men benefit from the family mode of production and from the social institution of paternity even though clearly not all are husbands or fathers. Similarly, the father may persist as a figure of power even though some individuals, women and men, do not know a father of their own, biological or otherwise. An important point is that fatherhood is a social institution, a hypothetical concretization. *Men* here refers to that gender class of people who so benefit from particular material relations around reproduction, housework, sexuality, violence, or emotional/care work beyond early child work. Thus men may be seen as simply the class that benefits from particular material relations over women. This is comparable to the bourgeois benefiting from capitalist relations over the proletariat, even though individual bourgeois may be in all sorts of material circumstances, including poverty and bankruptcy. The notion of class highlights the question of structural relations.

A modification of this gender class approach to men is to see men not as a class as such but as a shorthand for the aggregation of subclasses that exist semiautonomously in relative sexuality, fertility, child care, other care, and violence. For example, Mieli's (1980) analysis of the oppression of gays by nongays/heterosexuals introduces the notion of differentiation among men. Men are in effect "the sum of . . . particular class divisions, and the cumulative result of these divisions heaped on one another"

(Hearn, 1987, p. 64). Other differentiations, by class, ethnicity, age, and so on, complicate further any class relation of men with women.

Unities and Differences

According to this gender class view of men, we would expect to find different masculinities existing in terms of men's differential location in relation to these structured relations. For example, we might expect to find distinctions between gay, nonhierarchic heterosexual, and hierarchic heterosexual; between white and black; between nonfathers and fathers; unpaid careers, paid careers, and noncareers; and nonviolent, violent, and military (state violent) masculinities. Such masculinities may in turn be indicative or representative of men's relative stable locations with respect to structural relations, for example, as in the case of military masculinities, or of men's more temporary locations, for example, as temporary careers. As such, masculinities are about power relations, including power relations to women.

The possible unities between men are thus themselves complex; in addition there are the various debates on the problematic significance of the biological penis and the cultural phallus. It is still much more difficult to construct unities with respect to masculinities, diverse as they seem. Middleton (1989) notes this diversity and suggests:

> To speak legitimately of *a* discourse of *masculinity* [italics added] it would be necessary to show that a particular set of usages was located structurally within a clearly defined institution with its own methods, objects and practices. Otherwise the reference to discourses of masculinity is simply a reference to repeated patterns of linguistic usage, which may be significant, but cannot be theorised in the way some legal and medical discourses can. Masculinity is produced within some discourses in the stricter theoretical sense but most examples of "masculine" utterance are not structured discourses. They are not organised around specific knowledges. (p. 17)

Although we think that Middleton's assertions are substantively dubious, we do consider that he is indirectly making an important point on the unlikeliness of unified masculinity. Even if one considers masculinity/ masculinities with respect to the possible gender class of men, the possibility of unified masculinity seems remote. The traditions of supposedly universalizable masculinity-femininity scales and continua (Bem, 1977) seem in this context somewhat ridiculous.

Differences and Diversity

This moves us on, appropriately, to the consideration of diversity of and differences between men and masculinities. Here we are concerned with differences within the category of men, including different types of men and/or different relational positionings of different men at different times and places, and in different social sites. Thus in one sense these differences refer to types of men and masculinities; in another they refer to the interrelation of men/masculinities *with* other social divisions.

This section thus elaborates on Carrigan, Connell, and Lee's (1985) pluralizing of masculinity to masculinities. Their argument rests partly on a recognition of psychological differentiation and diversity among men and partly on the analysis of the importance of the reciprocal interrelationship of masculinities, albeit in the context of hegemonic masculinity. In keeping with this approach, there is a need to consider cultural and historical specificities; the integral interrelation of power, interpersonal relations, and psychodynamics; and, moreover, the interrelations of masculinities.

Kimmel and Messner's (1989) collection, *Men's Lives,* explicitly brings together readings on variations among men. These include differences in race and ethnicity, age, economic class, region, bodily state, sexuality, social arrangements, and relationships (see also Astrachan, 1986). Similarly, Middleton (1989) asserts: "There is no uniformity about men. The heterogeneity must be recognised, across age, class, race, religion, and world view. Yet these schisms are themselves reproduced through 'differential unities' between men" (p. 18; see, for example, Cockburn, 1983, on the relationship of the British trade unions, NGA and NATSOPA).

The theme of diversity is also explored in a recent political document that notes that it is an "illusion that masculinity is a single, uniform, and innate form." It continues: "Instead we want to emphasise . . . the sheer variety of masculine forms. These complex and often contradictory forms and relations are there in the specific histories of black, gay, bisexual, class-related, disabled, able-bodied, young and old, regional masculinities" (Men, Masculinities and Socialism Group, 1990, p. 18).

There are a number of different ways in which such differences may be conceptualized in relation to men and masculinities. A provisional exploration of these differences of (both) men and masculinities suggests attention to both the following types and their interrelations. Various men and masculinities may be defined in relation to other men, other masculinities, women, femininities, or some further difference(s). It is not possible to produce a complete taxonomy. Those listed next are merely examples of particular sources or references of identity that cut across notions of unified masculinity:

1. *Age,* or more precisely age-ness (referring to the social construction of age); thus there are young men, middle-aged men, old men, and many more particular types
2. *Appearance,* e.g., smart, transvestite, rough
3. *Bodily facility,* e.g., men with disabilities, able-bodied men, strong, weak
4. *Care,* e.g., professional, soft man, real man
5. *Economic class,* e.g., unemployed, working class, proletarian, shop floor, middle class, petit-bourgeois, manager, bourgeois
6. *Ethnicity,* e.g., black, white, Jewish, Chinese
7. *Fatherhood and relations to biological reproduction,* e.g., fathers, boys
8. *Leisure,* e.g., golfer, drinker
9. *Marital and kinship status,* e.g., husband, bachelor, divorcé, widower, uncle
10. *Mind,* e.g., bright, dumb
11. *Occupation,* e.g., fitter, salesman, fireman
12. *Place,* e.g., British, West Coast
13. *Religion,* e.g., Moslem, atheist
14. *Sexuality,* including gay, bisexual, narcissist, heterosexual, celibate
15. *Size,* e.g., tall, short, small, big
16. *Violence,* e.g., violent, sissy, military

Other-defined masculinities (other—masculinities)

In each of these cases, the general category of other social division, for example, economic class, may refer to different types of men in different social relations, for example, bourgeois men, and to different types of masculinities, for example, bourgeois masculinities. Differences between men and between masculinities may thus be produced by other social divisions, as when economic class is seen to produce different class-based masculinities (Tolson, 1977). In this formulation we may speak of *other-defined masculinities.* This other-definition may refer to a particular type of masculinities or it may refer to the way in which masculinities may be understood as a representation of being, say, working class or middle-aged. Masculinities may thus be understood as representations of particular locations within one or more social divisions. Either way, such other-defined masculinities may also be referred to or displayed by others not so defined. For example, nonbourgeois men may adapt forms of masculinity that refer to bourgeois masculinities—this may itself be in parody, emulation, or adaptation.

Masculinities-defined others (masculinities—other)

Conversely, masculinities may define other social divisions. For example, middle-agedness or working classness may be a representation of masculinities.

Interrelations of masculinities and others (masculinities/other)

In these and other ways, masculinities may reproduce other social divisions while at the same time those other social divisions reproduce masculinities. Thus as already noted, one needs not only consider diversity but also interrelations and contradictions. The exploration of the diversity of men and masculinities necessarily leads to considering the interrelation of gender divisions and other social divisions, by age, bodily facility, economic class, ethnicity, sexuality, and so on. Examples of such interrelations include assertions and resistance, mediation, and coexistence. First, masculinities may be simultaneously an *assertion* of a particular social location (sometimes of more than one such location simultaneously) and a form of *resistance* of one social division to another. An example of this is given by Sallie Westwood (1990) with respect to black masculinity as a form of resistance to the power of white people, say, in the form of the police.

Second, masculinities may be *mediations* between two or more other social divisions. For example, on the shop floor the humor of masculinity may mediate between young and old, single and married, bosses and workers, and moreover between those different forms of social divisions (Collinson, 1988, 1992; Hearn, 1985).

Underpinning shop-floor ribaldry and aggressive banter is often a real sense of and attempt at reinforcing self-differentiation from the group. So, for example, in the study by Collinson (1988), workers engaged in a variety of self-differentiating strategies. Boris highlighted his sexual prowess and his aspirations to progress into the office grades. Lenny insisted that owning a house rather than renting a council flat confirmed his difference from many of his colleagues. Others such as a man nicknamed Dirty Bar critically evaluated and looked down on those who he believed were "lazy bastards" and were not "pulling their weight." Others still openly criticized colleagues who they felt "couldn't take a joke." Yet the consequence of these strategies was to weaken further the power of the shop floor as a group in their dealings with management.

Third, one may simply see masculinities and other social divisions as coexisting, simultaneously and reciprocally referring to each other. For example, in the notions of the breadwinner or the paternalist relations of gender, among others shown are age and economic class.

Masculinities as Social Relations of Men

Those social forms, such as the breadwinner and the paternalist, that simultaneously show masculinities and other social divisions, such as father, husband, worker, and authoritarian, may also be looked at in another way. Although the breadwinner draws on a number of social divisions, most obviously around the family and waged work, it may also be seen as a form of masculinities derived from specific social relationships *between men*—that in this case are individualized and privatized. The paternalist is in contrast individualized, remote from other men, yet publicized (the father in public). By a similar argument what are referred to as macho masculinities are derived from relations between men, characterized by a combination of collectively shared and individually isolated relations.

Composite Masculinities and Multiple Identities

So far we have considered masculinities mainly in relation to one main other social division. However, masculinities are perhaps more accurately understood in terms of complex associations of more than one other social division. Thus we may recognize black middle-class masculinities, white gay masculinities, and so on. Such multiple identities are particularly important because tensions and schisms can arise between one identity (or aspect of identity) and another, both psychologically within the individual and socially between individuals and between collectivities. For example, is the individual foremost black, middle-class, or a man? How meaningful is such a question in different sites and situations? In a divided society it is very difficult, and probably impossible, to hold onto numerous composite identities equally at all times; some will be prioritized over others and their meanings may change over time. For example, a black middle-class man may prioritize being black in some situations, being middle-class in others, and being a man in still others. Composite masculinities, and their experiential form as multiple identities, reinforce the likelihood of simultaneous unities and differences within masculinities.

Interrelations of Masculinities

All the above forms themselves need to be understood in terms of their own interrelations with each other, in particular with respect to the construction of hegemonic and nonhegemonic masculinities. These should not be understood as fixed hierarchical relationships, but rather as existing in structured yet changing relations of power. The interrelations of masculinities and social divisions are not just a matter of different structural locations of men; it is also a question of specific individual experiences. These different references to forms of masculinities exist and interrelate at the different levels of personal biography. As the Men, Masculinities and Socialism Group (1990) puts it, "There is the daily antagonistic clashing between diverse masculine identities—like child-carer, authoritarian father, loving, supportive friend, single parent father, 'macho' manager, depressed unemployed worker, strong leader—struggling for overall supremacy" (p. 18).

What is interesting here is that political analysis and personal experience are confronting issues very similar to those of theoretical analysis. We find that the complexities of our own personal and biographical stories mirror these political and theoretical complexities. The interrogation of biography and autobiography is an important and necessary aspect of the interrogation of social divisions, in this case with respect to men and masculinities. Examples of this approach are David Morgan's (1987) autobiographically based analysis of life in the air force, drawing together divisions by age, class, manhood, and so on; and David Jackson's (1990) critical autobiography that retells stories of the interconnections of nation, boyhood, ethnicity, and sexuality.

Types of Men and Masculinities
and the Critique of Types

To illustrate some of the issues raised in the previous section, we will briefly consider a few examples. Categories such as "white heterosexual able-bodied men" (WHAM) (Shevills & Killingray, 1989), "white heterosexual men" (WHEM), and "heterosexual able-bodied men" (HAM) are sometimes used in derogatory ways; here we refer to them as descriptions just as "working class" or "professional" might be. To seriously discuss

WHAMs or WHEMs or HAMs (and indeed there is very little sociology of these social categories), one needs to consider them in their social contexts. For example, the social category of WHAMs may exist in ideology, interpersonal relations, and in institutional forms, such as state policies. The young WHAM is not spoken of, yet is a routine part of pop culture. In some representations, say, in advertising, the young WHAM may appear to transcend ethnicity and sexuality. The category of WHAMs can also be seen in a more structural sense—say, in the maintenance of hierarchic heterosexual patriarchy. They are produced in such a patriarchy and may reproduce such a patriarchy.

Another example is the social category of men managers. This may itself overlap and interrelate with WHAMs, WHEMs, and HAMs in specific sites. The category of men managers combines gender and economic class categorization. Like WHAMs, it is not a term in general sociological use. Although *women managers* and *women in management* are well-used terms, men managers is too much of a societal commonplace to have been of much sociological interest. Managers and management are usually presumed to be men, just as are writers and painters. The vast majority of managers are indeed men, but the social facts of social normality do not mean that men management is socially unproblematic. There are also important structural questions around the place of men managers within macrosocietal relations—of capitalism, public patriarchy, viriarchy (rule of adult males) (Waters, 1989), and fratriarchy. "Men managers" is a necessary social grouping within the contemporary forms of patriarchy. Then there are the many and various institutional and interpersonal associations of masculinities and management. Being a manager and a man may confirm facets of masculinity. Managers may adopt a variety of styles—"macho," authoritarian, entrepreneurial, democratic— and may even be against oppression. Some men managers may even be beginning to develop ways of leading that seek to undermine dominant forms of masculinities (Hearn, 1989a).

Having noted some examples of types of masculinities including some composite masculinities, it may be useful to look briefly at some of the limitations of an approach to masculinities in terms of types. This perspective on the relationship of men, masculinities, and social divisions has the advantage of stressing specificities—both for particular men and for particular social sites. On the other hand, an emphasis on specificities can degenerate to a diversified pluralism with insufficient attention to structures of power and oppression. The wheel can go full circle.

Another area of difficulty is the sheer complexity of the very large number of possible permutations and interrelations of types. The numerical combinations are themselves complicated by the diversity of ways in which interrelation can exist and develop. Linked to this point is the methodological question of the meaning of types of men and masculinities. They may refer to either structural or social relations or both and to individual men or groups of men. There is no necessary reason why, for example, white masculinities should operate in the same way structurally and personally.

However, perhaps the most important area of difficulty is how types exist in relation to men's lived experience. Men's experiences of masculinities may invoke types of masculinities and may deconstruct those types. Any of the categories that might be referred are deconstructable—for example, white masculinities are deconstructable and may indeed be simultaneously Irish, Jewish, and English; heterosexual masculinities may also be celibate, narcissistic, gay, bisexual; middle-class masculinities may be waged, salaried, unemployed. In short, types of men do not exist as separate categories or as separate in themselves.

A final general area of critique is the implications of the poststructuralist uses and critiques of difference, as applied in this case to men and masculinities. The issues of difference are relevant here in a number of ways. First, difference is one way of casting doubt on theories of gender class, in this case of men, or of any unified masculinity. Men are thus as socially variable as are women (see Moore, 1987). Second, there are the differences between the experiences of men compared with those of women, as in sexual difference, and between different men and types/groups/examples of men (see Barrett, 1987). Third, there is the use of difference in the work of Derrida (1976, 1978) to refer to that which is not present in any presence. In this sense references to differences between men are at best partial truths, at worst misleading falsehoods. They fail to address the sociality of the lives of men/masculinities. Fourth, there is the more wholesale (paradoxically foundationalist) antifoundationalist aspect of difference in which reference is not just made to many subjects but rather to the undermining of defining any bases for knowledge and epistemology (see Halbert, 1989, p. 7). A fifth major problem with treating masculinities in terms of types is the difficulty of adequately recognizing fluidity and change in social life.

Concluding Without Closing

In this chapter we have explored the interrelations of unities and differences between men and between masculinities. Accordingly, one of the major themes throughout our analysis has been the tension between the recognition of the gender class relations and experiences of men, and the questions of differences and diversity. We see our analysis of this as very provisional: The important point is to recognize that tension. Men and masculinities may involve simultaneous relations and experiences of both unities and differences, and moreover, those apparent differences between unities and differences may reinforce them both. Having recognized that, men and masculinities need to be deconstructed—both as a power bloc (as part of the sociology of superordination) and as unified masculinities. The gender class perspective is socially sustained in part by the mythology of unified Man, rational, knowing, centered (Brittan, 1989). Recognizing those unities is paradoxically part of their deconstruction. There is thus above all a need to both make explicit and (then) decenter the categories of men and masculinities. This paradoxical and contradictory way forward applies in sociology, as in other social sciences, in macrohistorical changes, and in microinteractionist sites.

These social processes, within and outside sociology, are of course themselves historical. They are features of social change, and also they present a means of understanding social change, both substantively and methodologically. In brief, an obvious and important question is: Why might the decentering of men (at last) be on agendas now? (Hearn 1989c). As already noted, much is due to the impact of feminism, and much is also due to the rate of change of globalization and the strange connections of the global and the personal. Social change may now, as ever, be about change in social divisions, but it may now be partly about the deconstruction or decomposition of social divisions, not toward equality, but toward the more complex recognition of differences, including differences of different types of differences. Yet of course the powers and dominations of men over women persist in many diverse ways, partly through these differences. We hope that this chapter will contribute to the opening of political and intellectual spaces for removing, if not those differences, then at least men's powers and dominations over and of differences.

References

Astrachan, A. (1986). *How men feel.* New York: Doubleday.

Barrett, M. (1987). The concept of "difference," *Feminist Review, 26,* 29-41.

Bem, S. (1977). On the utility of alternative procedures for assessing psychological androgyny. *Journal of Consulting and Clinical Psychology, 45*(2), 166-205.

Bologh, R. W. (1990). *Love or greatness? Max Weber and masculine thinking.* London & Boston: Unwin Hyman.

Braidotti, R. (1987). Envy: Or with my brains and your looks. In A. Jardine and P. Smith (Eds.). *Men in feminism* (pp. 233-241). London: Methuen.

Brittan, A. (1989). *Masculinity and power.* Oxford: Blackwell.

Brod, H. (1990, May). Emasculated masculinities: Jews and other others. Paper presented at Canadian Political Science Association Convention, Victoria, British Columbia.

Carrigan, T., Connell, R. W., & Lee, J. (1985). Toward a new sociology of masculinity. *Theory and Society, 14*(5), 551-604.

Chapman, R., & Rutherford, J. (Eds.). (1988). *Male order: Unwrapping masculinity.* London: Lawrence & Wishart.

Cockburn, C. K. (1983). *Brothers: Male dominance and technological change.* London: Pluto.

Collinson, D. L. (1988). Engineering humour: Masculinity, joking and conflict in shop-floor relations. *Organisation Studies, 9*(2), 181-199.

Collinson, D. L. (1992). *Managing the shopfloor: Subjectivity, masculinity and workplace culture.* Berlin: de Gruyter.

Connell, R. W. (1985). Theorising gender. *Sociology, 19*(2), 260-272.

Connell, R. W. (1987). *Gender and power.* Cambridge, UK: Polity.

Delphy, C. (1977). *The main enemy: A materialist analysis.* London: Women's Research and Resources Centre.

Delphy, C., & Leonard, D. (1986). Class analysis, gender analysis and the family. In R. Crompton & M. Mann (Eds.), *Gender and stratification* (pp. 57-73). Cambridge, UK: Polity.

Derrida, J. (1976). *Of grammatology.* Baltimore, MD: John Hopkins University Press.

Derrida, J. (1978). *Writing and difference.* London: Routledge & Kegan Paul.

Eichler, M. (1980). *The double standard: A feminist critique of feminist social science.* London: Tavistock.

Grint, K. (1988). Women and equality: The acquisition of equal pay in the Post Office, 1870-1961. *Sociology, 22*(1), 87-108.

Halbert, M. (1989). Feminist epistemology: An impossible project. *Radical Philosophy, 53,* 3-7.

Hanmer, J. (1990). Men, power and the exploitation of women. In J. Hearn & D. H. J. Morgan (Eds.), *Men, masculinities and social theory* (pp. 21-42). London & Boston: Unwin Hyman.

Hearn, J. (1985). Men's sexuality at work. In A. Metcalf & M. Humphries (Eds.), *The sexuality of men* (pp. 110-28). London: Pluto.

Hearn, J. (1987). *The gender of oppression: Men, masculinity and the critique of Marxism.* Brighton, UK: Wheatsheaf.

Hearn, J. (1989a). Men, masculinities and leadership: Changing patterns and new initiatives [Special issue]. *Equal Opportunities International, 8*(1).

Hearn, J. (1989b). Reviewing men and masculinities—or mostly boys' own papers. *Theory, Culture and Society, 6*(4), 665-689.

Hearn, J. (1989c). *Some sociological issues in researching men and masculinities* (Hallsworth Research Fellowship Working Paper No. 2). Manchester, UK: University of Manchester.

Hearn, J. (1992). *Men in the public eye: The construction and deconstruction of public men and public patriarchies.* London & New York: Routledge.

Hearn, J., & Morgan, D. H. J. (1990). Men, masculinities and social theory. In J. Hearn & D. H. J. Morgan (Eds.), *Men, masculinities and social theory* (pp. 1-18). London & Boston: Unwin Hyman.

Heward, C. (1988). *Making a man of him: Parents and their sons' education at an English public school, 1929-50.* London: Routledge.

Jackson, D. (1990). *Unmasking masculinity: A critical autobiography.* London & Boston: Unwin Hyman.

Kimmel, M., & Messner, M. (Eds.). (1989). *Men's lives.* New York: Macmillan.

MacKinnon, C. A. (1982). Feminism, Marxism, method and the state: An agenda for theory. *Signs, 7*(3), 515-544.

Men, Masculinities and Socialism Group. (1990). Changing men, changing politics. *Achilles Heel, 10,* 17-21.

Middleton, P. (1989). Socialism, feminism and men. *Radical Philosophy, 53,* 8-19.

Mieli, M. (1980). *Homosexuality and liberation: Elements of a gay critique* (D. Fernbach, Trans.). London: Gay Men's Press. (Original work published 1977)

Moore, H. (1987). *Feminism and anthropology.* Cambridge, UK: Cambridge University Press.

Morgan, D. H. J. (1987). *It will make a man of you.* Manchester, UK: University of Manchester, Studies in Sexual Politics.

Morgan, D. H. J. (1992). *Discovering men, sociology and masculinity.* London & New York: Routledge.

Morris, M. (1988). *The pirate's fiancée: Feminism, reading, postmodernism.* London: Verso.

O'Brien, M. (1979). Reproducing Marxist man. In L. Clark & L. Lange (Eds.), *The sexism of social and political thought* (pp. 99-116). Toronto: University of Toronto.

O'Brien, M. (1981). *The politics of reproduction.* London: Routledge & Kegan Paul.

OPCS. (1984a). *Census 1981: Household and family composition: England and Wales.* London: HMSO.

OPCS. (1984b). *Census 1981: Qualified manpower: Great Britain.* London: HMSO.

Shevills, J., & Killingray, J. (1989). Fraternally yours. Paper presented at Socialist Conference, Sheffield, UK.

Stanley, L. (1984). Whales and minnows: Some sexual theorists and their followers and how they contribute to making feminism invisible. *Women's Studies International Forum, 7*(1), 53-62.

Tolson, A. (1977). *The limits of masculinity.* London: Tavistock.

Walby, S. (1986). Gender, class and stratification: Towards a new approach. In R. Crompton & M. Mann (Eds.), *Gender and stratification* (pp. 23-29). Cambridge, UK: Polity.

Walker, C. R., & Guest, R. H. (1952). *The man on the assembly line.* Cambridge, MA: Harvard University Press.

Waters, M. (1989). Patriarchy and viriarchy. *Sociology, 23*(2), 193-211.

Weber, M. (1967). *The Protestant ethic and the spirit of capitalism*. London: Allen & Unwin.

Weeks, J. (1985). *Sexuality and its discontents*. London: Routledge & Kegan Paul.

Westwood, S. (1990). Racism, black masculinity and the politics of masculinity. In J. Hearn & D. H. J. Morgan (Eds.), *Men, masculinities and social theory* (pp. 55-71). London/Winchester, MA: Unwin Hyman.

Whyte, W. H. (1956). *Organization man*. New York: Simon & Schuster.

Willis, P. (1977). *Learning to labour*. Farnborough, Hampshire, UK: Saxon House.

7

Masculinity as Homophobia

Fear, Shame, and Silence
in the Construction of Gender Identity

MICHAEL S. KIMMEL

"Funny thing," [Curley's wife] said. "If I catch any one man, and he's
alone, I get along fine with him. But just let two of the guys get together
an' you won't talk. Jus' nothin' but mad." She dropped her fingers and
put her hands on her hips. "You're all scared of each other, that's what.
Ever'one of you's scared the rest is goin' to get something on you."

John Steinbeck, *Of Mice and Men* (1937)

We think of manhood as eternal, a timeless essence that resides deep in
the heart of every man. We think of manhood as a thing, a quality that one
either has or doesn't have. We think of manhood as innate, residing in the
particular biological composition of the human male, the result of androgens or the possession of a penis. We think of manhood as a transcendent
tangible property that each man must manifest in the world, the reward
presented with great ceremony to a young novice by his elders for having
successfully completed an arduous initiation ritual. In the words of poet

AUTHOR'S NOTE: This chapter represents a preliminary working out of a theoretical
chapter in my forthcoming book, *Manhood: The American Quest* (in press). I am grateful
to Tim Beneke, Harry Brod, Michael Kaufman, Iona Mara-Drita, and Lillian Rubin for
comments on earlier versions of the chapter.

119

Robert Bly (1990), "the structure at the bottom of the male psyche is still as firm as it was twenty thousand years ago" (p. 230).

In this chapter, I view masculinity as a constantly changing collection of meanings that we construct through our relationships with ourselves, with each other, and with our world. Manhood is neither static nor timeless; it is historical. Manhood is not the manifestation of an inner essence; it is socially constructed. Manhood does not bubble up to consciousness from our biological makeup; it is created in culture. Manhood means different things at different times to different people. We come to know what it means to be a man in our culture by setting our definitions in opposition to a set of "others"—racial minorities, sexual minorities, and, above all, women.

Our definitions of manhood are constantly changing, being played out on the political and social terrain on which the relationships between women and men are played out. In fact, the search for a transcendent, timeless definition of manhood is itself a sociological phenomenon—we tend to search for the timeless and eternal during moments of crisis, those points of transition when old definitions no longer work and new definitions are yet to be firmly established.

This idea that manhood is socially constructed and historically shifting should not be understood as a loss, that something is being taken away from men. In fact, it gives us something extraordinarily valuable—agency, the capacity to act. It gives us a sense of historical possibilities to replace the despondent resignation that invariably attends timeless, ahistorical essentialisms. Our behaviors are not simply "just human nature," because "boys will be boys." From the materials we find around us in our culture—other people, ideas, objects—we actively create our worlds, our identities. Men, both individually and collectively, can change.

In this chapter, I explore this social and historical construction of both hegemonic masculinity and alternate masculinities, with an eye toward offering a new theoretical model of American manhood.[1] To accomplish this I first uncover some of the hidden gender meanings in classical statements of social and political philosophy, so that I can anchor the emergence of contemporary manhood in specific historical and social contexts. I then spell out the ways in which this version of masculinity emerged in the United States, by tracing both psychoanalytic developmental sequences and a historical trajectory in the development of marketplace relationships.

Classical Social Theory
as a Hidden Meditation of Manhood

Begin this inquiry by looking at four passages from that set of texts commonly called classical social and political theory. You will, no doubt, recognize them, but I invite you to recall the way they were discussed in your undergraduate or graduate courses in theory:

The bourgeoisie cannot exist without constantly revolutionizing the instruments of production, and thereby the relations of production, and with them the whole relations of society. Conservation of the old modes of production in unaltered form, was, on the contrary, the first condition of existence for all earlier industrial classes. Constant revolutionizing of production, uninterrupted disturbance of all social conditions, everlasting uncertainty and agitation distinguish the bourgeois epoch from all earlier ones. All fixed, fast-frozen relations, with their train of ancient and venerable prejudices and opinions are swept away, all new-formed ones become antiquated before they can ossify. All that is solid melts into air, all that is holy is profaned, and man is at last compelled to face with sober senses, his real conditions of life, and his relation with his kind. (Marx & Engels, 1848/1964)

An American will build a house in which to pass his old age and sell it before the roof is on; he will plant a garden and rent it just as the trees are coming into bearing; he will clear a field and leave others to reap the harvest; he will take up a profession and leave it, settle in one place and soon go off elsewhere with his changing desires. . . . At first sight there is something astonishing in this spectacle of so many lucky men restless in the midst of abundance. But it is a spectacle as old as the world; all that is new is to see a whole people performing in it. (Tocqueville, 1835/1967)

Where the fulfillment of the calling cannot directly be related to the highest spiritual and cultural values, or when, on the other hand, it need not be felt simply as economic compulsion, the individual generally abandons the attempt to justify it at all. In the field of its highest development, in the United States, the pursuit of wealth, stripped of its religious and ethical meaning, tends to become associated with purely mundane passions, which often actually give it the character of sport. (Weber, 1905/1966)

We are warned by a proverb against serving two masters at the same time. The poor ego has things even worse: it serves three severe masters and does what it can to bring their claims and demands into harmony with one another. These claims are always divergent and often seem incompatible. No wonder that the ego so often fails in its task. Its three tyrannical masters are the external world, the super ego and the id. . . . It feels hemmed in on three sides, threatened by three kinds of danger, to which, if it is hard pressed, it reacts by generating anxiety. . . . Thus the ego, driven by the id, confined by the super ego, repulsed by reality, struggles to master its economic task of bringing about harmony among the forces and influences working in and upon it; and we can understand how it is that so often we cannot suppress a cry: "Life is not easy!" (Freud, "The Dissection of the Psychical Personality," 1933/1966)

If your social science training was anything like mine, these were offered as descriptions of the bourgeoisie under capitalism, of individuals in democratic societies, of the fate of the Protestant work ethic under the ever rationalizing spirit of capitalism, or of the arduous task of the autonomous ego in psychological development. Did anyone ever mention that in all four cases the theorists were describing men? Not just "man" as in generic mankind, but a particular type of masculinity, a definition of manhood that derives its identity from participation in the marketplace, from interaction with other men in that marketplace—in short, a model of masculinity for whom identity is based on homosocial competition? Three years before Tocqueville found Americans "restless in the midst of abundance," Senator Henry Clay had called the United States "a nation of self-made men."

What does it mean to be "self-made"? What are the consequences of self-making for the individual man, for other men, for women? It is this notion of manhood—rooted in the sphere of production, the public arena, a masculinity grounded not in landownership or in artisanal republican virtue but in successful participation in marketplace competition—this has been the defining notion of American manhood. Masculinity must be proved, and no sooner is it proved that it is again questioned and must be proved again— constant, relentless, unachievable, and ultimately the quest for proof becomes so meaningless than it takes on the characteristics, as Weber said, of a sport. He who has the most toys when he dies wins.

Where does this version of masculinity come from? How does it work? What are the consequences of this version of masculinity for women, for other men, and for individual men themselves? These are the questions I address in this chapter.

Masculinity as History
and the History of Masculinity

The idea of masculinity expressed in the previous extracts is the product of historical shifts in the grounds on which men rooted their sense of themselves as men. To argue that cultural definitions of gender identity are historically specific goes only so far; we have to specify exactly what those models were. In my historical inquiry into the development of these models of manhood[2] I chart the fate of two models for manhood at the turn of the 19th century and the emergence of a third in the first few decades of that century.

In the late 18th and early 19th centuries, two models of manhood prevailed. The *Genteel Patriarch* derived his identity from landownership. Supervising his estate, he was refined, elegant, and given to casual sensuousness. He was a doting and devoted father, who spent much of his time supervising the estate and with his family. Think of George Washington or Thomas Jefferson as examples. By contrast, the *Heroic Artisan* embodied the physical strength and republican virtue that Jefferson observed in the yeoman farmer, independent urban craftsman, or shopkeeper. Also a devoted father, the Heroic Artisan taught his son his craft, bringing him through ritual apprenticeship to status as master craftsman. Economically autonomous, the Heroic Artisan also cherished his democratic community, delighting in the participatory democracy of the town meeting. Think of Paul Revere at his pewter shop, shirtsleeves rolled up, a leather apron—a man who took pride in his work.

Heroic Artisans and Genteel Patriarchs lived in casual accord, in part because their gender ideals were complementary (both supported participatory democracy and individual autonomy, although patriarchs tended to support more powerful state machineries and also supported slavery) and because they rarely saw one another: Artisans were decidedly urban and the Genteel Patriarchs ruled their rural estates. By the 1830s, though, this casual symbiosis was shattered by the emergence of a new vision of masculinity, *Marketplace Manhood.*

Marketplace Man derived his identity entirely from his success in the capitalist marketplace, as he accumulated wealth, power, status. He was the urban entrepreneur, the businessman. Restless, agitated, and anxious, Marketplace Man was an absentee landlord at home and an absent father with his children, devoting himself to his work in an increasingly homosocial environment—a male-only world in which he pits himself against other men. His efforts at self-making transform the political and economic spheres, casting aside the Genteel Patriarch as an anachronistic feminized dandy—sweet, but ineffective and outmoded, and transforming the Heroic Artisan into a dispossessed proletarian, a wage slave.

As Tocqueville would have seen it, the coexistence of the Genteel Patriarch and the Heroic Artisan embodied the fusion of liberty and equality. Genteel

Patriarchy was the manhood of the traditional aristocracy, the class that embodied the virtue of liberty. The Heroic Artisan embodied democratic community, the solidarity of the urban shopkeeper or craftsman. Liberty and democracy, the patriarch and the artisan, could, and did, coexist. But Marketplace Man is capitalist man, and he makes both freedom and equality problematic, eliminating the freedom of the aristocracy and proletarianizing the equality of the artisan. In one sense, American history has been an effort to restore, retrieve, or reconstitute the virtues of Genteel Patriarchy and Heroic Artisanate as they were being transformed in the capitalist marketplace.

Marketplace Manhood was a manhood that required proof, and that required the acquisition of tangible goods as evidence of success. It reconstituted itself by the exclusion of "others"—women, nonwhite men, nonnative-born men, homosexual men—and by terrified flight into a pristine mythic homosocial Eden where men could, at last, be real men among other men. The story of the ways in which Marketplace Man becomes American Everyman is a tragic tale, a tale of striving to live up to impossible ideals of success leading to chronic terrors of emasculation, emotional emptiness, and a gendered rage that leave a wide swath of destruction in its wake.

Masculinities as Power Relations

Marketplace Masculinity describes the normative definition of American masculinity. It describes his characteristics—aggression, competition, anxiety—and the arena in which those characteristics are deployed— the public sphere, the marketplace. If the marketplace is the arena in which manhood is tested and proved, it is a gendered arena, in which tensions between women and men and tensions among different groups of men are weighted with meaning. These tensions suggest that cultural definitions of gender are played out in a contested terrain and are themselves power relations.

All masculinities are not created equal; or rather, we are all *created* equal, but any hypothetical equality evaporates quickly because our definitions of masculinity are not equally valued in our society. One definition of manhood continues to remain the standard against which other forms of manhood are measured and evaluated. Within the dominant culture, the masculinity that defines white, middle class, early middle-aged, heterosexual men is the masculinity that sets the standards for other men, against which other men are measured and, more often than not, found wanting. Sociologist Erving Goffman (1963) wrote that in America, there is only "one complete, unblushing male":

> a young, married, white, urban, northern heterosexual, Protestant father of college education, fully employed, of good complexion, weight and height, and a recent record in sports. Every American male tends to look out upon the world from this perspective. . . . Any male who fails to qualify in any one of these ways is likely to view himself . . . as unworthy, incomplete, and inferior. (p. 128)

This is the definition that we will call "hegemonic" masculinity, the image of masculinity of those men who hold power, which has become the standard in psychological evaluations, sociological research, and self-help and advice literature for teaching young men to become "real men" (Connell, 1987). The hegemonic definition of manhood is a man *in* power, a man *with* power, and a man *of* power. We equate manhood with being strong, successful, capable, reliable, in control. The very definitions of manhood we have developed in our culture maintain the power that some men have over other men and that men have over women.

Our culture's definition of masculinity is thus several stories at once. It is about the individual man's quest to accumulate those cultural symbols that denote manhood, signs that he has in fact achieved it. It is about those standards being used against women to prevent their inclusion in public life and their consignment to a devalued private sphere. It is about the differential access that different types of men have to those cultural resources that confer manhood and about how each of these groups then develop their own modifications to preserve and claim their manhood. It is about the power of these definitions themselves to serve to maintain the real-life power that men have over women and that some men have over other men.

This definition of manhood has been summarized cleverly by psychologist Robert Brannon (1976) into four succinct phrases:

1. "No Sissy Stuff!" One may never do anything that even remotely suggests femininity. Masculinity is the relentless repudiation of the feminine.
2. "Be a Big Wheel." Masculinity is measured by power, success, wealth, and status. As the current saying goes, "He who has the most toys when he dies wins."
3. "Be a Sturdy Oak." Masculinity depends on remaining calm and reliable in a crisis, holding emotions in check. In fact, proving you're a man depends on never showing your emotions at all. Boys don't cry.

4. "Give 'em Hell." Exude an aura of manly daring and aggression. Go for it. Take risks.

These rules contain the elements of the definition against which virtually all American men are measured. Failure to embody these rules, to affirm the power of the rules and one's achievement of them is a source of men's confusion and pain. Such a model is, of course, unrealizable for any man. But we keep trying, valiantly and vainly, to measure up. American masculinity is a relentless test.[3] The chief test is contained in the first rule. Whatever the variations by race, class, age, ethnicity, or sexual orientation, being a man means "not being like women." This notion of anti-femininity lies at the heart of contemporary and historical conceptions of manhood, so that masculinity is defined more by what one is not rather than who one is.

Masculinity as the Flight From the Feminine

Historically and developmentally, masculinity has been defined as the flight from women, the repudiation of femininity. Since Freud, we have come to understand that developmentally the central task that every little boy must confront is to develop a secure identity for himself as a man. As Freud had it, the oedipal project is a process of the boy's renouncing his identification with and deep emotional attachment to his mother and then replacing her with the father as the object of identification. Notice that he reidentifies but never reattaches. This entire process, Freud argued, is set in motion by the boy's sexual desire for his mother. But the father stands in the son's path and will not yield his sexual property to his puny son. The boy's first emotional experience, then, the one that inevitably follows his experience of desire, is fear—fear of the bigger, stronger, more sexually powerful father. It is this fear, experienced symbolically as the fear of castration, Freud argues, that forces the young boy to renounce his identification with mother and seek to identify with the being who is the actual source of his fear, his father. In so doing, the boy is now symbolically capable of sexual union with a motherlike substitute, that is, a woman. The boy becomes gendered (masculine) and heterosexual at the same time.

Masculinity, in this model, is irrevocably tied to sexuality. The boy's sexuality will now come to resemble the sexuality of his father (or at least the way he imagines his father)—menacing, predatory, possessive, and possibly punitive. The boy has come to identify with his oppressor; now he can become the oppressor himself. But a terror remains, the terror that the young man will be unmasked as a fraud, as a man who has not completely and irrevocably separated from mother. It will be other men who will do the unmasking. Failure will de-sex the man, make him appear as not fully a man. He will be seen as a wimp, a Mama's boy, a sissy.

After pulling away from his mother, the boy comes to see her not as a source of nurturance and love, but as an insatiably infantalizing creature, capable of humiliating him in front of his peers. She makes him dress up in uncomfortable and itchy clothing, her kisses smear his cheeks with lipstick, staining his boyish innocence with the mark of feminine dependency. No wonder so many boys cringe from their mothers' embraces with groans of "Aw, Mom! Quit it!" Mothers represent the humiliation of infancy, helplessness, dependency. "Men act as though they were being guided by (or rebelling against) rules and prohibitions enunciated by a moral mother," writes psychohistorian Geoffrey Gorer (1964). As a result, "all the niceties of masculine behavior—modesty, politeness, neatness, cleanliness—come to be regarded as concessions to feminine demands, and not good in themselves as part of the behavior of a proper man" (pp. 56, 57).

The flight from femininity is angry and frightened, because mother can so easily emasculate the young boy by her power to render him dependent, or at least to remind him of dependency. It is relentless; manhood becomes a lifelong quest to demonstrate its achievement, as if to prove the unprovable to others, because we feel so unsure of it ourselves. Women don't often feel compelled to "prove their womanhood"—the phrase itself sounds ridiculous. Women have different kinds of gender identity crises; their anger and frustration, and their own symptoms of depression, come more from being excluded than from questioning whether they are feminine enough.[4]

The drive to repudiate the mother as the indication of the acquisition of masculine gender identity has three consequences for the young boy. First, he pushes away his real mother, and with her the traits of nurturance, compassion, and tenderness she may have embodied. Second, he suppresses those traits in himself, because they will reveal his incomplete separation from mother. His life becomes a lifelong project to demonstrate that he possesses none of his mother's traits. Masculine identity is born in the renunciation of the feminine, not in the direct affirmation of the masculine, which leaves masculine gender identity tenuous and fragile.

Third, as if to demonstrate the accomplishment of these first two tasks, the boy also learns to devalue all women in his society, as the living embodiments of those traits in himself he has learned to despise. Whether or not he was aware of it, Freud also described the origins of sexism—the systematic devaluation of women—in the desperate efforts of the boy to separate from mother. We may *want* "a girl just like the girl that married dear old Dad," as the popular song had it, but we certainly don't want to *be like* her.

This chronic uncertainty about gender identity helps us understand several obsessive behaviors. Take, for example, the continuing problem of the school-yard bully. Parents remind us that the bully is the *least* secure about his manhood, and so he is constantly trying to prove it. But he "proves" it by choosing opponents he is absolutely certain he can defeat; thus the standard taunt to a bully is to "pick on someone your own size." He can't, though, and after defeating a smaller and weaker opponent, which he was sure would prove his manhood, he is left with the empty gnawing feeling that he has not proved it after all, and he must find another opponent, again one smaller and weaker, that he can again defeat to prove it to himself.[5]

One of the more graphic illustrations of this lifelong quest to prove one's manhood occurred at the Academy Awards presentation in 1992. As aging, tough guy actor Jack Palance accepted the award for Best Supporting Actor for his role in the cowboy comedy *City Slickers,* he commented that people, especially film producers, think that because he is 71 years old, he's all washed up, that he's no longer competent. "Can we take a risk on this guy?" he quoted them as saying, before he dropped to the floor to do a set of one-armed push-ups. It was pathetic to see such an accomplished actor still having to prove that he is virile enough to work and, as he also commented at the podium, to have sex.

When does it end? Never. To admit weakness, to admit frailty or fragility, is to be seen as a wimp, a sissy, not a real man. But seen by whom?

Masculinity as a Homosocial Enactment

Other men: We are under the constant careful scrutiny of other men. Other men watch us, rank us, grant our acceptance into the realm of manhood. Manhood is demonstrated for other men's approval. It is other men who evaluate the performance. Literary critic David Leverenz (1991) argues that "ideologies of manhood have functioned primarily in relation to the gaze of male peers and male authority" (p. 769). Think of how men boast to one another of their accomplishments—from their latest sexual conquest to the size of the fish they caught—and how we constantly parade the markers of manhood—wealth, power, status, sexy women—in front of other men, desperate for their approval.

That men prove their manhood in the eyes of other men is both a consequence of sexism and one of its chief props. "Women have, in men's minds, such a low place on the social ladder of this country that it's useless to define yourself in terms of a woman," noted playwright David Mamet. "What men need is men's approval." Women become a kind of currency that men use to improve their ranking on the masculine social scale. (Even those moments of heroic conquest of women carry, I believe, a current of homosocial evaluation.) Masculinity is a *homosocial* enactment. We test ourselves, perform heroic feats, take enormous risks, all because we want other men to grant us our manhood.

Masculinity as a homosocial enactment is fraught with danger, with the risk of failure, and with intense relentless competition. "Every man you meet has a rating or an estimate of himself which he never loses or forgets," wrote Kenneth Wayne (1912) in his popular turn-of-the-century advice book. "A man has his own rating, and instantly he lays it alongside of the other man" (p. 18). Almost a century later, another man remarked to psychologist Sam Osherson (1992) that "[b]y the time you're an adult, it's easy to think you're always in competition with men, for the attention of women, in sports, at work" (p. 291).

Masculinity as Homophobia

If masculinity is a homosocial enactment, its overriding emotion is fear. In the Freudian model, the fear of the father's power terrifies the young boy to renounce his desire for his mother and identify with his father. This model links gender identity with sexual orientation: The little boy's identification with father (becoming masculine) allows him to now engage in sexual relations with women (he becomes heterosexual). This is the origin of how we can "read" one's sexual orientation through the successful performance of gender identity. Second, the fear that the little boy feels does not send him scurrying into the arms of his mother to protect him from his father. Rather, he believes he will overcome his fear by identifying with its source. We become masculine by identifying with our oppressor.

But there is a piece of the puzzle missing, a piece that Freud, himself, implied but did not follow up.[6] If the pre-oedipal boy identifies with mother, he *sees the world through mother's eyes*. Thus, when he confronts father during his great oedipal crisis, he experiences a split vision: He sees his father as his mother sees his father, with a combination of awe, wonder, terror, *and desire*. He simultaneously sees the father as he, the boy, would like to see him—as the object not of desire but of emulation. Repudiating mother and identifying with father only partially answers his dilemma. What is he to do with that homoerotic desire, the desire he felt because he saw father the way that his mother saw father?

He must suppress it. Homoerotic desire is cast as feminine desire, desire for other men. Homophobia is the effort to suppress that desire, to purify all relationships with other men, with women, with children of its taint, and to ensure that no one could possibly ever mistake one for a homosexual. Homophobic flight from intimacy with other men is the repudiation of the homosexual within—never completely successful and hence constantly reenacted in every homosocial relationship. "The lives of most American men are bounded, and their interests daily curtailed by the constant necessity to prove to their fellows, and to themselves, that they are not sissies, not homosexuals," writes psychoanalytic historian Geoffrey Gorer (1964). "Any interest or pursuit which is identified as a feminine interest or pursuit becomes deeply suspect for men" (p. 129).

Even if we do not subscribe to Freudian psychoanalytic ideas, we can still observe how, in less sexualized terms, the father is the first man who evaluates the boy's masculine performance, the first pair of male eyes before whom he tries to prove himself. Those eyes will follow him for the rest of his life. Other men's eyes will join them—the eyes of role models such as teachers, coaches, bosses, or media heroes; the eyes of his peers, his friends, his workmates; and the eyes of millions of other men, living and dead, from whose constant scrutiny of his performance he will never be free. "The tradition of all the dead generations weighs like a nightmare on the brain of the living," was how Karl Marx put it over a century ago (1848/1964, p. 11). "The birthright of every American male is a chronic sense of personal inadequacy," is how two psychologists describe it today (Woolfolk & Richardson, 1978, p. 57).

That nightmare from which we never seem to awaken is that those other men will see that sense of inadequacy, they will see that in our own eyes we are not who we are pretending to be. What we call masculinity is often a hedge against being revealed as a fraud, an exaggerated set of activities that keep others from seeing through us, and a frenzied effort to keep at bay those fears within ourselves. Our real fear "is not fear of women but of being ashamed or humiliated in front of other men, or being dominated by stronger men" (Leverenz, 1986, p. 451).

This, then, is the great secret of American manhood: *We are afraid of other men.* Homophobia is a central organizing principle of our cultural definition of manhood. Homophobia is more than the irrational fear of gay men, more than the fear that we might be perceived as gay. "The word 'faggot' has nothing to do with homosexual experience or even with fears of homosexuals," writes David Leverenz (1986). "It comes out of the depths of manhood: a label of ultimate contempt for anyone who seems sissy, untough, uncool" (p. 455). Homophobia is the fear that other men will unmask us, emasculate us, reveal to us and the world that we do not measure up, that we are not real men. We are afraid to let other men see that fear. Fear makes us ashamed, because the recognition of fear in ourselves is proof to ourselves that we are not as manly as we pretend, that we are, like the young man in a poem by Yeats, "one that ruffles in a manly pose for all his timid heart." Our fear is the fear of humiliation. We are ashamed to be afraid.

Shame leads to silence—the silences that keep other people believing that we actually approve of the things that are done to women, to minorities, to gays and lesbians in our culture. The frightened silence as we scurry past a woman being hassled by men on the street. That furtive silence when men make sexist or racist jokes in a bar. That clammy-handed silence when guys in the office make gay-bashing jokes. Our fears are the sources of our silences, and men's silence is what keeps the system running. This might help to explain why women often complain that their male friends or partners are often so understanding when they are alone and yet laugh at sexist jokes or even make those jokes themselves when they are out with a group.

The fear of being seen as a sissy dominates the cultural definitions of manhood. It starts so early. "Boys among boys are ashamed to be unmanly," wrote one educator in 1871 (cited in Rotundo, 1993, p. 264). I have a standing bet with a friend that I can walk onto any playground in America where 6-year-old boys are happily playing and by asking one question, I can provoke a fight. That question is simple: "Who's a sissy around here?" Once posed, the challenge is made. One of two things is likely to happen. One boy will accuse another of being a sissy, to which that boy will respond that he is not a sissy, that the first boy is. They may have to fight it out to see who's lying. Or a whole group of boys will surround one boy and all shout "He is! He is!" That boy will either burst into tears and run home crying, disgraced, or he will have to take on several boys at once, to prove that he's not a sissy. (And what will his father or older brothers tell him if he chooses to run home crying?) It will be some time before he regains any sense of self-respect.

Violence is often the single most evident marker of manhood. Rather it is the willingness to fight, the desire to fight. The origin of our expression that one has a chip on one's shoulder lies in the practice of an adolescent boy in the country or small town at the turn of the century, who would literally walk around with a chip of wood balanced on his shoulder—a signal of his readiness to fight with anyone who would take the initiative of knocking the chip off (see Gorer, 1964, p. 38; Mead, 1965).

As adolescents, we learn that our peers are a kind of gender police, constantly threatening to unmask us as feminine, as sissies. One of the favorite tricks when I was an adolescent was to ask a boy to look at his fingernails. If he held his palm toward his face and curled his fingers back to see them, he passed the test. He'd looked at his nails "like a man." But if he held the back of his hand away from his face, and looked at his fingernails with arm outstretched, he was immediately ridiculed as a sissy.

As young men we are constantly riding those gender boundaries, checking the fences we have constructed on the perimeter, making sure that nothing even remotely feminine might show through. The possibilities of being unmasked are everywhere. Even the most seemingly insignificant thing can pose a threat or activate that haunting terror. On the day the students in my course "Sociology of Men and Masculinities" were scheduled to discuss homophobia and male-male friendships, one student provided a touching illustration. Noting that it was a beautiful day, the first day of spring after a brutal northeast winter, he decided to wear shorts to class. "I had this really nice pair of new Madras shorts," he commented. "But then I thought to myself, these shorts have lavender and pink in them. Today's class topic is homophobia. Maybe today is not the best day to wear these shorts."

Our efforts to maintain a manly front cover everything we do. What we wear. How we talk. How we walk. What we eat. Every mannerism, every movement contains a coded gender language. Think, for example, of how you would answer the question: How do you "know" if a man is homosexual? When I ask this question in classes or workshops, respondents invariably provide a pretty standard list of stereotypically effeminate behaviors. He walks a certain way, talks a certain way, acts a certain way. He's very emotional; he shows his feelings. One woman commented that she "knows" a man is gay if he really cares about her; another said she knows he's gay if he shows no interest in her, if he leaves her alone.

Now alter the question and imagine what heterosexual men do to make sure no one could possibly get the "wrong idea" about them. Responses typically refer to the original stereotypes, this time as a set of negative rules about behavior. Never dress that way. Never talk or walk that way. Never show your feelings or get emotional. Always be prepared to demonstrate sexual interest in women that you meet, so it is impossible for any woman to get the wrong idea about you. In this sense, homophobia, the fear of being perceived as gay, as not a real man, keeps men exaggerating all the traditional rules of masculinity, including sexual predation with women. Homophobia and sexism go hand in hand.

The stakes of perceived sissydom are enormous—sometimes matters of life and death. We take enormous risks to prove our manhood, exposing ourselves disproportionately to health risks, workplace hazards, and stress-related illnesses. Men commit suicide three times as often as women. Psychiatrist Willard Gaylin (1992) explains that it is "invariably because of perceived social humiliation," most often tied to failure in business:

> Men become depressed because of loss of status and power in the world of men. It is not the loss of money, or the material advantages that money could buy, which produces the despair that leads to self-destruction. It is the "shame," the "humiliation," the sense of personal "failure." . . . A man despairs when he has ceased being a man among men. (p. 32)

In one survey, women and men were asked what they were most afraid of. Women responded that they were most afraid of being raped and murdered. Men responded that they were most afraid of being laughed at (Noble, 1992, pp. 105-106).

Homophobia as a Cause of Sexism, Heterosexism, and Racism

Homophobia is intimately interwoven with both sexism and racism. The fear—sometimes conscious, sometimes not—that others might perceive us as homosexual propels men to enact all manner of exaggerated masculine behaviors and attitudes to make sure that no one could possibly get the wrong idea about us. One of the centerpieces of that exaggerated masculinity is putting women down, both by excluding them from the public sphere and by the quotidian put-downs in speech and behaviors that organize the daily life of the American man. Women and gay men become the "other" against which heterosexual men project their identities, against whom they stack the decks so as to compete in a situation in which they will always win, so that by suppressing them, men can stake a claim for their own manhood. Women threaten emasculation by representing the home, workplace, and familial responsibility, the negation of fun. Gay men have historically played the role of the consummate sissy in the American popular mind because homosexuality is seen as an inversion of normal gender development. There have been other "others." Through American history, various groups have represented the sissy, the non-men against whom American men played out their definitions of manhood, often with vicious results. In fact, these changing groups provide an interesting lesson in American historical development.

At the turn of the 19th century, it was Europeans and children who provided the contrast for American men. The "true American was vigorous, manly, and direct, not effete and corrupt like the supposed Europeans," writes Rupert Wilkinson (1986). "He was plain rather than ornamented, rugged rather than luxury seeking, a liberty loving common man or natural gentleman rather than an aristocratic oppressor or servile minion" (p. 96). The "real man" of the early 19th century was neither noble nor serf. By the middle of the century, black slaves had replaced the effete nobleman. Slaves were seen as dependent, helpless men, incapable of defending their women and children, and therefore less than manly. Native Americans were cast as foolish and naive children, so they could be infantalized as the "Red Children of the Great White Father" and therefore excluded from full manhood.

By the end of the century, new European immigrants were also added to the list of the unreal men, especially the Irish and Italians, who were seen as too passionate and emotionally volatile to remain controlled sturdy oaks, and Jews, who were seen as too bookishly effete and too physically puny to truly measure up. In the mid-20th century, it was also Asians—first the Japanese during the Second World War, and more recently, the Vietnamese during the Vietnam War—who have served as unmanly templates against which American men have hurled their gendered rage. Asian men were seen as small, soft, and effeminate—hardly men at all.

Such a list of "hyphenated" Americans—Italian-, Jewish-, Irish-, African-, Native-, Asian-, gay—composes the majority of American men. So manhood is only possible for a distinct minority, and the definition has been constructed to prevent the others from achieving it. Interestingly, this emasculation of one's enemies has a flip side—and one that is equally gendered. These very groups that have historically been cast as less than manly were also, often simultaneously, cast as hypermasculine, as sexually aggressive, violent rapacious beasts, against whom "civilized" men must take a decisive stand and thereby rescue civilization. Thus black men were depicted as rampaging sexual beasts, women as carnivorously carnal, gay men as sexually insatiable, southern European men as sexually predatory and voracious, and Asian men as vicious and cruel torturers who were immorally disinterested in life itself, willing to sacrifice their entire people for their whims. But whether one saw these groups as effeminate sissies or as brutal uncivilized savages, the terms with which they were perceived were gendered. These groups become the "others," the screens against which traditional conceptions of manhood were developed.

Being seen as unmanly is a fear that propels American men to deny manhood to others, as a way of proving the unprovable—that one is fully manly. Masculinity becomes a defense against the perceived threat of humiliation in the eyes of other men, enacted through a "sequence of postures"—things we might say, or do, or even think, that, if we thought carefully about them, would make us ashamed of ourselves (Savran, 1992, p. 16). After all, how many of us have made homophobic or sexist remarks, or told racist jokes, or made lewd comments to women on the street? How many of us have translated those ideas and those words into actions, by physically attacking gay men, or forcing or cajoling a woman to have sex even though she didn't really want to because it was important to score?

Power and Powerlessness in the Lives of Men

I have argued that homophobia, men's fear of other men, is the animating condition of the dominant definition of masculinity in America, that the reigning definition of masculinity is a defensive effort to prevent being emasculated. In our efforts to suppress or overcome those fears, the dominant culture exacts a tremendous price from those deemed less than fully manly: women, gay men, nonnative-born men, men of color. This perspective may help clarify a paradox in men's lives, a paradox in which men have virtually all the power and yet do not feel powerful (see Kaufman, 1993).

Manhood is equated with power—over women, over other men. Everywhere we look, we see the institutional expression of that power—in state and national legislatures, on the boards of directors of every major U.S. corporation or law firm, and in every school and hospital administration. Women have long understood this, and feminist women have spent the past three decades challenging both the public and the private expressions of men's power and acknowledging their fear of men. Feminism as a set of theories both explains women's fear of men and empowers women to confront it both publicly and privately. Feminist women have theorized that masculinity is about the drive for domination, the drive for power, for conquest.

This feminist definition of masculinity as the drive for power is theorized from women's point of view. It is how women experience masculinity. But it assumes a symmetry between the public and the private that does not conform to men's experiences. Feminists observe that women, as a group, do not hold power in our society. They also observe that individually, they, as women, do not feel powerful. They feel afraid, vulnerable. Their observation of the social reality and their individual experiences are therefore symmetrical. Feminism also observes that men, as a group, *are* in power. Thus, with the same symmetry, feminism has tended to assume that individually men must feel powerful.

This is why the feminist critique of masculinity often falls on deaf ears with men. When confronted with the analysis that men have all the power, many men react incredulously. "What do you mean, men have all the power?" they ask. "What are you talking about? My wife bosses me around. My kids boss me around. My boss bosses me around. I have no power at all! I'm completely powerless!"

Men's feelings are not the feelings of the powerful, but of those who see themselves as powerless. These are the feelings that come inevitably from the discontinuity between the social and the psychological, between the aggregate analysis that reveals how men are in power as a group and the pyschological fact that they do not feel powerful as individuals. They are the feelings of men who were raised to believe themselves entitled to feel that power, but do not feel it. No wonder many men are frustrated and angry.

This may explain the recent popularity of those workshops and retreats designed to help men to claim their "inner" power, their "deep manhood," or their "warrior within." Authors such as Bly (1990), Moore and Gillette (1991, 1992, 1993a, 1993b), Farrell (1986, 1993), and Keen (1991) honor and respect men's feelings of powerlessness and acknowledge those feelings to be both true and real. "They gave white men the semblance of power," notes John Lee, one of the leaders of these retreats (quoted in *Newsweek*, p. 41). "We'll let you run the country, but in the meantime, stop feeling, stop talking, and continue swallowing your pain and your hurt." (We are not told who "they" are.)

Often the purveyors of the mythopoetic men's movement, that broad umbrella that encompasses all the groups helping men to retrieve this mythic deep manhood, use the image of the chauffeur to describe modern man's position. The chauffeur appears to have the power—he's wearing the uniform, he's in the driver's seat, and he knows where he's going. So, to the observer, the chauffeur looks as though he is in command. But to the chauffeur himself, they note, he is merely taking orders. He is not at all in charge.[7]

Despite the reality that everyone knows chauffeurs do not have the power, this image remains appealing to the men who hear it at these weekend workshops. But there is a missing piece to the image, a piece concealed by the framing of the image in terms of the individual man's experience. That missing piece is that the person who is giving the orders is also a man. Now we have a relationship *between* men—between men giving orders and other men taking those orders. The man who identifies with the chauffeur is entitled to be the man giving the orders, but he is not. ("They," it turns out, are other men.)

The dimension of power is now reinserted into men's experience not only as the product of individual experience but also as the product of relations with other men. In this sense, men's experience of powerlessness is *real*—the men actually feel it and certainly act on it—but it is not *true,* that is, it does not accurately describe their condition. In contrast to women's lives, men's lives are structured around relationships of power and men's differential access to power, as well as the differential access to that power of men as a group. Our imperfect analysis of our own situation leads us to believe that we men need *more* power, rather than leading us to support feminists' efforts to rearrange power relationships along more equitable lines.

Philosopher Hannah Arendt (1970) fully understood this contradictory experience of social and individual power:

> Power corresponds to the human ability not just to act but to act in concert. Power is never the property of an individual; it belongs to a group and remains in existence only so long as the group keeps together. When we say of somebody that he is "in power" we actually refer to his being empowered by a certain number of people to act in their name. The moment the group, from

which the power originated to begin with . . . disappears, "his power" also vanishes. (p. 44)

Why, then, do American men feel so powerless? Part of the answer is because we've constructed the rules of manhood so that only the tiniest fraction of men come to believe that they are the biggest of wheels, the sturdiest of oaks, the most virulent repudiators of femininity, the most daring and aggressive. We've managed to disempower the overwhelming majority of American men by other means—such as discriminating on the basis of race, class, ethnicity, age, or sexual preference.

Masculinist retreats to retrieve deep, wounded, masculinity are but one of the ways in which American men currently struggle with their fears and their shame. Unfortunately, at the very moment that they work to break down the isolation that governs men's lives, as they enable men to express those fears and that shame, they ignore the social power that men continue to exert over women and the privileges from which they (as the middle-aged, middle-class white men who largely make up these retreats) continue to benefit—regardless of their experiences as wounded victims of oppressive male socialization.[8]

Others still rehearse the politics of exclusion, as if by clearing away the playing field of secure gender identity of any that we deem less than manly—women, gay men, nonnative-born men, men of color—middle-class, straight, white men can reground their sense of themselves without those haunting fears and that deep shame that they are unmanly and will be exposed by other men. This is the manhood of racism, of sexism, of homophobia. It is the manhood that is so chronically insecure that it trembles at the idea of lifting the ban on gays in the military, that is so threatened by women in the workplace that women become the targets of sexual harassment, that is so deeply frightened of equality that it must ensure that the playing field of male competition remains stacked against all newcomers to the game.

Exclusion and escape have been the dominant methods American men have used to keep their fears of humiliation at bay. The fear of emasculation by other men, of being humiliated, of being seen as a sissy, is the leitmotif in my reading of the history of American manhood. Masculinity has become a relentless test by which we prove to other men, to women, and ultimately to ourselves, that we have successfully mastered the part. The restlessness that men feel today is nothing new in American history; we have been anxious and restless for almost two centuries. Neither exclusion nor escape has ever brought us the relief we've sought, and there is no reason to think that either will solve our problems now. Peace of mind, relief from gender struggle, will come only from a politics of inclusion, not exclusion, from standing up for equality and justice, and not by running away.

Notes

1. Of course, the phrase "American manhood" contains several simultaneous fictions. There is no single manhood that defines all American men; "America" is meant to refer to the United States proper, and there are significant ways in which this "American manhood" is the outcome of forces that transcend both gender and nation, that is, the global economic development of industrial capitalism. I use it, therefore, to describe the specific hegemonic version of masculinity in the United States, that normative constellation of attitudes, traits, and behaviors that became the standard against which all other masculinities are measured and against which individual men measure the success of their gender accomplishments.

2. Much of this work is elaborated in *Manhood: The American Quest* (in press).

3. Although I am here discussing only American masculinity, I am aware that others have located this chronic instability and efforts to prove manhood in the particular cultural and economic arrangements of Western society. Calvin, after all, inveighed against the disgrace "for men to become effeminate," and countless other theorists have described the mechanics of manly proof. (See, for example, Seidler, 1994.)

4. I do not mean to argue that women do not have anxieties about whether they are feminine enough. Ask any woman how she feels about being called aggressive; it sends a chill into her heart because her femininity is suspect. (I believe that the reason for the enormous recent popularity of sexy lingerie among women is that it enables women to remember they are still feminine underneath their corporate business suit—a suit that apes masculine styles.) But I think the stakes are not as great for women and that women have greater latitude in defining their identities around these questions than men do. Such are the ironies of sexism: The powerful have a narrower range of options than the powerless, because the powerless can *also* imitate the powerful and get away with it. It may even enhance status, if done with charm and grace—that is, is not threatening. For the powerful, any hint of behaving like the powerless is a fall from grace.

5. Such observations also led journalist Heywood Broun to argue that most of the attacks against feminism came from men who were shorter than 5 ft. 7 in. "The man who, whatever his physical size, feels secure in his own masculinity and in his own relation to life is rarely resentful of the opposite sex" (cited in Symes, 1930, p. 139).

6. Some of Freud's followers, such as Anna Freud and Alfred Adler, did follow up on these suggestions. (See especially, Adler, 1980.) I am grateful to Terry Kupers for his help in thinking through Adler's ideas.

7. The image is from Warren Farrell, who spoke at a workshop I attended at the First International Men's Conference, Austin, Texas, October 1991.

8. For a critique of these mythopoetic retreats, see Kimmel and Kaufman, Chapter 14, this volume.

References

Adler, A. (1980). *Cooperation between the sexes: Writings on women, love and marriage, sexuality and its disorders* (H. Ansbacher & R. Ansbacher, Eds. & Trans.). New York: Jason Aronson.

Arendt, H. (1970). *On revolution.* New York: Viking.

Bly, R. (1990). *Iron John: A book about men.* Reading, MA: Addison-Wesley.

Brannon, R. (1976). The male sex role—and what it's done for us lately. In R. Brannon & D. David (Eds.), *The forty-nine percent majority* (pp. 1-40). Reading, MA: Addison-Wesley.

Connell, R. W. (1987). *Gender and power.* Stanford, CA: Stanford University Press.

Farrell, W. (1986). *Why men are the way they are.* New York: McGraw-Hill.

Farrell, W. (1993). *The myth of male power: Why men are the disposable sex.* New York: Simon & Schuster.

Freud, S. (1933/1966). *New introductory lectures on psychoanalysis* (L. Strachey, Ed.). New York: Norton.

Gaylin, W. (1992). *The male ego.* New York: Viking.

Goffman, E. (1963). *Stigma.* Englewood Cliffs, NJ: Prentice Hall.

Gorer, G. (1964). *The American people: A study in national character.* New York: Norton.

Kaufman, M. (1993). *Cracking the armour: Power and pain in the lives of men.* Toronto: Viking Canada.

Keen, S. (1991). *Fire in the belly.* New York: Bantam.

Kimmel, M. S. (in press). *Manhood: The American quest.* New York: HarperCollins.

Leverenz, D. (1986). Manhood, humiliation and public life: Some stories. *Southwest Review, 71,* Fall.

Leverenz, D. (1991). The last real man in America: From Natty Bumppo to Batman. *American Literary Review, 3.*

Marx, K., & F. Engels. (1848/1964). The communist manifesto. In R. Tucker (Ed.), *The Marx-Engels reader.* New York: Norton.

Mead, M. (1965). *And keep your powder dry.* New York: William Morrow.

Moore, R., & Gillette, D. (1991). *King, warrior, magician lover.* New York: HarperCollins.

Moore, R., & Gillette, D. (1992). *The king within: Accessing the king in the male psyche.* New York: William Morrow.

Moore, R., & Gillette, D. (1993a). *The warrior within: Accessing the warrior in the male psyche.* New York: William Morrow.

Moore, R., & Gillette, D. (1993b). *The magician within: Accessing the magician in the male psyche.* New York: William Morrow.

Noble, V. (1992). A helping hand from the guys. In K. L. Hagan (Ed.), *Women respond to the men's movement.* San Francisco: HarperCollins.

Osherson, S. (1992). *Wrestling with love: How men struggle with intimacy, with women, children, parents, and each other.* New York: Fawcett.

Rotundo, E. A. (1993). *American manhood: Transformations in masculinity from the revolution to the modern era.* New York: Basic Books.

Savran, D. (1992). *Communists, cowboys and queers: The politics of masculinity in the work of Arthur Miller and Tennessee Williams.* Minneapolis: University of Minnesota Press.

Seidler, V. J. (1994). *Unreasonable men: Masculinity and social theory.* New York: Routledge.

Symes, L. (1930). The new masculinism. *Harper's Monthly, 161,* January.

Tocqueville, A. de. (1835/1967). *Democracy in America.* New York: Anchor.

Wayne, K. (1912). *Building the young man.* Chicago: A. C. McClurg.

Weber, M. (1905/1966). *The Protestant ethic and the spirit of capitalism.* New York: Charles Scribner's.

What men need is men's approval. (1993, January 3). *The New York Times,* p. C-11.

Wilkinson, R. (1986). *American tough: The tough-guy tradition and American character.* New York: Harper & Row.

Woolfolk, R. L., & Richardson, F. (1978). *Sanity, stress and survival.* New York: Signet.

8

Men, Feminism, and Men's Contradictory Experiences of Power

MICHAEL KAUFMAN

In a world dominated by men, the world of men is, by definition, a world of power. That power is a structured part of the economies and systems of political and social organization; it forms part of the core of religion, family, forms of play, and intellectual life. On an individual level, much of what we associate with masculinity hinges on a man's capacity to exercise power and control.

But men's lives speak of a different reality. Though men hold power and reap the privileges that come with our sex, that power is tainted.[1]

There is, in the lives of men, a strange combination of power and powerlessness, privilege and pain. Men enjoy social power and many forms of privilege by virtue of being male. But the way we have set up that world of power causes immense pain, isolation, and alienation not only for women but also for men. This is not to equate men's pain with the systemic and systematic forms of women's oppression. Rather, it is to say that men's worldly power—as we sit in our homes or walk the street, apply ourselves at work or march through history—comes with a price for us. This combination of power and pain is the hidden story in the lives of men. This is men's contradictory experience of power.

The idea of men's contradictory experiences of power suggests not simply that there is both power and pain in men's lives. Such a statement would obscure the centrality of men's power and the roots of pain within that power. The key, indeed, is the relationship between the two. As we know, men's social power is the source of individual power and privilege, but as we shall see, it is also the source of the individual experience of

142

pain and alienation. That pain can become an impetus for the individual reproduction—the acceptance, affirmation, celebration, and propagation—of men's individual and collective power. Alternatively, it can be an impetus for change.[2]

The existence of men's pain cannot be an excuse for acts of violence or oppression at the hands of men. After all, the overarching framework for this analysis is the basic point of feminism—and here I state the obvious—that almost all humans currently live in systems of patriarchal power that privilege men and stigmatize, penalize, and oppress women.[3] Rather, knowledge of this pain is a means to better understand men and the complex character of the dominant forms of masculinity.

The realization of men's contradictory experiences of power allows us to better understand the interactions of class, race, sexual orientation, ethnicity, age, and other factors in the lives of men—which is why I speak of contradictory experiences of power in the plural. It allows us to better understand the process of gender acquisition for men. It allows us to better grasp what we might think of as the *gender work* of a society.

An understanding of men's contradictory experiences of power enables us, when possible, to reach out to men with compassion, even as we are highly critical of particular actions and beliefs and challenge the dominant forms of masculinity. It can be one vehicle to understand how good human beings can do horrible things and how some beautiful baby boys can turn into horrible adults. It can help us understand how the majority of men can be reached with a message of change. It is, in a nutshell, the basis for men's embrace of feminism.

This chapter develops the concept of men's contradictory experiences of power within an analysis of gender power, of the social-psychological process of gender development, and of the relation of power, alienation, and oppression. It looks at the emergence of profeminism among men, seeking explanations for this within an analysis of men's contradictory experiences of power. It concludes with some thoughts on the implications of this analysis for the development of counterhegemonic practices by profeminist men that can have a mass appeal and a mainstream social impact.

Men's Contradictory Experiences of Power

Gender and Power

Theorizing men's contradictory experiences of power begins with two distinctions: The first is the well-known, but too-often overlooked, distinction between biological sex and socially constructed gender. Derived from that is the second, that there is no single masculinity although there are hegemonic and subordinate forms of masculinity. These forms are based on men's social power but are embraced in complex ways by individual men who also develop harmonious and nonharmonious relationships with other masculinities.

The importance of the sex-gender distinction in this context is that it is a basic conceptual tool that suggests how integral parts of our individual identity, behavior, activities, and beliefs can be a social product, varying from one group to another and often at odds with other human needs and possibilities. Our biological sex—that small set of absolute differences between all males and all females—does not prescribe a set and static natural personality.[4] The sex-gender distinction suggests there are characteristics, needs, and possibilities within the potential as females or males that are consciously and unconsciously suppressed, repressed, and channeled in the process of producing men and women. Such products, the masculine and the feminine, the man and the woman, are what gender is all about.[5]

Gender is the central organizing category of our psyches. It is the axis around which we organize our personalities, in which a distinct ego develops. I can no more separate "Michael Kaufman—human" from "Michael Kaufman—man" than I can talk about the activities of a whale without referring to the fact that it spends its whole life in the water.

Discourses on gender have had a hard time shaking off the handy, but limited, notion of sex roles.[6] Certainly, roles, expectations, and ideas about proper behavior do exist. But the central thing about gender is not the prescription of certain roles and the proscription of others—after all, the range of possible roles is wide and changing and, what is more, are rarely adopted in a nonconflictual way. Rather, the key thing about gender is that it is a description of actual social relations of power between males and females and the internalization of these relations of power.

Men's contradictory experiences of power exist in the realm of gender. This suggests there are ways that gender experience is a conflictual one. Only part of the conflict is between the social definitions of manhood and possibilities open to us within our biological sex. Conflict also exists because of the cultural imposition of what Bob Connell calls hegemonic forms of masculinity.[7] Although most men cannot possibly measure up to the dominant ideals of manhood, these maintain a powerful and often unconscious presence in our lives. They have power because they describe and embody real relations of power between men and women *and* among men: Patriarchy exists as a system not simply of men's power over women but also of hierarchies of power among different groups of men and between different masculinities.

These dominant ideals vary sharply from society to society, from era to era, and, these days, from decade to decade. Each subgroup, based on race, class, sexual orientation, or whatever, defines manhood in ways that conform to the economic and social possibilities of that group. For example, part of the ideal of working-class manhood among white North American men stresses physical skill and the ability to physically manipulate one's environment, while part of the ideal of their upper-middle class counterparts stresses verbal skills and the ability to manipulate one's environment through economic, social, and political means. Each dominant image bears a relationship to the real-life possibilities of these men and the tools at their disposal for the exercise of some form of power.

Power and Masculinity

Power, indeed, in the key term when referring to hegemonic masculinities. As I argue at greater length elsewhere,[8] the common feature of the dominant forms of contemporary masculinity is that manhood is equated with having some sort of power.

There are, of course, different ways to conceptualize and describe power. Political philosopher C. B. Macpherson points to the liberal and radical traditions of the last two centuries and tells us that one way we have come to think of human power is as the potential for using and developing our human capacities. Such a view is based on the idea that we are doers and creators able to use rational understanding, moral judgment, creativity, and emotional connection.[9] We possess the power to meet our needs, the power to fight injustice and oppression, the power of muscles and brain, and the power of love. All men, to a greater or lesser extent, experience these meanings of power.

Power, obviously, also has a more negative manifestation. Men have come to see power as a capacity to impose control on others and on our own unruly emotions. It means controlling material resources around us. This understanding of power meshes with the one described by Macpherson because, in societies based on hierarchy and inequality, it appears that all people cannot use and develop their capacities to an equal extent. You have power if you can take advantage of differences between people. I feel I can have power only if I have access to more resources than you do. Power is seen as power over something or someone else.

Although we all experience power in diverse ways, some that celebrate life and diversity and others that hinge on control and domination, the two types of experiences are not equal in the eyes of men, for the latter is the dominant conception of power in our world. The equation of power with domination and control is a definition that has emerged over time in societies in which various divisions are central to the way we have organized our lives: One class has control over economic resources and politics, adults have control over children, humans try to control nature, men dominate women, and, in many countries, one ethnic, racial, or religious group, or group based on sexual orientation, has control over others. There is, though, a common factor to all these societies: All are societies of male domination. The equation of masculinity with power is one that developed over centuries. It conformed to, and in turn justified, the real-life domination of men over women and the valuation of males over females.

Individual men internalize all this into their developing personalities because, born into such a life, we learn to experience our power as a capacity to exercise control. Men learn to accept and exercise power this way because it gives us privileges and advantages that women or children do not usually enjoy. The source of this power is in the society around us, but we learn to exercise it as our own. This is a discourse of social power, but the collective power of men rests not simply on transgenerational and abstract institutions and structures of power but on the ways we internalize, individualize, and come to embody and reproduce these institutions, structures, and conceptualizations of men's power.

Gender Work

The way in which power is internalized is the basis for a contradictory relationship to that power.[10] The most important body of work that looks at this process is, paradoxically, that of one of the more famous of 20th-century intellectual patriarchs, Sigmund Freud. Whatever his miserable, sexist beliefs and confusions about women's sexualities, he identified the psychological processes and structures through which gender is created. The work of Nancy Chodorow, Dorothy Dinnerstein, and Jessica Benjamin and, in a different sense, the psychoanalytic writings of Gad Horowitz make an important contribution to our understanding of the processes by which gender is individually acquired.[11]

The development of individual personalities of "normal" manhood is a social process within patriarchal family relationships.[12] The possibility for the creation of gender lies in two biological realities, the malleability of human drives and the long period of dependency of children. On this biological edifice a social process is able to go to work for the simple reason that this period of dependency is lived out in society. Within different family forms, each society provides a charged setting in which love and longing, and support and disappointment become the vehicles for developing a gendered psyche. The family gives a personalized stamp to the categories, values, ideals, and beliefs of a society in which one's sex is a fundamental aspect of self-definition and life. The family takes abstract ideals and turns them into the stuff of love and hate. As femininity gets represented by the mother (or mother figures) and masculinity by the father (or father figures) in both nuclear and extended families, complicated conceptions take on flesh and blood form: We are no longer talking of patriarchy and sexism, and masculinity and femininity as abstract categories. I am talking about your mother and father, your sisters and brothers, your home, kin, and family.[13]

By 5 or 6 years old, before we have much conscious knowledge of the world, the building blocks of our gendered personalities are firmly anchored. Over this skeleton we build the adult as we learn to survive and, with luck, thrive within an interlocked set of patriarchal realities that includes schools, religious establishments, the media, and the world of work.

The internalization of gender relations is a building block of our personalities—that is, it is the individual elaboration of gender and our own subsequent contributions to replenishing and adapting institutions and social structures in a way that wittingly or unwittingly preserves patriarchal systems. This process, when taken in its totality, forms what I call the gender work of a society. Because of the multiple identities of individuals and the complex ways we all embody both power and powerlessness—as a result of the interaction of our sex, race, class, sexual orientation, ethnicity, religion, intellectual and physical abilities, and sheer chance—gender work is not a linear process. Although gender ideals exist in the form of hegemonic masculinities and femininities and although gender power is a social reality, when we live in heterogeneous societies, we each grapple with often conflicting pressures, demands, and possibilities.

The notion of gender work suggests there is an active process that creates and recreates gender. It suggests that this process can be an ongoing one, with particular tasks at particular times of our lives and that allows us to respond to changing relations of gender power. It suggests that gender is not a static thing that we become, but is a form of ongoing interaction with the structures of the surrounding world.

My masculinity is a bond, a glue, to the patriarchal world. It is the thing that makes that world mine, that makes it more or less comfortable to live in. Through the incorporation of a dominant form of masculinity particular to my class, race, nationality, era, sexual orientation, and religion, I gained real benefits *and* an individual sense of self-worth. From the moment when I learned, unconsciously, there were not only two sexes but a social significance to the sexes, my own self-worth became measured against the yardstick of gender. As a young male, I was granted a fantasy reprieve from the powerlessness of early childhood because I unconsciously realized I was part of that half of humanity with social power. My ability to incorporate not simply the roles, but to grasp onto this power—even if, at first, it existed only in my imagination—was part of the development of my individuality.

The Price

In more concrete terms the acquisition of hegemonic (and most subordinate) masculinities is a process through which men come to suppress a range of emotions, needs, and possibilities, such as nurturing, receptivity, empathy, and compassion, which are experienced as inconsistent with the power of manhood. These emotions and needs do not disappear; they are simply held in check or not allowed to play as full a role in our lives as would be healthy for ourselves and those around us. We dampen these emotions because they might restrict our ability and desire to control ourselves or dominate the human beings around us on whom we depend for love and friendship. We suppress them because they come to be associated with the femininity we have rejected as part of our quest for masculinity.

These are many things men do to have the type of power we associate with masculinity: We've got to perform and stay in control. We've got to conquer, be on top of things, and call the shots. We've got to tough it out, provide, and achieve. Meanwhile we learn to beat back our feelings, hide our emotions, and suppress our needs.

Whatever power might be associated with dominant masculinities, they also can be the source of enormous pain. Because the images are, ultimately, childhood pictures of omnipotence, they are impossible to obtain. Surface appearances aside, no man is completely able to live up to these ideals and images. For one thing we all continue to experience a range of needs and feelings that are deemed inconsistent with manhood. Such experiences become the source of enormous fear. In our society, this fear is experienced as homophobia or, to express it differently, homophobia is the vehicle that simultaneously transmits and quells the fear.

Such fear and pain have visceral, emotional, intellectual dimensions—although none of these dimensions is necessarily conscious—and the more we are the prisoners of the fear, the more we need to exercise the power we grant ourselves as men. In other words, men exercise patriarchal power not only because we reap tangible benefits from it. The assertion of power is also a response to fear and to the wounds we have experienced in the quest for power. Paradoxically, men are wounded by the very way we have learned to embody and exercise our power.

A man's pain may be deeply buried, barely a whisper in his heart, or it may flood from every pore. The pain might be the lasting trace of things that happened or attitudes and needs acquired 20, 30, or 60 years earlier. Whatever it is, the pain inspires fear for it means not being a man, which means, in a society that confuses gender and sex, not being a male. This means losing power and ungluing basic building blocks of our personalities. This fear must be suppressed for it itself is inconsistent with dominant masculinities.

As every woman who knows men can tell us, the strange thing about men's trying to suppress emotions is that it leads not to less but to more emotional dependency. By losing track of a wide range of our human needs and capacities and by blocking our need for care and nurturance, men lose our emotional common sense and our ability to look after ourselves. Unmet, unknown, and unexpected emotions and needs do not disappear but rather spill into our lives at work, on the road, in a bar, or at home. The very emotions and feelings we have tried to suppress gain a strange hold over us. No matter how cool and in control, these emotions dominate us. I think of the man who feels powerlessness who beats his wife in uncontrolled rage. I walk into a bar and see two men hugging each other in a drunken embrace, the two of them able to express their affection for each other only when plastered. I read about the teenage boys who go out gay-bashing and the men who turn their sense of impotence into a rage against blacks, Jews, or any who are convenient scapegoats.

Alternatively, men might direct buried pain against themselves in the form of self-hate, self-deprecation, physical illness, insecurity, or addictions. Sometimes this is connected with the first. Interviews with rapists and batterers often show not only contempt for women but also an even deeper hatred and contempt for oneself. It is as if, not able to stand themselves, they lash out at others, possibly to inflict similar feelings on another who has been defined as a socially acceptable target, possibly to experience a momentary sense of power and control.[14] We can think of men's pain as having a dynamic aspect. We might displace it or make it invisible, but in doing so we give it even more urgency. This blanking out of a sense of pain is another way of saying that men learn to wear a suit of armor, that is, to maintain an emotional barrier from those around us in order to keep fighting and winning. The impermeable ego barriers discussed in feminist psychoanalysis simultaneously protects men and keeps us locked in a prison of our own creation.

Power, Alienation, and Oppression

Men's pain and the way we exercise power are not just symptoms of our current gender order. Together they shape our sense of manhood, for masculinity has become a form of alienation. Men's alienation is our ignorance of our own emotions, feelings, needs, and potential for human connection and nurturance. Our alienation also results from our distance from women and our distance and isolation from other men. In his book *The Gender of Oppression,* Jeff Hearn suggests that what we think of as masculinity is the result of the way our power and our alienation combine. Our alienation increases the lonely pursuit of power and emphasizes our belief that power requires an ability to be detached and distant.[15]

Men's alienation and distance from women and other men takes on strange and rather conflicting forms. Robert Bly and those in the mythopoetic men's movement have made a lot out of the loss of the father and the distance of many men, in dominant North American cultures anyway, from their own fathers. Part of their point is accurate and simply reaffirms important work done over the past couple of decades on issues around fathers and fathering.[16] Their discussion of these points, however, lacks the richness and depth of feminist psychoanalysis that holds, as a central issue, that the absence of men from most parenting and nurturing tasks means that the masculinity internalized by little boys is based on distance, separation, and a fantasy image of what constitutes manhood, rather than on the type of oneness and inseparability that typifies early mother-child relationships.

The distance from other men is accentuated, in many contemporary heterosexual men's cultures at least, by the emotional distance from other males that begins to develop in adolescence. Men might have buddies, pals, workmates, and friends, but they seldom have the level of complete trust and intimacy enjoyed by many women. Our experience of friendship is limited by the reduced empathy that becomes the masculine norm.[17] As a result we have the paradox that most heterosexual men (and even many gay men) in the dominant North American culture are extremely isolated from other men. In fact, as I have argued elsewhere, many of the institutions of male bonding—the clubs, sporting events, card games, locker rooms, workplaces, professional and religious hierarchies—are a means to provide safety for isolated men who need to find ways to affirm themselves, find common ground with other men, and collectively exercise their power.[18] Such isolation means that each man can remain blind to his dialogue of self-doubt about making the masculine grade—the self-doubts that are consciously experienced by virtually all adolescent males and then consciously or unconsciously by them as adults. In a strange sense, this isolation is key in preserving patriarchy: To a greater or lesser extent it increases the possibility that all men end up colluding with patriarchy—in all its diverse myths and realities—because their own doubts and sense of confusion remain buried.

It is not only other men from whom most men, and certainly most straight men, remain distant. It is also from women. Here another important insight of feminist psychoanalysis is key: Boys' separation from their mother or mother figure means the erection of more or less impermeable ego barriers and an affirmation of distinction, difference, and opposition to those things identified with women and femininity. Boys repress characteristics and possibilities associated with mother/women/the feminine, unconsciously and consciously. Thus Bly and the mythopoetic theorists have it all wrong when they suggest that the central problem with contemporary men (and by this they seem to mean North American middle-class, young to middle-aged, white, straight urban men) is that they have become feminized. The problem as suggested above is the wholesale repression and suppression of those traits and possibilities associated with women.[19]

These factors suggest the complexity of gender identity, gender formation, and gender relations. It appears that we need forms of analysis that allow for contradictory relationships between individuals and the power structures from which they benefit. It is a strange situation when men's very real power and privilege in the world hinges not only on that power but also on an experience of alienation and powerlessness— rooted in childhood experiences but reinforced in different ways as adolescents and then adults. These experiences, in turn, become the spur at the individual level (in addition to the obvious and tangible benefits) to recreate and celebrate the forms and structures through which men exercise power.

But as we have seen, there is no single masculinity or one experience of being a man. The experience of different men, their actual power and privilege in the world, is based on a range of social positions and relations. The social power of a poor white man is different from a rich one, a working-class black man from a working-class white man, a gay man from a bisexual man from a straight man, a Jewish man in Ethiopia from a Jewish man in Israel, a teenage boy from an adult. Within each group, men usually have privileges and power relative to the women in that group, but in society as a whole, things are not always so straightforward.

The emergent discourses on the relation between oppression based on gender, racial, class, and social orientation are but one reflection of the complexity of the problem. These discussions are critical in the development of a new generation of feminist analysis and practice. The tendency, unfortunately, is often to add up categories of oppression as if they were separate units. Sometimes, such tallies are even used to decide who, supposedly, is the most oppressed. The problem can become absurd for two simple reasons: One is the impossibility of quantifying experiences of oppression; the other is that the sources of oppression do not come in discreet units. After all, think of an unemployed black gay working-class man. We might say this man is exploited as a working-class man, oppressed as a gay man, oppressed and the victim of racism because he is black, suffering terribly because he is out of work, but we are not going to say, oh, he's oppressed *as a man.* Of course he is not oppressed as a man, but I worry that the distinction is rather academic because none of the qualities used to describe him is completely separable from the others. After all, his particular sense of manhood, that is, his masculinity, is in part a product of those other factors. "Man" becomes as much an adjective modifying "black," "working-class," "out of work," and "gay" as these things modify the word "man." Our lives, our minds, our bodies simply are not divided up in a way that allows us to separate the different categories of our existence. This man's experiences, self-definition(s), and location in the hierarchies of power are codetermined by a multitude of factors. Furthermore, because masculinities denote relations of power among men, and not just men against women, a man who has little social power in the dominant society, whose masculinity is not of a hegemonic variety, who is the victim of tremendous social oppression, might also wield tremendous power in his own milieu and neighborhood vis-à-vis women of his own class or social grouping or other males, as in the case of a school-yard bully or a member of an urban gang who certainly does not have structural power in the society as a whole.

Our whole language of oppression is in need of overhaul for it is based on simplistic binary oppositions, reductionist equations between identity and social location, and unifocal notions of the self. What is important for us here is not to deny that men, as a group, have social power or even that men, within their subgroups, tend to have considerable power, but rather that there are different forms of structural power and powerlessness among men. Similarly, it is important not to deny the structural and individual oppression of women as a social group. Rather it is to recognize, as we have seen earlier, that there is not a linear relationship between a structured system of power inequalities, the real and supposed benefits of power, and one's own experience of these relations of power.

Men and Feminism

An analysis of men's contradictory experiences of power gives us useful insights into the potential relation of men to feminism. The power side of the equation is not anything new and, indeed, men's power and privileges form a very good reason for men to individually and collectively oppose feminism.

But we do know that an increasing number of men have become sympathetic to feminism (in content if not always in name) and have embraced feminist theory and action (although, again, more often in theory than in action). There are different reasons for a man's acceptance of feminism. It might be outrage at inequality; it might result from the influence of a partner, family member, or friend; it might be his own sense of injustice at the hands of other men; it might be a sense of shared oppression, say because of his sexual orientation; it might be his own guilt about the privileges he enjoys as a man; it might be horror at men's violence; it might be sheer decency.

Although the majority of men in North America would still not label themselves profeminist, a strong majority of men in Canada and a reasonable percentage of men in the United States would sympathize with many of the issues as presented by feminists. As we know, this sympathy does not always translate into changes of behavior, but, increasingly, ideas are changing and in some cases, behavior is starting to catch up.

How do we explain the growing number of men who are supportive of feminism and women's liberation (to use that term that was too hastily abandoned by the end of the 1970s)? Except for the rare outcast or iconoclast, there are few examples from history where significant numbers of a ruling group supported the liberation of those over whom they ruled and from whose subordination they benefited.

One answer is that the current feminist wave—whatever its weaknesses and whatever backlash might exist against it—has had a massive impact during the past two and a half decades. Large numbers of men, along with many women who had supported the status quo, now realize that the tide has turned and, like it or not, the world is changing. Women's rebellion against patriarchy holds the promise of bringing patriarchy to an end. Although patriarchy in its many different social and economic forms still has considerable staying power, an increasing number of its social, political, economic, and emotional structures are proving unworkable. Some men react with rearguard actions while others step tentatively or strongly in the direction of change.

This explanation of men's support for change catches only part of the picture. The existence of contradictory experiences of power suggests there is a basis for men's embrace of feminism that goes beyond swimming with a change in the tide.

The rise of feminism has shifted the balance between men's power and men's pain. In societies and eras in which men's social power went largely unchallenged, men's power so outweighed men's pain that the existence of this pain could remain buried, even nonexistent. When you rule the roost, call the shots, and are closer to God, there is not a lot of room left for pain, at least for pain that appears to be linked to the practices of masculinity. But with the rise of modern feminism, the fulcrum between men's power and men's pain has been undergoing a rapid shift. This is particularly true in cultures where the definition of men's power had already moved away from tight control over the home and tight monopolies in the realm of work.[20]

As men's power is challenged, those things that came as a compensation, a reward, or a lifelong distraction from any potential pain are progressively reduced or, at least, called into question. As women's oppression becomes problematized, many forms of this oppression become problems for men. Individual gender-related experiences of pain and disquietude among men have become increasingly manifest and have started to gain a social hearing and social expression in widely diverse forms, including different branches of the men's movement—from reactionary antifeminists, to the Bly-type mythopoetic movement, to profeminist men's organizing.

In other words, if gender is about power, then as actual relations of power between men and women and between different groups of men (such as straight and gay men) start to shift, then our experiences of gender and our gender definitions must also begin to change. The process of gender work is ongoing and includes this process of reformulation and upheaval.

Rising Support and Looming Pitfalls

The embrace of feminism by men is not, surprisingly, entirely new. As Michael Kimmel argues in his insightful introduction to *Against the Tide: Profeminist Men in the United States, 1796-1990. A Documentary History*, profeminist men have constituted a small but persistent feature of the U.S. sociopolitical scene for two centuries.[21]

What makes the current situation different is that profeminism among men (or at least acceptance of aspects of feminist critiques and feminist political action) is reaching such large-scale dimensions. Ideas that were almost unanimously discounted by men (and indeed by most women) only 25 years ago now have widespread legitimacy. It does not help to overstate the progress that has been made; many individuals remain staunchly propatriarchal and most institutions remain male dominated. But changes are visible. Affirmative action programs are widespread, many social institutions controlled by men—in education, the arts, professions, politics, and religion—are undergoing a process of sexual integration even though this usually requires not only ongoing pressure but often women's adapting to masculinist work cultures. In various countries the percentage of men favoring abortion rights for women equals or outstrips support by women. Male-dominated governments have accepted the need to adopt laws that have been part of the feminist agenda. (One of the most dramatic instances was in Canada in 1992 when the Conservative Party government completely recast the law on rape—following a process of consultation with women's groups. The new law stated that all sexual relations must be explicitly consensual, that "no means no" and that it takes a clearly stated and freely given "yes" to mean yes. Again, in Canada, one thinks of the way that feminist organizations insisted on their presence—and were accepted as key players—at the bargaining table in the 1991 and 1992 round of constitutional talks.) All such changes were a result of the hard work and impact of the women's movement; this impact on institutions controlled by men shows the increased acceptance by men of at least some of the terms of feminism, whether this acceptance is begrudging or welcome.

For those men and women interested in social change and speeding up the type of changes described above, some serious problems remain:

Although there are ever-increasing sympathies among men to the ideas of women's equality, and although some institutions have been forced to adopt measures promoting women's equality, there is still a lag between the ideas accepted by men and their actual behavior. Although many men might reluctantly or enthusiastically support efforts for change, profeminism among men has not yet reached mass organizational forms in most cases.

This brings us to the implications of the analysis of this chapter to the issue of profeminist organizing by men. Stimulated by the ever-widening impact of modern feminism, the past two decades have seen the emergence of something that, for lack of a better phrase, has been called the men's movement. There have been two major currents to the men's movements.[22] One is the mythopoetic men's movement. Coming to prominence in the late 1980s (in particular, with the success of Robert Bly's *Iron John*), it is actually the latest expression of an approach dating to the 1970s that focuses on the pain and costs of being men or of a masculinist politic dating almost a hundred years that sought to create homosocial spaces as an antidote to the supposed feminization of men.[23] A second has been the less prominent profeminist men's movement (within which I count my own activities) that has focused on the social and individual expressions of men's power and privileges, including issues of men's violence.

Unfortunately, the dominant expressions of these two wings of the men's movement have developed with their own deformities, idiosyncrasies, and mistakes in analysis and action. In particular, each has tended to grapple primarily with one aspect of men's lives—men's power, in the case of the profeminist movement, and men's pain, in the case of the mythopoetic. In doing so, they not only miss the totality of men's experience in a male-dominated society, but miss the crucial relationship between men's power and men's pain.[24]

The profeminist men's movement starts from the acknowledgment that men have power and privilege in a male-dominated society. Although I feel strongly that this must be our starting point, it is only a beginning, for there are many challenging issues: How can we build mass and active support for feminism among men? How can we encourage men to realize that support for feminism means more than supporting institutional and legal changes but also requires personal changes in their own lives? How can we link the struggles against homophobia and sexism and to realize in practice that homophobia is a major factor in promoting misogyny and sexism among men?

Within these questions are a set of theoretical, strategic, and tactical problems. If our goal is not simply to score academic or political debating points or to feel good about our profeminist credentials, but, alongside women, to actually affect the course of history, then, I would suggest, it is critical to take these questions very seriously. For me, several points emerge from this analysis.

Whether a man assumes that his most pressing concern is working in support of women's equality and challenging patriarchy, in challenging homophobia and encouraging a gay- and lesbian-positive culture, or in enhancing the lives of all men, our starting point as men must be a recognition of the centrality of men's power and privilege and a recognition of the need to challenge that power. This is not only in support of feminism, but it is a recognition that the social and personal construction of this power is the source of the malaise, confusion, and alienation felt by men in our era as well as an important source of homophobia.

The more we realize that some form of homophobia is central to the experience of men in most patriarchal societies, that homophobia and heterosexism shape the daily experiences of all men, and that such homophobia is central to the construction of sexism, the more we will be able to develop the understanding and the practical tools to achieve equality. The profeminist men's movement in North America, Europe, and Australia has provided men with a unique opportunity for gay, straight, and bisexual men to come together, to work together, to dance together. Yet I do not think that most straight profeminist men see confronting homophobia as a priority or, even if a part of a list of priorities, as something that has a central bearing on their own lives.[25]

The notion of contradictory experiences of power, in the plural, provides an analytical tool for integrating issues of race, class, and ethnicity into the heart of profeminist men's organizing. It allows us to sympathetically relate to a range of men's experiences, to understand that men's power is nonlinear and subject to a variety of social and psychological forces. It suggests forms of analysis and action that understand that the behavior of any group of men is the result of an often contradictory insertion into various hierarchies of power. It belies any notion that our identities and experiences as men can be separated from our identities and experiences based on the color of our skin or our class background. It therefore suggests that struggling against racism, anti-Semitism, and class privilege, for example, is integral to a struggle to transform contemporary gender relations.

We must follow the lead of the women's movement in asserting the importance not only of both personal and social change but of the relationship of the two. As men we need to advocate and actively organize in support of legal and social changes, from freedom of choice to child-care programs, from new initiatives to challenge men's violence to affirmative action programs at our workplaces. We must support and help build such changes not only at the level of macropolitics but in our own workplaces, trade unions, professional associations, places of worship, and communities. We must see these matters not simply as "women's issues" but issues that confront and affect us all.

Such work not only involves providing verbal, financial, and organizational support to the campaigns organized by women; it also requires men organizing campaigns of men aimed at men. Efforts such as Canada's White Ribbon Campaign[26] are critical to break men's silence on a range of feminist issues, to encourage men to identify with these concerns, and to productively use the resources to which men have disproportionate access. Such efforts must be carried out in dialogue and consultation with women's groups—and with respect for the leadership that women provide in this work—so that men will not come to dominate this work. At the same time we should not shrink from the importance of men taking up profeminist issues as our own: As perpetrators of violence against women, for example, men must be reached if we are to stop the problem—and because of sexism men can better reach other men.

At the same time as we engage in social activism, we need to learn to scrutinize and challenge our own behavior. This does not mean sinking into guilt or joining those men within the profeminist community who like the feel of a good hairshirt. After all, guilt is a profoundly conservative, demobilizing, and disempowering emotion. Rather it means understanding that our contribution to social change will be limited if we continue to interact with women on the basis of dominance; it will be limited if we do not actively challenge homophobia and sexism among our friends and workmates and in our ourselves. Change will be limited if we do not begin to create the immediate conditions for the transformation of social life, especially striving for equality in housework and child care.

Struggling for personal change can be done only if we are able to break our isolation with other men, something experienced most acutely by straight men but also by gay men. After all, uncontested assumptions about what it means to be a man combined with deep-set insecurities about making the masculine grade are essential props of the current patriarchal system and a basic reason why we construct and reconstruct personalities shaped by patriarchy. So developing a social action approach is entirely consistent with—and perhaps ultimately requires—men developing support groups. Such groups allow us to look at our individual process of gender work, how we have all been shaped by our patriarchal system. It allows us to examine our own contradictory relationships to men's power. It allows us to overcome the fear that prevents most men from speaking out and challenging sexism and homophobia. It can give us a new and different sense of strength.

In all this, in our public work, in our challenges to sexism and homophobia, to racism and bigotry in our daily lives, we must not shrink from a politics of compassion. This means never losing sight of the negative impact of contemporary patriarchy on men ourselves even if our framework sees the oppression of women as the central problem. It means looking at the negative impact of homophobia on all men. It means avoiding the language of guilt and blame and substituting for it the language of taking responsibility for change.

Such a politics of compassion is only possible if we begin from the sex-gender distinction. If patriarchy and its symptoms were a biological fiat then not only would the problems be virtually intractable, but punishment, repression, blame, and guilt would seem to be the necessary corollaries. But if we start with the assumption that the problems are ones of gender—and that gender refers to particular relations of power that are socially structured and individually embodied—then we are able to be simultaneously critical of men's collective power and the behavior and attitudes of individual men *and* to be male affirmative, to say that feminism will enhance the lives of men, that change is a win-win situation but that it requires men giving up forms of privilege, power, and control.

On the psychodynamic level—the realm in which we can witness the interplay between social movements and the individual psyche—the challenge of feminism to men is one of dislodging the hegemonic masculine psyche. This is not a psychological interpretation of change because it is the social challenge to men's power and the actual reduction of men's social power that is the source of change. What was once a secure relationship between power over others, control over oneself, and the suppression of a range of needs and emotions is under attack. What had felt stable, natural, and right is being revealed as both a source of oppression for others and the prime source of pain, anguish, and disquietude for men themselves.

The implication of all this is that the feminist challenge to men's power has the potential of liberating men and helping more men discover new masculinities that will be part of demolishing gender altogether. Whatever privileges and forms of power we will certainly lose will be increasingly compensated by the end to the pain, fear, dysfunctional forms of behavior, violence experienced at the hands of other men, violence we inflict on ourselves, endless pressure to perform and succeed, and the sheer impossibility of living up to our masculine ideals.

Our awareness of men's contradictory experiences of power gives us the tools to simultaneously challenge men's power and speak to men's pain. It is the basis for a politics of compassion and for enlisting men's support for a revolution that is challenging the most basic and long-lasting structures of human civilization.

Notes

1. Although it may be somewhat awkward for women readers, I often refer to men in the first person plural—we, us, our—to acknowledge my position within the object of my analysis.

2. My thanks to Harry Brod who several years ago cautioned me against talking about men's power and men's pain as two sides of the same coin, a comment that led me to focus on the relationship between the two. Thanks also to Harry and to Bob Connell for their comments on a draft of this article. I'd particularly like to express my appreciation to Michael Kimmel both for his comments on the draft and for our ongoing intellectual partnership and friendship.

3. Although there has been controversy over the applicability of the term *patriarchy*—see, for example, Michele Barrett and Mary MacIntosh's reservations in *The Anti-Social Family* (London: Verso, 1982)—I follow others who use it as a broad descriptive term for male-dominated social systems.

4. Even the apparently fixed biological line between males and females—fixed in terms of genital and reproductive differences—is subject to variation, as seen in the relatively significant number of males and females with so-called genital, hormonal, and chromosomal abnormalities that bend the sharp distinction between the sexes—rendering men or women infertile, women or men with secondary sex characteristics usually associated with the other sex, and women or men with different genital combinations. Nonetheless, the notion of biological sex is useful as shorthand and to distinguish sex from socially constructed gender. For an accessible discussion, particularly on the endocrinology of sex differentiation, see John Money and Anke A. Ehrhardt's, *Man & Woman, Boy & Girl* (Baltimore, MD: Johns Hopkins University Press, 1972).

5. The sex-gender distinction is ignored or blurred not only by reactionary ideologues or sociobiologists (of both liberal and conservative persuasion) who want to assert that the current lives, roles, and relations between the sexes are timeless, biological givens. At least one stream of feminist thought—dubbed cultural feminism or difference feminism by its critics—celebrates to varying degrees a range of supposedly timeless and natural female qualities. Similarly, those influenced by Jungian thought, such as Robert Bly and the mythopoetic thinkers, also posit essential qualities of manhood and woman-

hood. Even those feminists who accept the sex-gender distinction often use the term *gender* when what is meant is *sex*—as in "the two genders" and "the other gender" when in fact there are a multiplicity of genders, as suggested in the concepts of femininities and masculinities. Similarly, many feminist women and profeminist men refer erroneously to "male violence"—rather than "men's violence"—even though the biological category "male" (as opposed to the gender category "men") implies that a propensity to commit violence is part of the genetic mandate of half the species, a supposition that neither anthropology nor contemporary observation warrants.

6. For a critique of the limits of sex role theory, see, for example, Tim Carrigan, Bob Connell, and John Lee, "Hard and Heavy: Toward a New Sociology of Masculinity," in *Beyond Patriarchy: Essays by Men on Pleasure, Power and Change,* edited by Michael Kaufman (Toronto: Oxford University Press, 1987).

7. R. W. Connell, *Gender and Power* (Stanford, CA: Stanford University Press, 1987).

8. *Cracking the Armour: Power, Pain, and the Lives of Men* (Toronto: Viking Canada, 1993).

9. C. B. Macpherson, *Democratic Theory* (London: Oxford University Press, 1973).

10. Although I am referring here to men's contradictory relationships to masculine power, a parallel, although very different, discussion could also be conducted concerning women's relationship to men's power and to their own positions of individual, familial, and social power and powerlessness.

11. See Nancy Chodorow, *The Reproduction of Mothering* (Berkeley: University of California, 1978); Dorothy Dinnerstein, *The Mermaid and the Minotaur* (New York: Harper Colophon, 1977); Jessica Benjamin, *The Bonds of Love* (New York: Random House, 1988); and Gad Horowitz, *Repression: Basic and Surplus Repression in Psychoanalytic Theory* (Toronto: University of Toronto Press, 1977).

12. This paragraph is based on text in Kaufman, *Cracking the Armour,* op. cit.; and Kaufman, "The Construction of Masculinity and the Triad of Men's Violence," in *Beyond Patriarchy,* op. cit.

13. I am not implying that the nature of the relations or the conflicts are the same from one family form to another or, even that "the family" as such exists in all societies. See M. Barrett and M. McIntosh, *The Anti-Social Family,* op. cit.

14. See, for example, the accounts in Sylvia Levine and Joseph Koenig, eds., *Why Men Rape* (Toronto: Macmillan of Canada, 1980) and Timothy Beneke, *Men on Rape* (New York: St. Martin's, 1982).

15. Jeff Hearn, *The Gender of Oppression* (Brighton, UK: Wheatsheaf, 1987).

16. For numerous sources on fatherhood, see Michael E. Lamb, ed., *The Role of the Father in Child Development* (New York: John Wiley, 1981); Stanley H. Cath, Alan R. Gurwitt, and John Munder Ross, *Father and Child* (Boston: Little, Brown, 1982). Also see Michael W. Yogman, James Cooley, & Daniel Kindlon, "Fathers, Infants, Toddlers: Developing Relationship" and others in Phyllis Bronstein and Carolyn Pape Cowan, *Fatherhood Today* (New York: John Wiley, 1988); and Kyle D. Pruett, "Infants of Primary Nurturing Fathers," in *The Psychoanalytic Study of the Child,* vol. 38, 1983; and for a different approach, see Samuel Osherson, *Finding our Fathers* (New York: Free Press, 1986).

17. Lillian Rubin, *Intimate Strangers* (New York: Harper Colophon, 1984). See also Peter M. Nardi, ed., *Men's Friendships* (Newbury Park: Sage, 1992).

18. Kaufman, *Cracking the Armour,* op. cit.

19. The mythopoetic framework is discussed at length by Michael Kimmel and Michael Kaufman in chapter 14 of this volume.

20. One fascinating account of total patriarchal control of the home is Naguib Mahfouz's 1956 book *Palace Walk* (New York: Anchor Books, 1990).

21. Michael Kimmel and Tom Mosmiller, eds., *Against the Tide: Profeminist Men in the United States, 1776-1990. A Documentary History* (Boston: Beacon, 1992).

22. A third is the antifeminist and, at times, unashamedly misogynist, men's rights movement, which does not concern us in this chapter.

23. In the 1970s and early 1980s, books and articles by men such as Herb Goldberg and Warren Farrell spoke of the lethal characteristics of manhood—in particular in the ways it was lethal against men. By the time Robert Bly's *Iron John* made it to the top of the best-seller lists at the end of 1990, vague analyses had crystalized into a broad North American movement with a newspaper, *Wingspan,* men's retreats, groups, drumming circles, regional newsletters, and a string of books that has yet to abate.

There are some positive and potentially progressive aspects to this approach and the work of the thousands of men who participate in some sort of men's group within this framework. One is the simple, but significant, acknowledgment of men's pain; another is the participation of men in men's groups and the decision by men (usually, but not always, straight men) to break their isolation from other men and seek collective paths of change.

On the other hand, as Michael Kimmel and I argue at length elsewhere in this volume, the theoretical framework of this movement virtually ignores men's social and individual power (and its relation to pain), ignores what we have called the mother wound (following the insights of feminist psychoanalysis), crudely attempts to appropriate a hodgepodge of indigenous cultures, and pulls men away from the social (and possibly the individual) practices that will challenge patriarchy. My thanks to Michael for the formulation of masculinist politics creating new homosocial space.

24. Although categorizing these two wings of the men's movement makes a useful tool for discussion, there are no hard and fast boundaries between the two. A number of the men (more so in Canada than in the United States) attracted to Robert Bly and the mythopoetic movement are sympathetic to feminism and the contemporary struggles of women. Meanwhile, most men pulled toward the profeminist framework are also concerned about enhancing the lives of men. Men, particularly in the latter category, are concerned with the impact of homophobia on all men.

25. My favorite story about the reluctance of many straights to identify with the need to publicly challenge homophobia is told by a colleague who, in Toronto in the early 1980s, was teaching a course on social change. At the student pub after class one night, one of the students was lamenting that he didn't live in another era. It would have been great to live in the late 1930s, he said, so he could have gone off and fought in the Spanish revolution. My colleague said, "Well you know, dozens of gay bathhouses were raided by the police this week and there have been big demonstrations almost every night. You could join those." The student looked at him and said, "But I'm not gay," to which my colleague responded, "I didn't know you were Spanish."

On the relationship of homophobia to the construction of "normal" masculinity see Michael Kimmel, Chapter 7, this volume, and Kaufman, *Cracking the Armour,* op. cit. Also see Suzanne Pharr, *Homophobia: A Weapon of Sexism* (Little Rock: Chardon Press, 1988).

26. The White Ribbon Campaign focuses on men's violence against women. A small group of us began the campaign in late 1991 and within a week tens of thousands of men across Canada (hundreds of thousands a year later) wore a white ribbon for a week as a pledge they would not "commit, condone or remain silent about violence against women." The campaign, aimed to break men's silence and to mobilize the energy and resources of men, enjoys support across the social and political spectrum and has begun to spread to other countries. To receive an information packet on the campaign ($2) please write: The White Ribbon Campaign, 220 Yonge Street, Suite 104, Toronto, Canada M5B 2H1 or telephone (416) 596-1513 or fax (416) 596-2359.

PART TWO

Theorizing *MASCULINITIES*

9

Theater of War

Combat, the Military, and Masculinities

DAVID H. J. MORGAN

I found it very difficult to speak to my wife about my experiences. The only way that I could ever let her know how I felt was actually to tell the story to other people but to make sure that she was within earshot, and I consciously did this on several occasions. This conflict has been working on inside me for some time, but I'm glad to say I've managed to get it out and tell her exactly how I felt, and I feel better for it.

I was left with the feeling of the absurdity of war. It's a message that has been said many times before. War is hell, believe me.

Lt. Cdr. Patrick Kettle (Bilton & Kosminsky, 1990, pp. 94-95)

Of all the sites where masculinities are constructed, reproduced, and deployed, those associated with war and the military are some of the most direct. Despite far-reaching political, social, and technological changes, the warrior still seems to be a key symbol of masculinity. In statues, heroic

AUTHOR'S NOTE: My initial thinking on this topic was very much aided by a British Economic and Social Research Council award, G00242047, which enabled me to explore some of the complexities linking masculinities and violence. I should also like to thank the editors of this volume, Harry Brod and Michael Kaufman, for their detailed and most helpful comments on the original draft of this chapter.

paintings, comic books, and popular films the gendered connotations are inescapable. The stance, the facial expressions, and the weapons clearly connote aggression, courage, a capacity for violence, and, sometimes, a willingness for sacrifice. The uniform absorbs individualities into a generalized and timeless masculinity while also connoting a control of emotion and a subordination to a larger rationality.

Such links are very widespread and deeply embedded. The gendered associations of war and soldiering have been, at least until very recently, one of the most abiding features of the sexual division of labor. In all types of society, state or stateless, simple or complex, men are expected to fight or to be prepared to fight, to enlist for military service, and to undergo some form of military training. Conversely, women are often formally barred from such activities. As in other aspects of gendered divisions of labor, such expectations and prohibitions define not only who *does* what but who *is* what; the very nature of gender itself seems to be forged and reproduced in such socially constructed but very widespread and deeply pervasive divisions.

This is, of course, seen in its most heightened form at times of war, especially the mass wars of the 20th century. As war became "democratized" and involved greater numbers of its citizens more normally accustomed to the routines of civilian life, so grew one of the most central and poignant images associated with combat: the ordinary soldier saying goodbye to family and loved ones. Such images multiplied during the 19th century (Hichberger, 1988) and continue effortlessly into wars of more recent times—the Falklands/Malvinas struggle and the Gulf War. In the farewell at the airstrip or the dockside there is the convergence of the protector and the protected, of the public and the private, and of masculinity and femininity—each strong in its own, but very different, way.

Traditionally, then, combat and military experience separate men from women while binding men to men. It is a separation that reaches deep into a man's sense of identity and self, as the quotation at the beginning of this chapter illustrates. However, these dual processes of separation and unity have another face. If war and the military often highlight key and frequently sacred themes within society and appear effortlessly to weave these themes around constructions of masculinity and femininity, it is also important to note the darker, less publicly celebrated associations of such institutions and events. As has often been noted, rape and war are almost inevitably linked (Brownmiller, 1976), and sexual aggression is often an integral part of the training and the bonding of soldiers (Theweleit, 1987). Military authorities, with varying degrees of covertness, will seek to provide outlets for the sexual needs of their men, again highlighting other well-established gendered contrasts between active masculine animality and female passivity.

A Body of Men and Men's Bodies

One way of understanding military life and its relationships with gender is in terms of the construction of the masculine body. Training involves the disciplining, controlling, and occasional mortification of the body. The individual body and the self that is identified with that body are shaped into the collective body of men. Drill instructors during my period of basic training in the late 1950s often claimed that they would "make you or break you," an unambiguously physical description of a social process. The shaping may often be almost literal in the sculpting of the close haircut and the enclosure into uniforms. At times of combat, the body is placed at risk, threatened with danger or damage, and subjected to unmediated physicality in confined quarters, deprivation of food or sleep, and exposure to fire or the elements. Physicality may become finality in the remains enclosed in a body bag.

The informal cultures that elaborate in the course of military training and beyond similarly revolve, to a very large extent, around socially constructed bodily needs and functions that are linked to strong and hegemonic definitions of masculinity. Chiefly, of course, these revolve around the construction of heterosexuality. The ubiquitous pin-ups establish direct links between the bodies of women and the bodily needs of men. British National Servicemen were quickly introduced to the rumor that "they" put bromide into the tea in order to reduce sexual desires and learned that their beds were known as "wanking chariots." Conversely, this heterosexist culture also, at least at the more overt level, generated homophobia with references to queers and "arse bandits" and warnings about not bending over in the presence of those whose heterosexual masculinity might be in question.

Such emphases on aggressive heterosexism and homophobia seem to lend support to the argument that masculine group solidarities organized around violence (legitimized or otherwise) serve as a defense against homosexuality. It cannot be denied that this is part of the story, especially where young men are coming to terms with or to an understanding of their own sexuality away from home and in the company of other men, sometimes under conditions of extreme discomfort. Much of the debate about the legalization and recognition of homosexual relations within the armed services bears witness to these fears and uncertainties. But it is not the whole story. The less official accounts of military life suggest the operation of a double standard, the toleration of homosexual relationships so long as they did not threaten the wider patterns of good order and discipline (see, for example, Royle, 1986, pp. 120-121). If in the armed services one finds an ideological emphasis on homosociability and heterosexuality, it is, as is so often the case in a complex society, a complex ideological unity compounded of several, sometimes contradictory, strands.

It could be argued that war and the military represent one of the major sites where direct links between hegemonic masculinities and men's bodies are forged. Indeed, it is the disciplining and control of the body and exposure to risk and sheer physicality that distinguishes many features of military life from everyday civilian life. Insofar as masculinity continues to be identified with physicality, then there are strong reasons for continuing to view military life as an important site in the shaping and making of masculinities. However, this should not be overstated. For one thing, there are several other areas of life where the links between physicality and masculinity may be stressed: Other occupations, such as the police, deep-sea fishing, or mining—or in a modern, more leisure-oriented society, sport—may come to replace the military as a major site linking embodiment with masculinities. Further, there are factors serving to weaken the links between military life, embodiment, and masculinities.

Boundedness and Pervasiveness

Modern societies are characterized as possessing a multitude of more or less distinct and identifiable cultures, senses of collective identity, and "we-ness." These bases for identity may be examined along two dimensions, one to do with a sense of boundedness, the other to do with the wider pervasiveness or influence of that culture. In the first case one is concerned with the extent to which clear distinctions between "us" and "them" are created, while in the second case one is concerned with the extent to which the central features of a given culture become prized or dominant within the wider society. These two dimensions may be seen as varying independently and could be the basis for comparative analysis. The strength and clarity of the boundaries are consequential for the identities of those subsumed within the boundaries. The extent to which the values or practices of a given culture pervade the wider social order is of consequence for those outside that culture. Thus, under certain conditions, military values may come to dominate civilians as well as soldiers.

Military institutions appear to be, in a multiplicity of ways, highly and strongly bounded, certainly in the context of modern societies. This boundedness has a very direct and spatial representation in the guarded military camps, clearly controlling access from the outside world. In a modern society, themes of secrecy are similarly bound up with the activities associated with defense and the military. Further, the very activities associated with the military life, ultimately to do with the taking of life and the exposure to extreme physical danger, serve to establish an almost unbridgeable gulf between the world of the soldier and the world of the civilian (Bilton & Kosminsky, 1990). No civilian, it is argued repeatedly, can ever really know what it is like. Military personnel, returning from the field of combat, often feel a sense of estrangement from the civilian society to which they are returning. Thus, formally and experientially, the military life appears as a highly bounded one, and this sense of boundedness might seem to make it a particularly appropriate site for the generation of masculinities. However, there are processes at work undermining this sense of boundedness.

The pervasiveness of military culture and values within the wider society is more obviously variable. Although military leaders are often given public heroic status, and although military victories form pivotal points for the construction of national histories, these alone do not mean that a particular society can be labeled as "militaristic" or "warlike." Clearly, whether or not a particular society is currently in a state of war or war preparedness will be influential, but it is not the only factor. One needs also to consider the extent to which military training is seen as a necessary feature of the training of all male citizens, the extent to which political leaders have military backgrounds and continue to enjoy military rank, and the extent to which military uniforms are a persistent and widespread feature of public spaces. There are also economic variables to be considered, such as the proportion of national resources devoted to all forms of military expenditure, including research, weapons and vehicle production, salaries, pensions, toxic waste disposal, and so on.

Other things being equal, the military will be the more closely associated with the construction of masculinities in societies where it is both highly bounded and highly pervasive. In the former dimension, military life will function as a "total institution" (Goffman, 1968), shaping and molding masculinities of those internal to the system. In the latter dimension, these militaristic forms of masculinity will become hegemonic, shaping not only the construction of desired masculinities but the whole order of gender relations. In terms of the earlier discussion of embodiment, there will be links made between the construction of the masculine body in the military career and the understanding of the wider "body politic." The image of the warrior will come to personify the society, and individual soldiers will be called on to identify their occupation with the core values of the nation. However, such a high degree of fit or overlap between military values and practices and societal values and practices may not always exist. Discussions of the varying degrees and kinds of boundedness and pervasiveness may be a point of entry into the complexities of the connections between masculinities and the military in modern society.

The Limits of Militarism

Although there are good reasons to see war and military experience as important, perhaps central, sites for the creations of masculinities, there are also some clear and growing limitations to this understanding. A major consideration today is the increasing formal participation of women in military activities. Throughout history the apparent absolute masculine monopoly of war and soldiering has in fact been breached, often covertly and sometimes openly (Wheelwright, 1989). However, in the 20th century, especially since the Second World War, the participation of women in all branches of the armed services has increased and has, to some degree, been normalized. Although the actual extent and range of activities varies considerably between countries and services, the increases, although marked, have not generally extended to the higher echelons of military power and have tended to avoid those areas where the taking of human life might seem to be a probability. However, one of the features of modern warfare is the blurring of the boundaries between combat and noncombat, and the absence of a direct fighting role for women does not necessarily mean an avoidance of actual physical danger. This was particularly apparent, on the anti-Iraq side, in the recent Gulf War (Shaw, 1991, p. 212).

It is clear that such moves in the direction of the deployment of women in the armed services have provided a variety of contradictory responses. It is perhaps no accident that some of the most passionate debates about the roles of men and women in modern society have focused on religion, the military, and sport, each site dealing in some measure with aspects of the sacred, the body, and gendered identity. In the cases of the military, the kinds of issues that are at stake here include the extent to which women, especially in a combat situation, might be defined as weakening or polluting; the extent to which feminine skills or aptitudes for caring and nurturing will be diminished through such participations; as well as the more openly expressed questions as to whether women would be able to cope with the rigors and deprivations of war and training. Other major concerns have been whether men will obey women officers and whether men will endanger themselves by protecting women in combat situations. But running through all these concerns and coloring them at every point is a concern with the overall symbolic order, the apparent loosening of boundaries between women and men, and the weakening of the links between nation, the military, and gendered identities. To put it graphically: What difference does it make if the person parting at the dockside or the airstrip is a woman and the person left behind is a man? Such themes began to emerge in public and publicized forms during the Gulf War.

The increasing, if uneven, participation of women in the military is one much heralded trend that potentially problematizes the traditional link-ages between masculinity and legitimized violence. However, a less heralded but equally important trend is the growth of peace and pacifist movements (e.g., Sager, 1980) and, possibly, a wider, more diffused, and ambiguous distaste for war and things military. Where these movements have been noted and discussed, the emphasis (at least in recent years) has been on the role of women in such movements in, for example, the First World War or the peace camps outside the U.S. military base at Greenham Common, England. Although many of the feminist discussions of such movements have understood these connections in gendered terms (some-times to an extent that has given rise to concerns about a possible essentialism, that is, the notion that women are naturally more peaceful than men), the participation of men in peace movements has rarely been interpreted in gendered terms.

One possible counterexample is provided by one of the U.S. 1960s antiwar slogans: "Women say yes to men who say no." In terms of the prevailing gender order, such participations constitute an anomaly. During the 20th century, for example, potential conscientious objectors were often presented with the hypothetical dilemma, "What would you do if you saw a German (etc.) about to rape your sister/wife/daughter?" It might be noted also that the deprivations ranging from ostracism to imprison-ment experienced by many pacifists in time of war often equaled and sometimes exceeded those experienced by enlisted men.

Thus the links between masculinity and war may be seen as being called into question by the increasing participation of women and the somewhat less heralded role of men in peace movements. A more abiding way in which the links might be questioned is the fact that, for those in Western Europe, North America, and parts of Asia, wars are not all that frequent and that actual battles form only a small part of any given war (Shaw, 1991, p. 44). A journalist reflecting on some aspects of the Gulf War writes:

> Sometimes, late at night, Dad would tell his war stories. . . . His war, he said, comprised six years of boredom interspersed with one or two moments of sheer terror. I gathered the impression of war as one vast lottery, with the merest fluke distinguishing between the heroic and the dead. (Engel, 1991)

It might be argued that the moments of combat or action, infrequent though they might be, are of such an intensity and at such variance with everyday routine that they are enough to underline the role of the military in the making of masculinities. However, it is clear that combat itself remains a somewhat slim basis for such gendered constructions and that one has to examine the whole military experience, with all its possible contradictions, to pursue the links between it and gender.

One also has to consider the argument that long-term trends have contributed to the erosion of the warrior image and its association with heroic masculinity (Morgan, 1990). These trends include the complex process of technological and organizational rationalization, establishing a greater distance between the soldier and the means of destruction. Further, whether or not it is possible to talk of a general civilizing process in relation to the military and the conduct of war, it is certainly the case that military establishments become more and more affected by civilian values. This is reflected in the domestication of many aspects of service life, the reduction of the distance between service personnel and their families, and the attempts to present many military roles as being just like any other civilian job. Other indications such as the relatively muted nature of the celebrations at the end of the Falklands and the Gulf conflicts and the continuing problem facing injured war veterans in the context of an overwhelming civilian society point in the same direction: toward a weakening of connections between nation-state, the military, and heroic masculinities. Two major factors in the United States in the past two decades have been the U.S. withdrawal from Vietnam and the counter-hegemonic role of the counterculture and the antiwar movement.

In an important recent study Martin Shaw has written of the development of a "post-military society" (Shaw, 1991). He establishes a model of "classical militarism" as a feature of the 19th century, "which reached its peak in the two world wars of the first half of the twentieth century" (p. 64). Such a form of militarism was associated with the rise of the nation-state, industrialization, state bureaucracy, and "new means of mass ideological diffusion" (p. 64). In a variety of complex ways and for a variety of reasons, this period of classical militarism is on the wane at least in those countries conventionally defined as the West. In Western terms, this has meant a decline in the overall pervasiveness of the military and some more ambiguous trends in terms of its boundedness. On the one hand, it becomes more open to civilian practices, influences, and careers. On the other hand, as it declines in size, it becomes more closed and more professional. Although Shaw does not fully develop the gender implications of his argument, it is clear that the advent of something like a postmilitary society would entail the weakening of some of the strong linkages between gender constructions and war and the military that could be seen more properly as a feature of the period of classical militarism.

One way of viewing this transition in gender terms is perhaps not so much in terms of a straightforward weakening of the links between masculinity and the military, but more in terms of an increasingly diverse range of masculinities converging on the sites of war and military action. For example, during the Gulf War there was the familiar masculine rhetoric of "kicking ass." But there was also the fascination with technology, the apparent sense of mastery over nature conveyed in missiles and precision bombing, the near orgasmic excitement of nighttime explosions presented on television screens across the world. Such excitement in the power of technology and the control over massively destructive forces was very much part of the culture in which atomic weapons were developed and tested (Easlea, 1983).

Contradictions Within Military Life

Apart from these long-term trends that have, at least in some parts of the world, had the effect of weakening the links between hegemonic masculinities and the military, there have often been contradictions within military life that certainly point to a more complex model. Most of these contradictions are recognized in sociological and personal accounts of war and the military and certainly need to be taken into consideration in more detailed analyses. Indeed, it is possible that such analyses will have a wider applicability, pointing to potential complexities in all sites involved in the making of masculinities. I shall simply provide some brief indications of these contradictions.

The group and the individual. Traditionally, there have been two contrasting models of heroism, one focusing on the warrior, the heroic individual, and the other focusing on "brothers in arms." It has also often been noted that one of the long-term trends has been in favor of the latter at the expense of the former. Whether or not warfare ever allowed scope for the deployment of heroic individualism is a matter for some debate, but it is clear that the rationalizations of modern combat allow much less scope for this. Further, the group solidarities developed in the course of training and combat may inhibit or stigmatize any displays of individual heroism. Heroism may become identified with particular units or sections of the military—the marines, the paratroops, the SAS—rather than with any one individual. War memorials celebrate abstracted unknown soldiers rather than the heroic deeds of identifiable persons.

Modern day armies, therefore, seem to be ideal sites for the construction of abstracted masculinities. However, such trends seem to come up against other trends in modern societies, namely, that modernization involves identification with growing individualism and a stress on the self. In this context at least, military values do not seem to be all pervasive and might, indeed, serve to heighten the boundaries between military and civilian life. However, techniques exist of resolving this apparent contradiction. Public accounts of war may focus on human interest stories (e.g., Bilton & Kosminsky, 1990) or on the individual eccentricities or even heroisms of military leaders (Sandy Woodward and Norman Schwarzkopf, for example).

Thus in the context of modern war and the role of the military in liberal democracies there seems to be the possibility and indeed the requirement for the elaboration of a range of masculinities rather than a single hegemonic masculinity. Such a range is obviously not without bounds and some masculinities are more hegemonic than others. However, the military cannot be seen straightforwardly as a site for the construction of a single embodied masculinity.

Hierarchies and organizations. I have already referred to the themes of bureaucratization and rationalization that form central strands in accounts of the changing patterns of the military and warfare. Clearly, such changes stand in sharp contrast to heroic models of masculinity, especially those of the more individualistic type. However, perhaps this should not be seen as a weakening of the military/masculinity linkage, but more as a source of increasing complexity. Insofar as organizations generally tend to be dominated and run by men and insofar as bureaucratic rationalities themselves may be seen as incorporating certain historically constructed masculine values (Bologh, 1990; Seidler, 1989), these long-term trends may be seen as the reshaping and pluralization of these linkages rather than their simple erosion. Military organizations become complex, overdetermined, and sometimes contradictory mixes of the warrior and the bureaucratic ethos, combining to produce a complex range of masculinities.

By definition, bureaucracies are also hierarchies, and where you get hierarchies you also get the creation of group solidarities at all levels. At the lower levels, as sociologists of work and organizations have demonstrated, such solidarities may run counter to the official ethos of the organization as a whole. In the case of the military, the group loyalties among lower participants may, indeed, lead to mutinies or to firing on one's own officers. More routinely there may be a diffuse sense of "them" and "us" with at least an overt code of rejecting formal military values and of sanctioning those soldiers who show excessive enthusiasm for smartness, patriotism, or military values in general. It is not masculine values that are rejected here but certain officially sponsored models of masculinity.

Matters become further complicated when it is recognized that military hierarchies very often reflect values and divisions within the wider society. Thus different masculinities in terms of social class or ethnicity may be superimposed on or interact with the hierarchies of military organizations, especially the differences between officers and "men." The traditional bracketing of the terms *officer and a gentleman* neatly encapsulates the interplay between class and military masculinities.

Regulars and conscripts. Clearly the nature of military experience will in some measure be shaped by the mode of recruitment and the distinctions between those for whom the military life is part of a long-term career with all the associated involvements and commitments and those for whom the involvement is a temporary, possibly unwelcome, interruption of an otherwise civilian life course. Certainly the European experience shows an uneven but clear shift away from any form of conscription (Mather, 1991). One likely consequence of these trends, so long as they are not reversed, would be the waning influence of military values, as fewer and fewer generations become touched by the experience or memories of military service. Again, this may be seen as a weakening of the links between military life and the making of masculinities.

These remarks need to be modified in a couple of ways. In the first place the connections between conscription and militarism are by no means straightforward. It is not immediately obvious, for example, that Sweden, which retains conscription (albeit with ample opportunities for alternative service), is more militaristic than Britain, which has abandoned national service. Also, in societies with high rates of unemployment and with marked class or ethnic divisions, the degree to which a man may be said to have chosen military service may be open to question. Further, there are differences within the ranks of the regulars between those who have opted for a more or less life-long military career and those for whom a minimum period of enlistment may be seen as a short-term economic strategy. Again, it is the interplay between military cultures and factors in the wider society as a whole that shape masculinities, rather than simply the military culture in isolation.

Combat and noncombat. This is a dynamic and fluid distinction, and individuals may move between these military positions according to circumstances. More important, it can be maintained that the distinction becomes harder and harder to draw in the context of modern war just as the distinction between soldier and civilian becomes more blurred. People may be able to inflict considerable destruction without being in any immediate physical danger themselves, or, alternatively, they may be exposed to considerable risk without directly encountering the enemy.

Although technology plays a major role in this blurring of distinction between combat and noncombat, other sociopolitical developments will also be of significance. This is particularly the case where troops may be engaged in what are at times, and sometimes controversially, described as peace-keeping roles or in counterterrorism. There are, one might reasonably suppose, considerable differences between the relatively short-lived, if often intense, battles of the Falklands War and the continued uncertainties and tensions involved in maintaining a military presence in Northern Ireland.

Contradictions within battle. If soldiering is supposed to be the central site in the construction of masculinity and if the experience of battle is supposed to lie at the heart of the military life in this connection, then one should also be aware of the multiple contradictions that are found at this supposed core of masculine experience. At the very least one should remember that dominant models of masculinity are subject to considerable historical and cultural variation. "Big boys don't cry" has been repeatedly cited as signifying the masculine inability to deal with feelings, yet tears are found at the heart of the military experience:

> After Goose Green I insisted that we bury our dead and give the soldiers time to grieve. It's important. A hole was dug by a bulldozer on the side of a hill and we literally carried each of our friends and put them down side by side and we said our prayers and cried. It was a pretty bad moment. Then we left and got on with the war. (Bilton & Kosminsky, 1990, p. 220)

In a different context and with different nuances of meaning, a genre known as "shooting and crying" literature has been noted as emerging from the experiences of Israeli soldiers (Margalit, 1988).

War provides the opportunity for the display of other characteristics more conventionally associated with the feminine than with the masculine. These include open and physical displays of mutual concern and care, a willingness to show fear and pain, and a contempt for the abstractions to do with patriotism and fighting for democracy or the cause that may be promulgated far from the actual field of battle. The good padre, for example, is the one who shows a willingness to share in the trials of the frontline troops rather than someone apparently interested only in more abstract notions of morality or morale. Some of the strongest antiwar sentiments have come from full-time soldiers. The previous account came from a Major Chris Keble writing of his Falklands experience. The account concludes with these words: "I don't think there were any best moments. The whole affair is one of tragedy. War is a messy dirty business. We should never allow ourselves to go to war" (Bilton & Kosminsky, 1990, p. 220).

One has only, therefore, to listen to some actual accounts of war and battle to be aware of a model of masculinity more complex and contradictory than the one that generally emerges from much of the recent literature on men and their identities. It is likely, indeed, that there has always been a distinction between a straightforward capacity for violence on the one hand and the construction of a masculine identity in which controlled violence may well be a feature but not the central feature.

Rhetoric and reality. There is no doubt that masculinities form a major element in the construction of military identities and that much of this will appear as aggressive, threatening, and deeply misogynist. Although there are occasions for tears and tenderness in the military life as elsewhere, it can hardly be maintained that these are central features of any military culture. Further, there is no doubt that military life provides not only many of the resources out of which misogynies are constructed (group solidarities, all-male bondings, a relatively limited age range, a cult of hardness and actual physical deprivations) but also, from time to time, the opportunity for such misogynies to be given open, physical expression without sanction or retribution. However, much of the misogynist rhetoric is not peculiar to military cultures and may be a feature of many all-male work situations or, indeed, leisure activities in which danger and group solidarities are involved.

Even where military cultures may continue to be relatively bounded and where their values continue to have a degree of pervasiveness, it may be argued that it is possible to overstate the links between army life and the constructions of masculinities. One feature of modern life is, as many theorists have acknowledged, the ability and the need to move between a range of different worlds and to provide performances that are appropriate for these different contexts. It is certainly the case that there are often strong pressures for men in military life to develop a particularly hard style, to be able to swear, to hold one's drink, and to display a sexual knowingness. This is as true in the officers' mess as it is in the barracks. In such contexts it is difficult for individuals to avoid participating in these presentations without appearing to express some kind of moral superiority, something that goes against the egalitarianism of men sharing a common fate.

But it is also the case that the individual who overplays the masculine culture may be an object of mild contempt. It is one thing to use sexual swear words at times of annoyance or frustration. It is another thing to use them three or four times within a single sentence. It is one thing to claim sexual experience; it is another to give graphic details of each and every sexual encounter, real or imagined. There is some degree of awareness that a masculine culture is being created, some possibility for ironic role-distance, some room for maneuver and negotiation. More important is the fact that there is some recognition that this masculine culture is in some respects confined to military life and is not to be extended to the wider society. Cautionary tales are told of servicemen who forget themselves in civilian company and who use expressions that are not usually expected outside the barracks. More serious, there is the often noted fates of veterans in a dominantly civilian society, their deeds forgotten and their wounds and their medals a source of embarrassment or boredom.

Conclusion

This chapter has suggested that the nexus linking masculinity, violence, and the military, although providing some of the most dominant gendered images in many cultures, is far from being a straightforward one. Indeed, the apparently simple linkages represent a major cultural achievement rather than a natural ordering of things. These dominant cultural understandings have influenced not only the powerful, in whose interests it might be to maintain such a dominant model, but also those who seek to challenge conventional models of masculinity or the institutions of war. In particular, men, seeking the best of reasons to distance themselves from dominant and harmful models of masculinity, may have unwittingly perpetuated a one-dimensional and quasi-naturalistic model of "man the warrior."

In contrast, I have argued that the linkages between masculinity, violence, and the military are rarely, if ever, as straightforward as the dominant model suggests or that they come together in straightforward and direct ways only under certain specific circumstances. There are also good reasons to suppose that the linkages have become even weaker and more complex in many modern societies. The linkages have been eroded by two interrelated movements. One is a widespread, if uneven and certainly incomplete, set of challenges to the gender order. The second, the focus of this chapter, is a widespread challenge to and restructuring of the military and its overall position within society.

Whether one talks of a civilizing process or of the advent of a postmilitary society is still a matter for considerable debate. Certainly, Martin Shaw's construction of the latter has much to tell us about the weakening of this gendered and embodied nexus in societies where militarism takes on more ideological and cultural forms (Shaw, 1991, p. 126). In the terminology developed earlier, military values become less pervasive while military institutions become more or less clearly bounded. Insofar as they become more open to civilian values and practices, the boundaries become weakened. But insofar as they become more specialized, more limited in scope and recruitment, and apparently more marginal to the day-to-day world, so they become more closely bounded. There are clearly dangers in the developing isolation of relatively closed military groups from the rest of society, dangers that become apparent at the time of military atrocities.

However one characterizes the movements, the changes in the military and the changes in the gender order are mutually dependent. Changes in the military and the conduct of war have an effect on dominant images of embodied masculinities. Changes in the gender order, for example, in the widespread employment of women, in their turn have an effect on how the military is conceived and constructed. These interacting changes have underlined the need to see the military as a site for the development of a plurality of masculinities rather than a single, dominant, and highly embodied masculinity.

In referring to such a need I also indicate the need for a more wide-ranging comparative perspective. In a very crude way, this need is highlighted by contrasting the rhetorics engaged during the Gulf War: on one side talk of "Americans swimming in their own blood," on the other talk of "kicking ass." In the former, one has a frank recognition that war entails the taking and the loss of life linked elsewhere to a wider political/religious rhetoric that is also highly gendered. In the latter, one has a rhetoric that masks or obscures the real nature of violence. Yet it, too, with its strong echoes of the locker room, is highly gendered, if drawing on different traditions and images of masculinity.

Shaw's account lays the ground for the development of such a comparative perspective. He proposes a "three-tier model of states." In the first place there are the richer and more technologically advanced states that "can afford to rely more on sophisticated weaponry than manpower" (Shaw, 1991, p. 100). Here one finds a considerable weakening of many of the main strands of militarism. In the second place, he distinguishes some of the poorest and most populous states of south Asia or Africa that can afford little in the way of systematic or large-scale military defense, although retaining some elements of traditional militarism. Third, there are a large number of states in many parts of the world that cannot rely largely on technology but import a wide range of weapons and maintain conscription in some degree or another. "These are the countries in which traditional militarism flourishes" (p. 100).

Although Shaw does not develop the gender theme in making this classification, there is little doubt that these differing relationships between militarism, military institutions, and nation-states also entail different ways in which masculinities are drawn on and shaped around themes that involve war and the military. Roughly speaking, I hypothesize that in the first group of states one finds a weakening of the straightforward linkages between gender and militarism, probably in the direction of the development of a plurality of masculinities evolving in military contexts. In the case of the third group of states I suggest that the links may be relatively straightforward although probably still subject to some variation and contradiction. In the middle group of states one shall probably find the greatest range of variation in terms of the links between gender orders, military institutions, and values. I stress that these are only suggestions concerning the links between masculinities and military orders and that a fuller, more comparative analysis is very much needed.

Finally, although there is a clear need to depart from simple equations of masculinity and violence around the site of the military, this should not lead to the idea of a straightforward evolutionary progression. For one thing, as previously suggested, the military can become the site for other, less directly embodied models of masculinity. More important, global trends are by no means uniform. For example, the developments of nationalisms in many parts of Europe may have the effect of reinforcing or elaborating existing linkages between gender and legitimized violence, the mass rapes reported in Bosnia being only one of the more blatant recent examples. Similarly, in the same area of the world, the issues of racism and xenophobia may lead to the further elaboration of quasi-military institutions within societies where such linkages have been more generally and more formally weakened. One should welcome the weakening of such linkages where this takes place without ignoring the fact that other masculinities are being forged or that such weakenings may not be inevitable. There is a need for a much more detailed, finely nuanced, and systematic comparative analysis of the constructions of masculinities around the sites of war, combat, and military life.

References

Bilton, M., & Kosminsky, P. (1990). *Speaking out: Untold stories from the Falklands War.* London: Grafton.

Bologh, R. (1990). *Love or greatness: Max Weber and masculine thinking.* London: Unwin Hyman.

Brownmiller, S. (1976). *Against our will: Men, women and rape.* Harmondsworth, UK: Penguin.

Easlea, B. (1983). *Fathering the unthinkable: Masculinity, scientists and the nuclear arms race.* London: Pluto.

Engel, M. (1991, March 16-17). A hack at the house of Saud. *Weekend Guardian,* pp. 4-6.

Goffman, E. (1968). *Asylums.* Harmondsworth, UK: Penguin.

Hichberger, J. W. M. (1988). *Images of the army: The military in British art 1815-1914.* Manchester, UK: Manchester University Press.

Margalit, A. (1988, November 24). The kitsch of Israel. *New York Review of Books,* pp. 20-24.

Mather, I. (1991, April 19/21). The last call-up? *The European,* p. 9.

Morgan, D. (1990). No more heroes? Masculinity, violence and the civilising process. In L. Jamieson & H. Corr (Eds.), *State, private life and political change*. Basingstoke, UK: Macmillan.

Royle, T. (1986). *The best years of their lives: The national service experience, 1945-63*. London: Michael Joseph.

Sager, W. (1980). The social origins of Victorian pacifism. *Victorian Studies, 23*, 211-236.

Seidler, V. J. (1989). *Rediscovering masculinity: Reason, language and sexuality*. London: Routledge.

Shaw, M. (1991). *Post-military society*. Cambridge, UK: Polity.

Theweleit, K. (1987). *Male fantasies* (Vol. 1). Cambridge, UK: Cambridge University Press.

Wheelwright, J. (1989). *Amazons and military maids: Women who dressed as men in the pursuit of life, liberty and the pursuit of happiness*. London: Pandora.

10

The Making of
Black English Masculinities

MAIRTIN MAC AN GHAILL

The white man hates the black man. In Africa they tried to destroy us, you know. The white Christians had a problem. All men were supposed to be equal. But they were enslaving the black man. So the white man thought, well blacks are not real men. And this is still going on in Africa, here and everywhere today. So the black man is always under pressure, has to make sure they don't wipe our race out. And now the younger ones have to defend our families, defend our people. The whites know we are strong because we have always fought back and they are afraid of us.

Leonard—a black student

White English researchers have tended to see Afro-Caribbean young men as constituting a threatening racial underclass and have explained this in terms of various theories of cultural deprivation. Missing from such theories has been an understanding of the inner cultural meanings that inform these young people's social behavior and understanding of the social world. In an earlier study (Mac an Ghaill, 1988) I examined the social relations between white male adults and English-born black young

AUTHOR'S NOTE: Thanks to Clyde Chitty, Lynne Davies, Mairead Dunne, Chris Griffin, and Bev Skeggs for reading earlier drafts. Also thanks to Michael Kaufman and Harry Brod.

men within an inner-city secondary boys school. In this chapter I develop this work by focusing on the young men's social practices, beliefs, and self-representations in their masculine formation. I illustrate this more specifically by a case study of the gender relations between authoritarian white male adults and a group of Afro-Caribbean young men, called the Rasta Heads, who were seen as projecting an antiauthority form of masculinity. I shall explore a number of interrelated issues: the effects of differentiated curriculum tracks, the social functions of the Rasta Heads' subculture, the relationship to their parents, changing local labor market opportunities, interpeer male group relations, and white male teachers' ambivalent responses to young black masculinities.

Differentiated Curriculum Tracks and Differentiated Masculinities

A number of writers have talked about the processes of stereotyping involved in the essentialization of black men (hooks, 1991; Segal, 1990). Westwood (1990) has described how for black men of African descent:

> . . . stereotypes have been fixed on the body, on physicality, physical strength, and as a site for European fantasies about black male sexuality. . . . The fixity of these stereotypes places 'races', genders, motivations and behaviours in such a way that they become naturalized and a substitute for the complex realities they seek to describe. (p. 57)

These processes of naturalization and objectification were most immediately experienced by the Kilby School students through the dominant systems by which teachers maintained and projected their own racial and gender beliefs. Such attitudes and practices formed the basis of creating an ethnic and racial hierarchy of students that was of central significance in shaping black students' masculinities. This was most visibly expressed in terms of the development of negative Afro-Caribbean and positive Asian caricatured racial images. It is important to stress that there were diverse responses from different subject teachers. However, the Afro-Caribbeans were evaluated solely in behavioral terms and were not placed in cognitive categories, because as a group they were assumed to be of low ability.

In contrast, the Rasta Heads recalled that they were among some of the brightest students in the school, who had been demoted from the top track during their secondary school career. English state schools traditionally have provided social mobility for working-class young men to develop a middle-class mode of masculinity, based on values of competitive individualism and careerism. However, the Rasta Heads refused to allow a black masculine elite to be created from among them.

M. M.: Why have you gone from the top stream to a lower one?

Neville: Teachers always saying we expect this from you, you are different, you work hard. I don't think we're different. We're all the same. I mean we should all be treated the same, shouldn't we?

Kevin: Like Leonard him got brains, like Leslie him got brains and all of them, but teachers they try to divide, separate friends.

Recently Connell (1989, p. 291) has argued that the institutionalized structure of schooling creates the strongest effects on the construction of masculinity. At Kilby School the highly stratified curriculum was of primary importance in structuring differentiated individual and collective ethnic masculine identities. The link between the construction of differentiated ethnic masculinities and the stratification of black student school careers was seen most clearly in the Rasta Heads' overrepresentation in practical-based, vocational subject areas (Gillborn, 1990). These low-status nonacademic curriculum tracks had a specific male ethos that helped to shape specific black working-class masculine identities. This included teachers' adopting more authoritarian modes of interaction with these students. There was vigilant policing of the antischool students' clothes, footwear, and hairstyles, resulting in their being more frequently suspended for not wearing the school uniform. Most of their teachers were nonacademic subject specialists and a high number of those responsible for their pastoral care were former physical education teachers. The cumulative effect of these differentiated curriculum practices was to create a pedagogical culture that reflected the masculine world of manual work, with its "distinctive complex of chauvinism, toughness and machismo" (Willis, 1977, p. 53). In short, "tough white teachers" were producing "tough young black men."

Gilroy: The teachers say we're aggressive but they're much worse than us. They have all the power. They try and scare you and threaten you and cause trouble all the time.

Andrew: We get the really bad teachers to try and control us. Some of the teachers are scared of us. You see they think they can't teach us anything, so they'll just control us. They must be fucking joking.

Once you learn to read and write in the primary school, what else do you learn? It's like a prison, just keeping you in. We do our own business.

Connell (1989) has persuasively argued in relation to the institutionalization of academic failure via competitive grading and streaming: "The reaction of the 'failed' is likely to be a claim to other sources of power, even other definitions of masculinity. Sporting prowess, physical aggression or sexual conquest may do" (p. 295). For the Rasta Heads, "doing their own business" involved an active construction of a black masculinity within the interrelated nexus of state institutions "that do nothing but boss them about" (Corrigan, 1979). It involved their survivalist peer-group culture, an adolescent psychosexual development, and the anticipation of their future location in low-skilled labor markets. Their inversion of models of dominant white adult masculinities was developed from within the security of their own subculture.

The Rasta Heads:
A Black Masculine Subculture

Brake (1980) suggests that subcultures emerge as "attempts to resolve collectively experienced problems arising from the contradictions in the social structure, and that they generate a form of collective identity from which an individual identity can be achieved" (p. 36). A major condition of the emergence of the Rasta Heads was their alienating experience of English society, from which they were excluded. Black youth systematically encounter among white sectors of the population situations of degradation and violence that serve to deny their black identity. For the Rasta Heads this ranged from local fascists who verbally and physically assaulted them; state officials, including teachers and social workers, operating with reified conceptions of "race" that constructed them as problems and victims; and an occupying police force that was seen as using power in an arbitrary and racially discriminatory manner that was causal of the Kilby urban "riots" (Cohen & Bains, 1986). It was against the background of this pervasive racial exclusion and the contrasting security of their peer group that a black masculine apprenticeship was developed. The Rasta Heads' collective masculinity was most crucially shaped against state systems of white authoritarianism and the resulting dominant cultural misrecognitions of black history and culture.

M. M.:   Say black people were accepted as English, would you want to be classed as English?

Andrew: No, you can never change just like that. Long time, it cannot be the same. I don't feel English because everything that goes in Britain it's not really for black people. It's against black people, so how can you join it, become part of that?

Leslie: How can you call it your country when you've got racialists against you. You can't even get a job in their country. So how can you call it your country?

For large sectors of working-class young men, their experience of English society can be read in terms of the building of a defensive culture of masculine survival against social marginalization. It is within this culture that they construct and live out images of what it means to be a man. A central component of the Rasta Heads survival was their projection and amplification of a specific form of masculinity that overemphasized "toughness." In this process, they can be seen as active gender makers. Dodd (1978) cogently captures this social development:

> The culture of these "black marginals" is based like any "culture of poverty" upon survival; but its emphasis is upon style, movement and talk. This may be confusing to the visitor until he realises that, in this culture, this is precisely how you survive. Roles and career follow accordingly. The black street perspective, a profound contemporary influence on Afro-Caribbean youth in England and the Caribbean look to its history in the highly symbolic histories of Marcus Garvey, Haile Selassie and nameless rebel slaves. Rebellion in fact is a primary concept in building a visible street identity. . . . It is a taken for granted assumption about their manhood and place in society. (p. 599)

The Rasta Heads' vocabulary of masculinity stressed the physical, solidarity, and territorial control. Their projected machismo image to those in authority and to overt white racists on the streets was justified as a necessary strategic tactic. They were aware that it had won them space within the school. Equally important, they knew that their collective toughness had protected them from the recent increase in racist attacks that many Asian youths were suffering with the reemergence of the perniciously labeled "Paki-bashing" as a cultural form of white racial violence. However, their toughness was not merely based on physical criteria.

M. M.:   Is it important to act tough?

Christopher: In this country, yeah. You gotta survive don't you? You can't let the white man use you all the time.

M. M.:   Do you think you sometimes act tough when you don't necessarily feel that way?

Christopher: Yeah, yeah that's true. You see it's the image. You've got to act tough to survive here, to survive in this country. If you are being picked on, do you understand? I mean you've got to act tough. Like say two white kids right call you a black bastard, what are you gonna say? Are you gonna walk on? Truth and rights I wouldn't. I'd give them the same. I'd give them, you white this, you white bastard, back the same way. It's the same with teachers and especially the beesman [policeman]. He tries to make you feel low. You gotta stand up for your rights.

M. M.:   Does a black guy have to be tough?

Kevin: It depends. You gotta act kind of tough. I mean there's two kinds of toughness. You can talk right and you can be physical. If you're just physical, I wouldn't mix with that somebody. I want somebody who can talk and is physical right. I don't want to mix with a stupid head-case. He will cause you unnecessary trouble. Most of my friends they have sense. You got to talk to the man [someone in authority].

In their cultural dissociation from mainstream society the Rasta Heads developed a positive subcultural association, central to which was a process of Africanization, which underpinned their resistance to state authoritarianism. Of particular significance was the ideological influence of Rastafari in building a black cultural nationalism. They were aware of the historical contradictions of black masculinity as a subordinated masculinity, with the denial of the patriarchal privileges of power, control, and authority that are ascribed to the white male role (Mercer & Julien, 1988, p. 112). Their adoption of hypermasculine codes of contestation and resistance may be read as attempts to challenge current white institutional practices that they see as attempting to "emasculate them."

Andrew: White men have always tried to keep us down. African men have had their balls cut off from slavery onwards. They are doing it now in different ways. So, we have to fight them. We have to, just to let the white man know they can't keep cutting our balls off. We have to work this out for ourselves.

Kevin: You see a man he's supposed to have respect, right. Well the black man can't get respect in this society. So what are we supposed to do? We have to let them know that we exist, that we exist as a people.

The Rasta Heads' generation of style helped to make visible their hypermasculinity to those in authority. This included their dress, hairstyle, body posture, language, and the wearing of Rastafari colors. In response the school authorities made vocal their opposition to Rastafari, a philosophy that for black students made popular their concern with "roots history." The school created a moral panic concerning the imagined threat of the Rasta Heads to the school's social order that was linked to the coercive policing policy introduced in the local area following the inner-city Kilby "riots." As the teachers increased coercive disciplinary measures against the Rasta Heads, they became a direct target of the students' subcultural opposition. It was within this warlike arena of mutual distrust, increased tension, and overt conflict that the Rasta Heads developed specific masculine practices that were expressed in their language in terms of "standing up for your rights" and "refusing to be shamed up by the white man." Furthermore, with so few women teachers on the staff, this took place within the contextual atmosphere of a men-only military club. There was much talk among the authoritarian male teachers of "frontline troops," "law and order," "territorial imperatives," "winning ground," and "taking out the student leaders."

Leonard: I'll tell Mr. Keegan [headteacher] right, how can you run a school on fear alone? Most of them, like first years are frightened to go to Keegan. . . . In my mind I say, if Keegan laid a hand on me I swear to god I'd thump him down.

M. M.:   But you wouldn't?

Leonard: I would, truth and rights. I'd thump him back, don't care he's just a normal man.

Relationship to Parents

As Hollands (1990) has indicated, "The power position within the working-class household is crucial in forming masculine identities" (p. 10). Of equal importance to the formation of the Rasta Heads was their relationship to the parent culture. Black local community workers dismissed the explanations common among white officials that pathologized the Afro-Caribbean family structure. For example, white officials spoke of Afro-Caribbean young men's "deviant behavior" in terms of a generational conflict with their parents, who objected to their involvement in oppositional youth subcultures. More specific, they claimed that the assumed high rate of lone-parent, mother-headed families created difficulties for gender identity among the young black men, who had no masculine role models. Hence, it was argued that these youths, who lacked appropriate male discipline in their home lives, developed aggressive masculine attitudes with white male authority figures. A local black youth worker explained the limitations of these views and the social functions that they served:

Mr. Wallace: It's like I said to you before, it's the old rulers' principle of divide and rule. It's got a long colonial history of dividing up different sections of the community. With slavery one of the main divisions was that between men and women. We weren't allowed to look after our families in a normal way and then they used this to say we weren't real men because we were irresponsible. Today young black men are selectively abused by white authorities and if they defend themselves, they are accused of being aggressive. And then invidiously, the whites blame black families for not disciplining the kids, and particularly mothers are blamed. There are increased tensions in some black families, but as you know black parents support their kids, knowing how vulnerable they are, especially the boys.

The Rasta Heads also rejected the concept of being "caught between two cultures" that white race relations experts predicted would lead to the need to choose between their parents' culture or that of their country of birth. The young black men offered a more sophisticated analysis. On one hand they responded positively to their parents in terms of intergenerational ethnic identity. On the other, they spoke of the intergenerational gender conflicts and strains in relation to the domestic division of labor and their parents', particularly their mothers', authority in making demands on their independence. Nava (1992, p. 45) writes of the different placement of girls and boys to their adulthood and the generational specificity for young masculinities with their ambiguous relation to social power. She suggests that the implications of young men's identification of the temporary nature of their subordination as youth may inform their contentious transition into adulthood. I may add that for young black men's racially subordinated masculinity there are potential increased intergenerational tensions. For some of the Rasta Heads, like white working-class subordinated masculinities, one way of attempting to resolve these tensions was to displace onto their mothers and sisters their experiences of social inferiority as men in the wider society (Mac an Ghaill, in press).

Local Labor Market Opportunities: *"Black Men Need Not Apply"*

A third aspect that was of importance in the formulation of the Rasta Heads' masculine identity was the changing material conditions of the local political economy (Hollands, 1990). At a time of structural unemployment black male adults within Kilby were disproportionately affected by the destruction of the regional manufacturing base because they were concentrated in the declining metal industries. For black youth the situation was even worse. During the research period there was a 50% reduction in the total numbers entering employment within the region. In Kilby one of every two white male youths who left school found work compared to less than one in three black male youths. There was much talk by local politicians of the development of a hi-tech service sector. As one of the Rasta Heads stated: "The only area of service growth was the opening of government unemployment offices." Tolson (1977) and Willis (1977) have shown how work is central to white working-class boys' masculine self-representation in their preparation for adulthood. As a result of a long history of mass unemployment, the Rasta Heads' masculine identity did not have the same cultural investment in manual waged labor. As they indicate below, the logic of their subculture was not one of failure, inability to do examinations, or cultural deficiency, but one of questioning the validity of academic qualifications in relation to job prospects. At the same time, teachers were dismissed as being unable to advise them on "real" masculine jobs because of the association of teaching with "feminized" mental work.

M. M.:   Do you think qualifications are important?

Leslie: Put it this way, I know friends who have qualifications and some of them have left school for two or three years and they haven't got nowhere. The teachers don't know what it's like out here. How can they? They may build up your hopes and you go looking for jobs and they just look at you and you know, go away nigger. When our parents came to England, they had notices up that they didn't want blacks living in their areas. Now when there is little work left in England, they are saying the same to us about work. They don't want us.

Kevin: Like the careers teacher will give you advice on how to get a job. But what the fuck do teachers know? Their job's a piece of piss. They've never had to work out here on the street. You know, the real thing. They wouldn't know how to survive. They're more like a woman staying at home looking after the kids. It's just soft, soft work.

The relationship between the Rasta Heads' world view and their own preparation for work was further highlighted by the question of their rejection of contemporary forms of employment. Black men's subordinate position in the labor market was explicitly linked to British imperialism. At the same time they were aware of the need to build alternative ways of developing a masculine identity.

Leonard: I don't see why I should work for England because England hasn't done anything for me. You can't say we're supposed to do good and work for England. And you did this for us and this. You came to my descendent country, right, of your own free will. We couldn't stop it because you have the guns and all that. It's because of the white man, slavery, Africa. Because of slavery and that's the mostest thing about it. Teachers make you think it slavery was in the past, well in this country there's a new slavery of bad work. . . . I wouldn't work for no white man. It's going to be difficult without money from a proper job to be independent from your parents and to look after your girlfriend and all that business. But you aren't going to get your rightful respect as a black man in a job. So you have to look at other things, you know what I mean? Like some of us have a thing going in the music scene. You are among your own people and you can grow up better and build a good future.

Male Student and Male Teacher Relations

A final aspect of the Rasta Heads' masculine formation concerns their relationship with other male students and white male teachers' ambivalent responses to the Rasta Heads. A range of masculinities are developed within institutional contexts in relation to and against each other. Among other antischool male students, the Rasta Heads and an Asian peer group called the Warriors were seen as the best organized and toughest gangs and so were respected or feared by different students. Among antischool students both gangs had high status and were particularly admired for challenging white teachers' and police authoritarianism. The Warriors strongly identified with the Rasta Heads, overtly associating with the Afro-Caribbean rude boy subculture. Hebdige (1979) describes the rude boy as an archetypal rebel. He writes: "The rude boys formed a deviant sub-culture in Jamaica in the mid to late 60s. Flashy, urban, 'rough and tough,' they were glamourised in a string of reggae and rocky steady hits" (pp. 16-17). As is indicated by their choice of name, the Warriors wished to project a tough image that challenged the dominant stereotype of the feminized passive Asian male. They claimed that the Rasta Heads were important male role models for younger Asians and Afro-Caribbeans in opposing white racist practices.

Parminder: The Rasta Heads are hated by the teachers and the police because they are stronger than them. It's like Amerjit said they're like a strong organization like the IRA. They stick together and look after each other. It's good for the kids in the lower classes to learn from the Rastas. To learn that authority is not a good thing. It's to keep the Asian and black man down. That's important for us [Asians] because we are seen as soft by whites but things are changing. If racialism gets worse in the future it's us, young Asian and black men that have to look after our own communities, isn't it?

Earlier ethnographic studies of white antischool males have failed to acknowledge how the latter's resistance also acted as a form of oppression for other students, most notably for young women and conformist male students (see McRobbie, 1991). For the more conformist male students at Kilby School, both the Rasta Heads and the Warriors were seen as troublemakers, either in directly bullying them or in their constant disruption of lessons. As Mayes (1986) makes clear in writing of the culture of school masculinities, "A masculine ideal which allows competition and aggressive individualism may take its toll. The alternative status sought by the boys who fail in the system may result in an aggressively 'macho' stance, dangerous to themselves and others" (p. 29).

In a previous study (Mac an Ghaill, 1991, p. 301) of young black and white gay students, one of them recalled the masculine codes through which male teachers and students colluded in constructing dominant forms of straight masculinity that operated to devalue and threaten femininities and subordinated masculinities.

Sean: I always loved football but there was something about it that I didn't like. I really enjoyed playing the game but it was all the rest of it. You see it wasn't just a game. I came to see that it was about proving yourself as a man. All the boys together, acting tough, bragging about sexual conquests, putting down women and all the macho fooling around in the showers. They had to keep telling each other that they were the real men. We had the fit bodies, we had the strength, we had the power. The male teachers and pupils measured everyone against us, though this was usually hidden.

Similarly at Kilby School, in order to enhance and amplify their own masculinity, the Rasta Heads were overtly sexist to young women and female staff and aggressive to male students who did not live up to their prescribed masculine norms. They adopted a number of collective social practices in their attempt to regulate and normalize gender/sexual boundaries. They were particularly vindictive to a small group of Afro-Caribbean academic students who overtly distanced themselves from the Rasta Heads' antischool strategies. For the Rasta Heads, the academic group's "overconcern" with literature and drama resulted in their being labeled "botty men" (a homophobic comment). As Mercer and Julien (1988) point out, a further contradiction in subordinated black masculinities occurs "when black men subjectively internalise and incorporate aspects of the dominant definitions of masculinity in order to contest the conditions of dependency and powerlessness which racism and racial oppression enforce" (p. 112). Ironically, the Rasta Heads, in distancing themselves from the racist school structures, adopted survival strategies of hypermasculine heterosexuality that threatened other Afro-Caribbean students, adding further barriers to their gaining academic success. Consequently, this made it more difficult for academic black students to gain social mobility via a professional job and the accompanying middle-class mode of masculinity. The Rasta Heads made clear their own assessment of the pro-school black students' career aspirations.

Gilroy: You see you have soft boys here and they don't know about life. Black men must stick together. The white man tries to divide us up. Like they'll say, you're good blacks, you can have little jobs. You're bad blacks, so you can't have any. And then they can blame us for having no work. You see it's clever. We have to teach the soft boys, if you go their way, you'll become white but you'll never be accepted as white. So you will end up as choc-ices, black on the outside and white on the inside.

In developing these oppressive gender and sexual practices the Rasta Heads assumed that they had the support of most male teachers and exploited the latter's ambiguous gendered responses to themselves. At one level, the macho male teacher confronted the macho male student in the attempt to maintain social control. This was a school for the making of real men (Beynon, 1989). In the process the male teachers acted out their responses within an arena where they took for granted the legitimacy of dominant masculine authority forms.

At another level, the male authoritarian teachers colluded with the antischool Afro-Caribbean Rasta Heads' contestation of schooling, which functioned to confirm and celebrate a normative macho mode of masculinity with which the teachers intuitively identified. The Rasta Heads projected working-class masculine forms consisting of such themes as independence, toughness, and aggression (Tolson, 1977). These cultural forms found a resonance with such teachers, many of whom had working-class origins. In contrast, these teachers privately were critical and suspicious of the more conformist middle-class Asian students for the assumed deceitfulness and unmanliness that the teachers attributed to them. Furthermore, the authoritarian teachers conflated these imputed negative traits with femininity in order to ridicule these students. For the male teachers, derogative references to the boys' gender, with such comments as "you're acting like little girls," were a common disciplinary technique of social control that operated to maintain and regulate gender boundaries. At the same time, one could see the intersection of gender and sexual school codes that were shared by the teachers and the Rasta Heads. Within the "rampant heterosexual" atmosphere of the school's macho culture, the "conformist" Asian students' behavior acquired a connotation of femininity in that they were not acting like "normal men" (Arnot, 1984; Cockburn, 1987). The misogyny and homophobia that were pervasive throughout the school circumscribed the teachers' and antischool students' masculine bonding (Mac an Ghaill, 1991). It served to maintain the dominant belief that "boys will be and must be boys" all of their lives. The Rasta Heads spoke of the white teachers' contradictory racial and gender responses involved in their masculine identification with themselves.

Michael: When it comes to all the school work, what you call academic, the teachers prefer the Asians. But when it comes to other things, like sport and all that, they prefer us [Afro-Caribbeans].

M. M.:   How do you know this?

Michael: Well they wouldn't tell you this, you just know in the way they act. It's like this a boys' school, right. But it's like in every situation you have people to act as girls and some acting as men. Well, the teachers, the men teachers prefer us because we're the men here. . . . And you hear them saying things to the Asian kids like, stop acting like a group of little girls, stop acting like nancies [a homophobic comment]. Really putting them down.

At Kilby School the male teacher-student collusion was most visibly mediated through the culturally exalted forms of masculine sport (Walker, 1988). Carrington and Wood (1983) reported in their research that "teachers sponsored the involvement of the allegedly 'motor-minded' (Afro-Caribbean) pupils in sport, and utilised, particularly in the case of nonacademic males, extra curricular sports involvement as a mechanism of social control" (p. 37). Similar forms of official sponsorship of Afro-Caribbean males into sport were evident at Kilby School with a disproportionately high number of Afro-Caribbean students in the high-status sporting areas of football and athletics. For example, all of the Rasta Heads, at some time in their school career, had represented the school at football. The male teachers' rationalization of the Afro-Caribbeans' overrepresentation in sporting activities illustrates their ambivalent and contradictory responses to these students. On the one hand, their racist and gender beliefs juxtaposed the Afro-Caribbean males' assumed innate physical superiority with their assumed low academic capacity and achievement. On the other hand, this social subordination was accompanied by contradictory elements of the male teachers' emotional investment in masculine sport (Segal, 1990).

Clive: I think that the teachers, especially the ones that take us for sport would think we are more together, them and us, than the soft kids, who don't like football and that. . . . I mean the teachers are a lot different when you're doing sport together, they really change. It's probably what they really enjoy more than all the books and learning that the other kids are into.

For the white male teachers there was admiration, pride, and desire as well as jealousy of the Afro-Caribbeans' sporting display and celebration of a version of working-class masculinity, which the teachers valued highly but with which they felt unable to compete. Similar contradictory white working-class male cultural responses were acted out at the local football ground. White supporters combined racist chants toward the opposition's black players with a standing ovation for the highly skilled young black player who had just joined their club (see Fanon, 1970; Henriques, 1984). It was within this complex arena of social-cultural structures and processes that the Rasta Heads negotiated a collective black masculine identity.

Kevin: The white man doesn't know who he is. It is true that he hates the black man and he's got the power but also he wishes he could do the things that black men do. It's like here, we are free and the whites are trapped. Do you know what I mean? They need to sort themselves out badly.

Conclusion

This chapter has illustrated the multiple determination of power in the interplay between a state institution, racism, and the cultural formation of a black masculine identity. As Walkerdine (1990) has stated in her study of boys' resistance in a nursery school:

> The gender and the ages of the particular participants clearly have major effects that serve to displace other variables. . . . Since the boys are both children and male, and the teacher is both teacher and female, they can enter as subjects in a variety of discourses, some of which render them powerful and some of which render them powerless. (pp. 4-5)

A main theme of this narrative concerns a group of black working-class male youths' response to and negotiation with the official institutional ambivalence to their subordinated masculinity. They provide a case study illustrative of a broader question of how contemporary institutions are active, constituent social forces in the cultural production of a hierarchically ordered range of masculinities and femininities. For progressive social activists located within this arena, there are political and pedagogical spaces within which collectively to identify and challenge current dominant social practices (Mac an Ghaill, 1993, in press). In so doing, one may build on the feminist project of reconstructing new forms of masculinity and femininity.

References

Arnot, M. (1984). How shall we educate our sons? In R. Deem (Ed.), *Co-education reconsidered* (pp. 37-57). Milton Keynes, UK: Open University Press.

Beynon, J. (1989). A school for men: An ethnographic case study of routine violence in schooling. In S. Walker & L. Barton (Eds.), *Politics and the processes of schooling* (pp. 191-217). Milton Keynes, UK: Open University Press.

Brake, M. (1980). *The sociology of youth culture and youth sub-cultures.* London: Routledge & Kegan Paul.

Carrington, B., & Wood, E. (1983). Body talk: Images of sport in a multiracial school. *Multiracial Education, 11*(2), 29-38.

Cockburn, C. (1987). *Two-track training: Sex inequalities and the YTS.* London: Macmillan.

Cohen, P., & Bains, H. (1986). *Multi-racist Britain.* London: Hutchinson.

Connell, R. W. (1989). Cool guys, swots and wimps: The inter-play of masculinity and education. *Oxford Review of Education, 15*(3), 291-303.

Corrigan, P. (1979). *Schooling the smash street kids.* London: Macmillan.

Dodd, A. (1978). Police and thieves on the streets of London. *New Society, 16,* 598-600.

Fanon, F. (1970). *Black skin, white masks.* London: Paladin.

Gillborn, D. (1990). *Race, ethnicity and education: Teaching and learning in multi-ethnic schools.* London: Unwin Hyman.

Hebdige, D. (1979). *Subculture: The meaning of style.* London: Methuen.

Henriques, J. (1984). Social psychology and the politics of racism. In J. Henriques, W. Hollway, C. Urwin, C. Venn, & V. Walkerdine (Eds.), *Changing the subject: Psychology, social regulation and subjectivity* (pp. 60-90). London: Methuen.

Hollands, R. (1990). *The long transition: Class, culture and youth training.* London: Macmillan.

hooks, b. (1991). *Yearning: Race, gender and cultural politics.* London: Turaround.

Mac an Ghaill, M. (1988). *Young, gifted, and black: Student-teacher relations in the schooling of black students.* Milton Keynes, UK: Open University Press.

Mac an Ghaill, M. (1991). Schooling, sexuality and male power: Towards an emancipatory curriculum. *Gender and Education, 3*(3), 291-309.

Mac an Ghaill, M. (1993, in press). *Acting like men: Masculinities, sexualities, and schooling.* Milton Keynes, UK: Open University Press.

Mayes, P. (1986). *Gender.* London: Longman.

McRobbie, A. (1991). *Feminism and youth culture.* London: Macmillan.

Mercer, K., & Julien, I. (1988). Race, sexual politics and black masculinity: A dossier. In J. Rutherford & R. Chapman (Eds.), *Male order: Unwrapping masculinity* (pp. 97-164). London: Lawrence & Wishart.

Nava, M. (1992). *Changing cultures: Feminism, youth and consumerism.* London: Sage Ltd.

Segal, L. (1990). *Slow motion: Changing masculinities, changing men.* London: Virago.

Tolson, A. (1977). *The limits of masculinity.* London: Tavistock.

Walker, J. (1988). *Louts and legends: Male youth cultures in an inner-city school.* London: Allen & Unwin.

Walkerdine, V. (1990). *Schoolgirl fictions.* London: Verso.

Westwood, S. (1990). Racism, black masculinity and the politics of space. In J. Hearn & D. Morgan (Eds.), *Men, masculinities and social theory* (pp. 55-71). London: Unwin Hyman.

Willis, P. (1977). *Learning to labour: How working class kids get working class jobs.* London: Saxon House.

11

Gender Displays and Men's Power

The "New Man" and the Mexican Immigrant Man

PIERRETTE HONDAGNEU-SOTELO
MICHAEL A. MESSNER

In our discussions about masculinity with our students (most of whom are white and upper-middle class), talk invariably turns to critical descriptions of the "macho" behavior of "traditional men." Consistently, these men are portrayed as "out there," not in the classroom with us. Although it usually remains an unspoken subtext, at times a student will actually speak it: Those men who are still stuck in "traditional, sexist, and macho" styles of masculinity are black men, Latino men, immigrant men, and working-class men. They are not us; we are the New Men, the Modern, Educated, and Enlightened Men. The belief that poor, working-class, and ethnic minority men are stuck in an atavistic, sexist "traditional male role," while white, educated middle-class men are forging a more sensitive egalitarian "New," or "Modern male role," is not uncommon. Social scientific theory and research on men and masculinity, as well as the "men's movement," too often collude with this belief by defining masculinity almost entirely in terms of gender display (i.e., styles of talk, dress, and bodily comportment), while ignoring men's structural positions of power and privilege over women and the subordination of certain groups of men to other men (Brod, 1983-1984). Our task in this chapter is to explore and explicate some links between contemporary men's gender

The authors thank Harry Brod, Scott Coltrane, and Michael Kaufman for helpful comments on earlier versions of this chapter.

displays and men's various positions in a social structure of power. Scott Coltrane's (1992) comparative analysis of gender display and power in 93 nonindustrial societies provides us with an important starting point. Coltrane found that men's "fierce public displays and denigration of women . . . competitive physical contests, vociferous oratory, ceremonies related to warfare, exclusive men's houses and rituals, and sexual violence against women" are common features in societies where men control property and have distant relations with young children (Coltrane, 1992, p. 87). By contrast, "in societies in which women exercise significant control over property and men have close relationships with children, men infrequently affirm their manliness through boastful demonstrations of strength, aggressiveness, and sexual potency" (p. 86). This research suggests that men's public gender displays are not grounded in some essential "need" for men to dominate others but, instead, tend to vary according to the extent of power and privilege that men hold vis-à-vis women. Put another way, the micropolitics of men's and women's daily gender displays and interactions both reflect and reconstruct the macropolitical relations between the sexes (Henley, 1977).

But in modern industrial societies, the politics of gender are far more complex than in nonindustrial societies. Some men publicly display verbal and physical aggression, misogyny, and violence. There are public institutions such as sport, the military, fraternities, and the street where these forms of gender display are valorized (Connell, 1991a, 1992b; Lyman, 1987; Martin & Hummer, 1989; Messner, 1992; Sabo, 1985). Other men, though, display more "softness" and "sensitivity," and this form of gender display has been recently lauded as an emergent "New Masculinity."

In this chapter, we will contrast the gender display and structural positions of power (in both public and domestic spheres of life) of two groups of men: class-privileged white men and Mexican immigrant men. We will argue that utilizing the concepts of Modern (or New) and Traditional men to describe these two groups oversimplifies a complex reality, smuggles in racist and classist biases about Mexican immigrant men, and obscures the real class, race, and gender privileges that New Men still enjoy. We will argue that the theoretical concepts of hegemonic, marginalized, and subordinated masculinities best capture the dynamic and shifting constellation of contemporary men's gender displays and power (Brod, 1987; Connell, 1987; Kaufman, 1987; Segal, 1990). We will conclude by arguing that a critical/feminist sociology of men and masculinity should decenter and problematize hegemonic masculinity by proceeding from the standpoint of marginalized and subordinated masculinities.

The "New Man" as Ideological Class Icon

Today there is a shared cultural image of what the New Man looks like: He is a white, college-educated professional who is a highly involved and nurturant father, "in touch with" and expressive of his feelings, and egalitarian in his dealings with women. We will briefly examine two fragments of the emergent cultural image of the contemporary New Man: the participant in the mythopoetic men's movement and the New Father.[1] We will discuss these contemporary images of men both in terms of their larger cultural meanings and in terms of the extent to which they represent any real shift in the ways men live their lives vis-à-vis women and other men. Most important, we will ask if apparent shifts in the gender displays of some white, middle-class men represent any real transformations in their structural positions of power and privilege.

Zeus Power and the Mythopoetic Men's Movement

A recently emergent fragment of the cultural image of the New Man is the man who attends the weekend "gatherings of men" that are at the heart of Robert Bly's mythopoetic men's movement. Bly's curious interpretations of mythology and his highly selective use of history, psychology, and anthropology have been soundly criticized as "bad social science" (e.g., Connell, 1992a; Kimmel, 1992; Pelka, 1991). But perhaps more important than a critique of Bly's ideas is a sociological interpretation of why the mythopoetic men's movement has been so attractive to so many predominantly white, college-educated, middle-class, middle-aged men in the United States over the past decade. (Thousands of men have attended Bly's gatherings, and his book was a national best-seller.) We speculate that Bly's movement attracts these men *not* because it represents any sort of radical break from "traditional masculinity" but precisely because it is so congruent with shifts that are already taking place within current constructions of hegemonic masculinity. Many of the men who attend Bly's gatherings are already aware of some of the problems and limits of narrow conceptions of masculinity. A major preoccupation of the gatherings is the poverty of these men's relationships with their fathers and with other men in workplaces. These concerns are based on very real and often very painful experiences. Indeed, industrial capitalism undermined much of the structural basis of middle-class men's emotional bonds with each other as wage labor, market competition, and instrumental rationality largely supplanted primogeniture, craft brotherhood, and inter-generational mentorhood (Clawson, 1989; Tolson, 1977). Bly's "male initiation" rituals are intended to heal and reconstruct these masculine bonds, and they are thus, at least on the surface, probably experienced as largely irrelevant to men's relationships with women.

But in focusing on how myth and ritual can reconnect men with each other and ultimately with their own "deep masculine" essences, Bly manages to sidestep the central point of the feminist critique—that men, as a group, benefit from a structure of power that oppresses women as a group. In ignoring the social structure of power, Bly manages to convey a false symmetry between the feminist women's movement and his men's movement. He assumes a natural dichotomization of "male values" and "female values" and states that feminism has been good for women in allowing them to reassert "the feminine voice" that had been suppressed. But Bly states (and he carefully avoids directly blaming feminism for this), "the masculine voice" has now been muted—men have become "passive . . . tamed . . . domesticated." Men thus need a movement to reconnect with the "Zeus energy" that they have lost. "Zeus energy is male authority accepted for the good of the community" (Bly, 1990, p. 61).

The notion that men need to be empowered *as men* echoes the naïveté of some 1970s men's liberation activists who saw men and women as "equally oppressed" by sexism (e.g., Farrell, 1975). The view that everyone is oppressed by sexism strips the concept of oppression of its political meaning and thus obscures the social relations of domination and subordination. Oppression is a concept that describes a relationship between social groups; for one group to be oppressed, there must be an oppressor group (Freire, 1970). This is not to imply that an oppressive relationship between groups is absolute or static. To the contrary, oppression is characterized by a constant and complex state of play: Oppressed groups both actively participate in their own domination and actively resist that domination. The state of play of the contemporary gender order is characterized by men's individual and collective oppression of women (Connell, 1987). Men continue to benefit from this oppression of women, but, significantly, in the past 20 years, women's compliance with masculine hegemony has been counterbalanced by active feminist resistance.

Men do tend to pay a price for their power: They are often emotionally limited and commonly suffer poor health and a life expectancy lower than that of women. But these problems are best viewed not as "gender oppression," but rather as the "costs of being on top" (Kann, 1986). In fact, the shifts in masculine styles that we see among some relatively privileged men may be interpreted as a sign that these men would like to stop paying these costs, but it does not necessarily signal a desire to cease being "on top." For example, it has become commonplace to see powerful and successful men weeping in public—Ronald Reagan shedding a tear at the funeral of slain U.S. soldiers, basketball player Michael Jordan openly crying after winning the NBA championship. Most recent, the easy manner in which the media lauded U.S. General Schwartzkopf as a New Man for shedding a public tear for the U.S. casualties in the Gulf War is indicative of the importance placed on *styles of masculine gender display* rather than the institutional *position of power* that men such as Schwartzkopf still enjoy.

This emphasis on the significance of public displays of crying indicates, in part, a naive belief that if boys and men can learn to "express their feelings," they will no longer feel a need to dominate others. In fact, there is no necessary link between men's "emotional inexpressivity" and their tendency to dominate others (Sattel, 1976). The idea that men's "need" to dominate others is the result of an emotional deficit overly psychologizes a reality that is largely structural. It does seem that the specific type of masculinity that was ascendent (hegemonic) during the rise of entrepreneurial capitalism was extremely instrumental, stoic, and emotionally inexpressive (Winter & Robert, 1980). But there is growing evidence (e.g., Schwartzkopf) that today there is no longer a neat link between class-privileged men's emotional inexpressivity and their willingness and ability to dominate others (Connell, 1991b). We speculate that a situationally appropriate public display of sensitivity such as crying, rather than signaling weakness, has instead become a legitimizing sign of the New Man's power.[2]

Thus relatively privileged men may be attracted to the mythopoetic men's movement because, on the one hand, it acknowledges and validates their painful "wounds," while guiding them to connect with other men in ways that are both nurturing and mutually empowering.[3] On the other hand, and unlike feminism, it does not confront men with the reality of how their own privileges are based on the continued subordination of women and other men. In short, the mythopoetic men's movement may be seen as facilitating the reconstruction of a new form of hegemonic masculinity—a masculinity that is less self-destructive, that has revalued and reconstructed men's emotional bonds with each other, and that has learned to feel good about its own Zeus power.

The New Father

In recent years Western culture has been bombarded with another fragment of the popular image of the New Man: the involved, nurturant father. Research has indicated that many young heterosexual men do appear to be more inclined than were their fathers to "help out" with housework and child care, but most of them still see these tasks as belonging to their wives or their future wives (Machung, 1989; Sidel, 1990). Despite the cultural image of the "new fatherhood" and some modest increases in participation by men, the vast majority of child care, especially of infants, is still performed by women (Hochschild, 1989; La Rossa, 1988; Lewis, 1986; Russell, 1983).

Why does men's stated desire to participate in parenting so rarely translate into substantially increased involvement? Lynn Segal (1990) argues that the fact that men's apparent attitudinal changes have not translated into widespread behavioral changes may be largely due to the fact men that may (correctly) fear that increased parental involvement will translate into a loss of their power over women. But she also argues that increased paternal involvement in child care will not become a widespread reality unless and until the structural preconditions—especially economic equality for women—exist. Indeed, Rosanna Hertz (1986) found in her study of upper-middle class "dual career families" that a more egalitarian division of family labor sometimes developed as a rational (and constantly negotiated) response to a need to maintain his career, her career, and the family. In other words, career and pay equality for women was a structural precondition for the development of equality between husbands and wives in the family.

However, Hertz notes two reasons why this is a very limited and flawed equality. First, Hertz's sample of dual-career families in which the women and the men made roughly the same amount of money is still extremely atypical. In two-income families, the husband is far more likely to have the higher income. Women are far more likely than men to work part-time jobs, and among full-time workers, women still earn about 65 cents to the male dollar and are commonly segregated in lower paid, lower status, dead-end jobs (Blum, 1991; Reskin & Roos, 1990). As a result, most women are not in the structural position to be able to bargain with their husbands for more egalitarian divisions of labor in the home. As Hochschild's (1989) research demonstrates, middle-class women's struggles for equity in the home are often met by their husbands' "quiet resistance," which sometimes lasts for years. Women are left with the choice of either leaving the relationship (and suffering not only the emotional upheaval, but also the downward mobility, often into poverty, that commonly follows divorce) or capitulating to the man and quietly working her "second shift" of family labor.

Second, Hertz observes that the roughly egalitarian family division of labor among some upper-middle class dual-career couples is severely shaken when a child is born into the family. Initially, new mothers are more likely than fathers to put their careers on hold. But eventually many resume their careers, as the child care and much of the home labor is performed by low-paid employees, almost always women, and often immigrant women and/or women of color. The construction of the dual-career couple's "gender equality" is thus premised on the family's privileged position within a larger structure of social inequality. In other words, some of the upper-middle class woman's gender oppression is, in effect, bought off with her class privilege, while the man is let off the hook from his obligation to fully participate in child care and housework. The upper-middle class father is likely to be more involved with his children today than his father was with him, and this will likely enrich his life. But given the fact that the day-to-day and moment-to-moment care and nurturance of his children is still likely to be performed by women (either his wife and/or a hired, lower-class woman), "the contemporary revalorisation of fatherhood has enabled many men to have the best of both worlds" (Segal, 1990, p. 58). The cultural image of the New Father has given the middle-class father license to choose to enjoy the emotional fruits of parenting, but his position of class and gender privilege allow him the resources with which he can buy or negotiate his way out of the majority of second shift labor.

In sum, as a widespread empirical reality, the emotionally expressive, nurturant, egalitarian New Man does not actually exist; he is an ideological construct, made up of disparate popular images that are saturated with meanings that express the anxieties, fears, and interests of relatively privileged men. But this is not to say that some changes are not occurring among certain groups of privileged men (Segal, 1990). Some men are expressing certain feelings that were, in the past, considered outside the definition of hegemonic masculinity. Some men are reexamining and changing their relationships with other men. Some men are participating more—very equitably in some cases, but marginally in many others—in the care and nurturance of children. But the key point is that when examined within the context of these men's positions in the overall structure of power in society, these changes do not appear to challenge or undermine this power. To the contrary, the cultural image of the New Man and the partial and fragmentary empirical changes that this image represents serve to file off some of the rough edges of hegemonic masculinity in such a way that the possibility of a happier and healthier life for men is created, while deflecting or resisting feminist challenges to men's institutional power and privilege. But because at least verbal acceptance of the "New Woman" is an important aspect of this reconstructed hegemonic masculinity, the ideological image of the New Man requires a counterimage against which to stand in opposition. Those aspects of traditional hegemonic masculinity that the New Man has rejected—overt physical and verbal displays of domination, stoicism and emotional inexpressivity, overt misogyny in the workplace and at home—are now increasingly projected onto less privileged groups of men: working-class men, gay body-builders, black athletes, Latinos, and immigrant men.

Mexican Immigrant Men

According to the dominant cultural stereotype, Latino men's "machismo" is supposedly characterized by extreme verbal and bodily expressions of aggression toward other men, frequent drunkenness, and sexual aggression and dominance expressed toward normally "submissive" Latinas. Manuel Peña's (1991) research on the workplace culture of male undocumented Mexican immigrant agricultural workers suggests that there is a great deal of truth to this stereotype. Peña examined the Mexican immigrant male's participation in *charritas coloradas* (red jokes) that characterize the basis of the workplace culture. The most common basis of humor in the *charritas* is sexualized "sadism toward women and symbolic threats of sodomy toward other males" (Paredes, 1966, p. 121).

On the surface, Peña argues, the constant "half-serious, half playful duels" among the men, as well as the images of sexually debased "perverted wenches" and "treacherous women" in the *charritas,* appear to support the stereotype of the Mexican immigrant male group as being characterized by a high level of aggressive masculine posturing and shared antagonisms and hatred directed toward women. But rather than signifying a fundamental hatred of women, Peña argues that these men's public displays of machismo should be viewed as a defensive reaction to their oppressed class status:

> As an expression of working-class culture, the folklore of machismo can be considered a realized signifying system [that] points to, but simultaneously displaces, a class relationship and its attendant conflict. At the same time, it introduces a third element, the gender relationship, which acts as a mediator between the signifier (the folklore) and the signified (the class relationship). (Peña, 1991, p. 40)

Undocumented Mexican immigrant men are unable to directly confront their class oppressors, so instead, Peña argues, they symbolically displace their class antagonism into the arena of gender relations. Similar arguments have been made about other groups of men. For instance, David Collinson (1988) argues that Australian male blue-collar workers commonly engage in sexually aggressive and misogynist humor, as an (ultimately flawed) means of bonding together to resist the control of management males (who are viewed, disparagingly, as feminized). Majors and Billson (1992) argue that young black males tend to embody and publicly display a "cool pose," an expressive and often sexually aggressive style of masculinity that acts as a form of resistance to racism. These studies make important strides toward building an understanding of how subordinated and marginalized groups of men tend to embody and publicly display styles of masculinity that at least symbolically resist the various forms of oppression that they face within hierarchies of intermale dominance. These studies all share the insight that the public faces of subordinated groups of men are *personally and collectively constructed performances of masculine gender display.* By contrast, the public face of the New Man (his "sensitivity," etc.) is often assumed to be one-and-the-same with who he "is," rather than being seen as a situationally constructed public gender display.

Yet in foregrounding the oppression of men by men, these studies risk portraying aggressive, even misogynist, gender displays primarily as liberatory forms of resistance against class and racial oppression (e.g., Mirandé, 1982). Though these studies view microlevel gender display as constructed within a context of structured power relations, macrolevel gender relations are rarely viewed as a constituting dynamic within this structure. Rather gender is commonly viewed as an epiphenomenon, an effect of the dominant class and/or race relations. What is obscured, or even drops out of sight, is the feminist observation that masculinity itself is a form of domination over women. As a result, women's actual experiences of oppression and victimization by men's violence are conspicuously absent from these analyses, thus leaving the impression that misogyny is merely a symbolic displacement of class (or race) antagonism. What is needed, then, is an examination of masculine gender display and power within the context of intersecting systems of class, race, and gender relations (Baca Zinn, Cannon, Higgenbotham, & Dill, 1986; Collins, 1990). In the following section we will consider recent ethnographic research on Mexican immigrant communities that suggests that gender dynamics help to constitute the immigration process and, in turn, are reconstituted during and following the immigrant settlement process.

The Rhetoric of Return Migration as Gender Display

Mexican immigrant men who have lived in the United States for long periods of time frequently engage in the rhetoric of return migration. These stated preferences are not necessarily indicative of what they will do, but they provide some telling clues to these men's feelings and perceptions about their lives as marginalized men in the United States. Consider the following statements:[4]

> I've passed more of my life here than in Mexico. I've been here for thirty-one years. I'm not putting down or rejecting this country, but my intentions have always been to return to Mexico . . . I'd like to retire there, perhaps open a little business. Maybe I could buy and sell animals, or open a restaurant. Here I work for a big company, like a slave, always watching the clock. Well I'm bored with that.

> I don't want to stay in the U.S. anymore. [Why not?] Because here I can no longer find a good job. Here, even if one is sick, you must report for work. They don't care. I'm fed up with it. I'm tired of working here too. Here one must work daily, and over there with my mother, I'll work for four, maybe five months, and then I'll have a four or five month break without working. My mother is old and I want to be with the family. I need to take care of the rancho. Here I have nothing, I don't have my own house, I even share the rent! What am I doing here?

> I would like to return, but as my sons are born here, well that is what detains me here. Otherwise, I would go back to Mexico . . . Mexico is now in a very inflationary situation. People come here not because they like it, but because the situation causes them to do so, and it makes them stay here for years and years. As the song says, this is a cage made of gold, but it is still a cage.

These statements point to disappointments with migration. In recent years, U.S.-bound migration has become institutionalized in many areas of Mexico, representing a rite of passage for many young, single men

(Davis, 1990; Escobar, Gonzalez de la Rocha, & Roberts, 1987). But once in the United States the accomplishment of masculinity and maturity hinges on living up to the image of a financially successful migrant. If a man returns homes penniless, he risks being seen as a failure or a fool. As one man explained: "One cannot go back without anything, because people will talk. They'll say 'oh look at this guy, he sacrificed and suffered to go north and he has nothing to show for it.' "

Although most of these men enjoyed a higher standard of living in the United States than in Mexico, working and settling in the United States significantly diminished their patriarchal privileges. Although the men compensated by verbally demonstrating their lack of commitment to staying in the United States, most of these men realized that their lives remained firmly anchored in the United States and that they lacked the ability to return. They could not acquire sufficient savings in the public sphere to fund return migration, and in the domestic sphere, they did not command enough authority over their wives or children, who generally wished to remain in the United States, to coerce the return migration of their families. Although Mexican immigrant men blamed the terms of U.S. production as their reason for wanting to return to Mexico, we believe that their diminished patriarchal privileges significantly fueled this desire to return.[5] Here, we examine the diminution of patriarchy in three arenas: spatial mobility, authority in family decision-making processes, and household labor.

Mexican immigrant men, especially those who were undocumented and lacked legal status privileges, experienced limited spatial mobility in their daily lives and this compromised their sense of masculinity (Rouse, 1990). As undocumented immigrants, these men remained fearful of apprehension by the Immigration Naturalization Service and by the police.[6] In informal conversations, the men often shared experiences with police harassment and racial discrimination. Merely "looking Mexican," the men agreed, was often cause for suspicion. The jobs Mexican immigrant men commonly took also restricted their spatial mobility. As poor men who worked long hours at jobs as gardeners, dishwashers, or day laborers, they had very little discretionary income to afford leisure activities. As one man offered, "Here my life is just from work to the home, from work to the home."

Although the men, together with their families, visited parks, shops, and church, the public spaces open to the men alone were typically limited to street corners and to a few neighborhood bars, pool halls, and doughnut shops. As Rouse (1990) has argued, Mexican immigrant men, especially those from rural areas, resent these constrictions on their public space and mobility and attempt to reproduce public spaces that they knew in Mexico in the context of U.S. bars and pool halls. In a California immigrant community Rouse observed that "men do not come to drink alone or to meet with a couple of friends . . . they move from table to table, broadening the circuits of information in which they participate and modulating social relationships across the widest possible range." Although these men tried to create new spaces where they might recapture a public sense of self, the goal was not so readily achieved. For many men, the loss of free and easy mobility signified their loss of publicly accorded status and recognition. One man, a junkyard assembler who had worked in Mexico as a rural *campesino* (peasant), recalled that in his Mexican village he enjoyed a modicum of public recognition: "I would enter the bars, the dances, and when I entered everyone would stand to shake my hand as though I were somebody—not a rich man, true, but I was famous. Wherever you like, I was always mentioned. Wherever you like, everyone knew me back there." In metropolitan areas of California, anonymity replaced public status and recognition.

In Mexico many of these men had acted as the undisputed patriarchs in major family decision-making processes, but in the United States they no longer retained their monopoly on these processes. When families were faced with major decisions—such as whom to seek for legal help, whether or not to move to another town, or the decision to lend money or make a major purchase—spousal negotiation replaced patriarchal exertions of authority. These processes did not go uncontested, and some of the decision-making discussions were more conflictual than harmonious, but collaboration, not domination, characterized them.

This trend toward more egalitarian patterns of shared authority often began with migration. In some families, men initially migrated north alone, and during their absences, the women acted decisively and autonomously as they performed a range of tasks necessary to secure family sustenance. Commentators have referred to this situation as one in which "thousands of wives in the absence of their husbands must 'take the reigns' " (Mummert, 1988, p. 283) and as one in which the wives of veteran migrants experience "a freedom where woman command" *(una libertad donde mujeres mandan)* (Baca & Bryan, 1985). This trend toward more shared decision making continued after the women's migration and was also promoted by migration experiences as well as the relative increase in women's and the decrease in men's economic contributions to the family (Hondagneu-Sotelo, 1992). As the balance of relative resources and contributions shifted, the women assumed more active roles in key decision-making processes. Similar shifts occurred with the older children, who were now often reluctant to subordinate their earnings and their autonomy to a patriarchal family hierarchy. As one man somewhat reluctantly, but resignedly, acknowledged: "Well, each person orders one's self here, something like that . . . Back there [Mexico], no. It was still whatever I said. I decided matters."

The household division of labor is another arena that in some cases reflected the renegotiation of patriarchal relations. Although most families continued to organize their daily household chores along fairly orthodox, patriarchal norms, in some families—notably those where the men had lived for many years in "bachelor communities" where they learned to cook, iron, and make tortillas—men took responsibility for some of the housework. In these cases, men did part of the cooking and housework, they unself-consciously assumed the role of host in offering guests food and beverages, and in some instances, the men continued to make tortillas on weekends and special occasions. These changes, of course, are modest if judged by ideal standards of feminist egalitarianism, but they are significant when compared to patriarchal family organization that was normative before immigration.

This movement toward more egalitarian divisions of labor in some Mexican immigrant households cannot be fully explained by the men's acquisition of household skills in bachelor communities. (We are reminded, for instance, of several middle-class male friends of ours who lived in "bachelor" apartments during college, and after later marrying, conveniently "forgot" how to cook, wash clothes, and do other household chores.) The acquisition of skills appears to be a necessary, but not a sufficient, condition for men's greater household labor participation in reunited families.

A key to the movement toward greater equality within immigrant families was the change in the women's and men's relative positions of power and status in the larger social structure of power. Mexican immigrant men's public status in the United States is very low, due to racism, insecure and low-paying jobs, and (often) illegal status. For those families that underwent long periods of spousal separation, women often engaged in formal- or informal-sector paid labor for the first time, developed more economic skills and autonomy, and assumed control over household affairs. In the United States nearly all of the women sought employment, so women made significant economic contributions to the family. All of these factors tend to erode men's patriarchal authority in the family and empower women to either directly challenge that authority or at least renegotiate "patriarchal bargains" (Kandiyoti, 1988) that are more palatable to themselves and their children.

Although it is too hasty to proclaim that gender egalitarianism prevails in interpersonal relations among undocumented Mexican immigrants, there is a significant trend in that direction. This is indicated by the emergence of a more egalitarian household division of labor, by shared decision-making processes, and by the constraints on men's and expansion of women's spatial mobility. Women still have less power than men, but they generally enjoy more than they previously did in Mexico. The stereotypical image of dominant macho males and submissive females in Mexican immigrant families is thus contradicted by actual research with these families.

Masculine Displays and Relative Power

We have suggested that men's overt public displays of masculine bravado, interpersonal dominance, misogyny, embodied strength, and so forth are often a sign of a lack of institutional power and privilege, vis-à-vis other men. Though it would be a mistake to conclude that Mexican immigrant men are not misogynist (or, following Peña, that their misogyny is merely a response to class oppression), there is considerable evidence that their actual relations with women in families—at least when measured by family divisions of labor and decision-making processes— are becoming more egalitarian than they were in Mexico. We have also argued that for more privileged men, public displays of sensitivity might be read as signs of class/race/gender privilege and power over women and (especially) over other men (see Table 11.1 for a summary comparison of these two groups).

Coltrane (1992) argues that in nonindustrial societies, "men's displays of dominance confirm and reinforce existing property relations rather than compensate for a lack of control over valued resources" (pp. 102-103). His claim that men's *control* (rather than lack of control) of resources is correlated with more extreme microdisplays of masculinity seems, at first, to contradict findings by Peña, Collinson, and Billson and Majors, who claim that in industrial societies, *lack* of access to property and other material resources by Mexican immigrant, working-class, and black males

Table 11.1 Comparison of Public and Domestic Gender Displays of White, Class-Privileged Men and Mexican Immigrant Men

| | Public | | Domestic | |
	Power/Status	*Gender Display*	*Power/Status*	*Gender Display*
White, class-privileged men	High, built into position	"Sensitive," little overt misogyny	High, based on public status/ high income	"Quiet control"
Mexican immigrant men	Low (job status, pay, control of work, legal rights, public status)	"Hombre": verbal misogyny, embodied toughness in work/ peer culture	Contested, becoming more egalitarian	Exaggerated symbols of power and authority in family

are correlated with more overt outward displays of aggressive, misogynist masculinity. The key to understanding this apparent contradiction is that Coltrane is discussing societies where women enjoy high social status, where men are highly involved in child care, and where women have a great deal of control over property and other material resources. In these types of societies, men do not "need" to display dominance and masculine bravado. But in complex, stratified societies where the standards of hegemonic masculinity are that a man should control resources (and other people), men who do not have access to these standards of masculinity thus tend to react with displays of toughness, bravado, "cool pose," or "hombre" (Baca Zinn, 1982).

Marginalized and subordinated men, then, tend to overtly display exaggerated embodiments and verbalizations of masculinity that can be read as a desire to express power over others within a context of relative powerlessness. By contrast, many of the contemporary New Man's highly celebrated public displays of sensitivity can be read as a desire to project an image of egalitarianism within a context where he actually enjoys considerable power and privilege over women and other men. Both groups of men are "displaying gender," but the specific forms that their masculine displays take tend to vary according to their relative positions in (a) the social structure of men's overall power relationship to women and (b) the social structure of some men's power relationships with other men.

Conclusion

We have argued for the importance of viewing microlevel gender displays of different groups of men within the context of their positions in a larger social structure of power. Too often critical discussions of masculinity tend to project atavistic hypermasculine, aggressive, misogynist masculinity onto relatively powerless men. By comparison, the masculine gender displays of educated, privileged New Men are too often uncritically applauded, rather than skeptically and critically examined. We have suggested that when analyzed within a structure of power, the gender displays of the New Man might best be seen as strategies to reconstruct hegemonic masculinity by projecting aggression, domination, and misogyny onto subordinate groups of men. Does this mean that all of men's changes today are merely symbolic and ultimately do not contribute to the types of changes in gender relations that feminists have called for? It may appear so, especially if social scientists continue to collude with this reality by theoretically framing shifts in styles of hegemonic masculinity as indicative of the arrival of a New Man, while framing marginalized men as Other—as atavistic, traditional men. Instead, a critical/feminist analysis of changing masculinities in the United States might begin with a focus on the ways that marginalized and subordinated masculinities are changing.

This shift in focus would likely accomplish three things: First, it would remove hegemonic masculinity from center stage, thus taking the standpoints of oppressed groups of men as central points of departure. Second, it would require the deployment of theoretical frameworks that examine the ways that the politics of social class, race, ethnicity, and sexuality interact with those of gender (Baca Zinn, Cannon, Higgenbotham, & Dill, 1986; Collins, 1990; Harding, 1986; Hondagneu-Sotelo, 1992; Messner, 1990). Third, a sociology of masculinities that starts from the experience of marginalized and subordinated men would be far more likely to have power and politics—rather than personal styles or lifestyles—at its center. This is because men of color, poor and working-class men, immigrant men, and gay men are often in very contradictory positions at the nexus of intersecting systems of domination and subordination. In short, although they are oppressed by class, race, and/or sexual systems of power, they also commonly construct and display forms of masculinity as ways of resisting other men's power over them, as well as asserting power and privilege over women. Thus, to avoid reverting to the tendency to view masculinity simply as a defensive reaction to other forms of oppression, it is crucial in such studies to keep women's experience of gender oppression as close to the center of analysis as possible. This sort of analysis might inform the type of progressive coalition building that is necessary if today's changing masculinities are to contribute to the building of a more egalitarian and democratic world.

Notes

1. This section of the chapter is adapted from Messner (1993).

2. It is significant, we suspect, that the examples cited of Reagan, Jordan, and Schwartzkopf publicly weeping occurred at moments of *victory* over other men in war and sport.

3. Our speculation on the class and racial bias of the mythopoetic men's movement and on the appeal of the movement to participants is supported, in part, by ongoing (but as yet unpublished) research by sociologist Michael Schwalbe. Schwalbe observes that the "wounds" of these men are very real, because a very high proportion of them are children of alcoholic parents and/or were victims of childhood sexual abuse or other forms of violence. Many are involved in recovery programs.

4. Material in this section is drawn from Hondagneu-Sotelo's study of long-term undocumented immigrant settlers, based on 18 months of field research in a Mexican undocumented immigrant community. See Hondagneu-Sotelo, (1994). *Gendered Transitions: Mexican Experiences of Immigrants.* Berkelely: University of California Press.

5. For a similar finding and analysis in the context of Dominican immigrants in New York City, see Pessar (1986).

6. This constraint was exacerbated by passage of the Immigration Reform and Control Act of 1986, which imposed employer sanctions and doubly criminalized undocumented immigrants' presence at the workplace.

References

Baca, R., & Bryan, D. (1985). Mexican women, migration and sex roles. *Migration Today, 13,* 14-18.

Baca Zinn, M. (1982). Chicano men and masculinity. *Journal of Ethnic Studies, 10,* 29-44.

Baca Zinn, M., Cannon, L. W., Higgenbotham, E., & Dill, B. T. (1986). The costs of exclusionary practices in women's studies. *Signs: Journal of Women in Culture and Society, 11,* 290-303.

Blum, L. M. (1991). *Between feminism and labor: The significance of the comparable worth movement.* Berkeley: University of California Press.

Bly, R. (1990). *Iron John: A book about men.* Reading, MA: Addison-Wesley.

Brod, H. (1983-1984). Work clothes and leisure suits: The class basis and bias of the men's movement. *Changing Men, 11,* 10-12, 38-40 (Winter)

Brod, H. (Ed.). (1987). *The making of masculinities: The new men's studies.* Boston: Allen & Unwin.

Clawson, M. A. (1989). *Constructing brotherhood: Class, gender, and fraternalism.* Princeton, NJ: Princeton University Press.

Collins, P. H. (1990). *Black feminist thought: Knowledge, consciousness, and the politics of empowerment.* Boston: Unwin Hyman.

Collinson, D. L. (1988). "Engineering humor": Masculinity, joking and conflict in shop-floor relations. *Organization Studies, 9,* 181-199.

Coltrane, S. (1992). The micropolitics of gender in nonindustrial societies. *Gender & Society, 6,* 86-107.

Connell, R. W. (1987). *Gender and power.* Stanford, CA: Stanford University Press.

Connell, R. W. (1991a). Live fast and die young: The construction of masculinity among young working-class men on the margin of the labour market. *Australian & New Zealand Journal of Sociology, 27,* 141-171.

Connell, R. W. (1991b). *Men of reason: Themes of rationality and change in the lives of men in the new professions.* Unpublished paper.

Connell, R. W. (1992a). Drumming up the wrong tree. *Tikkun, 7,* 517-530.

Connell, R. W. (1992b). Masculinity, violence, and war. In M. S. Kimmel & M. A. Messner (Eds.), *Men's lives* (2nd ed., pp. 176-182). New York: Macmillan.

Davis, M. (1990). *Mexican voices, American dreams: An oral history of Mexican immigration to the United States.* New York: Henry Holt.

Escobar, A. L., Gonzalez de la Rocha, M., & Roberts, B. (1987). Migration, labor markets, and the international economy: Jalisco, Mexico and the United States. In J. Eades (Ed.), *Migrants, workers, and the social order* (pp. 42-64). London: Tavistock.

Farrell, W. (1975). *The liberated man.* New York: Bantam.

Freire, P. (1970). *Pedagogy of the oppressed.* New York: Herder & Herden.

Harding, S. (1986). *The science question in feminism.* Ithaca, NY: Cornell University Press.

Henley, N. M. (1977). *Body politics: Power, sex, and nonverbal communication.* Englewood Cliffs, NJ: Prentice Hall.

Hertz, R. (1986). *More equal than others: Women and men in dual career marriages.* Berkeley: University of California.

Hochschild, A. (1989). *The second shift: Working parents and the revolution at home.* New York: Viking.

Hondagneu-Sotelo, P. (1992). Overcoming patriarchal constraints: The reconstruction of gender relations among Mexican immigrant women and men. *Gender & Society, 6,* 393-415.

Kandiyoti, D. (1988). Bargaining with patriarchy. *Gender & Society, 2,* 274-290.

Kann, M. E. (1986). The costs of being on top. *Journal of the National Association for Women Deans, Administrators, & Counselors, 49,* 29-37.

Kaufman, M. (Ed.). (1987). *Beyond patriarchy: Essays by men on pleasure, power, and change.* Toronto: Oxford University Press.

Kimmel, M. S. (1992). Reading men: Men, masculinity, and publishing. *Contemporary Sociology, 21,* 162-171.

La Rossa, R. (1988). Fatherhood and social change. *Family Relations, 37,* 451-457.

Lewis, C. (1986). *Becoming a father.* Milton Keynes, UK: Open University Press.

Lyman, P. (1987). The fraternal bond as a joking relation: A case study of the role of sexist jokes in male group bonding. In M. Kimmel (Ed.), *Changing men: New directions in research on men and masculinities* (pp. 148-163). Newbury Park, CA: Sage.

Machung, A. (1989). Talking career, thinking job: Gender differences in career and family expectations of Berkeley seniors. *Feminist Studies, 15.*

Majors, R., & Billson, J. M. (1992). *Cool pose: The dilemmas of black manhood in America.* New York: Lexington.

Martin, P. Y., & Hummer, R. A. (1989). Fraternities and rape on campus. *Gender & Society, 3,* 457-473.

Messner, M. A. (1990). Men studying masculinity: Some epistemological questions in sport sociology. *Sociology of Sport Journal, 7,* 136-153.

Messner, M. A. (1992). *Power at play: Sports and the problem of masculinity.* Boston: Beacon.

Messner, M. A. (1993). "Changing men" and feminist politics in the U.S. *Theory & Society, 22,* 723-737.

Mirandé, A. (1982). Machismo: Rucas, chingasos y chagaderas. *De Colores: Journal of Chicano Expression and Thought, 6*(1/2), 17-31.

Mummert, G. (1988). Mujeres de migrantes y mujeres migrantes de Michoacán: Nuevo papeles para las que se quedan y para las que se van. In T. Calvo & G. Lopez (Eds.), *Movimientos de población en el occident de Mexico* (pp. 281-295). Mexico, DF: Centre de'etudes mexicaines et centroamericaines and El colegio de Mexico.

Paredes, A. (1966). The Anglo-American in Mexican folklore. In R. B. Browne & D. H. Wenkelman (Eds.), *New voices in American studies.* Lafayette, IN: Purdue University Press.

Pelka, F. (1991). Robert Bly and Iron John: Bly romanticizes history, trivializes sexist oppression and lays the blame for men's "grief" on women. *On the Issues, 19,* 17-19, 39.

Peña, M. (1991). Class, gender and machismo: The "treacherous woman" folklore of Mexican male workers. *Gender & Society, 5,* 30-46.

Pessar, P. (1986). The role of gender in Dominican settlement in the United States. In J. Nash & H. Safa (Eds.), *Women and change in Latin America* (pp. 273-294). South Hadley, MA: Bergin & Garvey.

Reskin, B. F., & Roos, P. A. (1990). *Job queues, gender queues: Explaining women's inroads into male occupations.* Philadelphia: Temple University Press.

Rouse, R. (1990, March 14). *Men in space: Power and the appropriation of urban form among Mexican migrants in the United States.* Paper presented at the Residential College, University of Michigan, Ann Arbor.

Russell, G. (1983). *The changing role of fathers.* London: University of Queensland.

Sabo, D. F. (1985). Sport, patriarchy, and male identity: New questions about men and sport. *Arena Review, 9,* 1-30.

Sattel, J. W. (1976). The inexpressive male: Tragedy or sexual politics? *Social Problems, 23,* 469-477.

Segal, L. (1990). *Slow motion: Changing masculinities, changing men.* New Brunswick, NJ: Rutgers University.

Sidel, R. (1990). *On her own: Growing up in the shadow of the American dream.* New York: Penguin.

Tolson, A. (1977). *The limits of masculinity: Male identity and women's liberation.* New York: Harper & Row.

Winter, M. F., & Robert, E. R. (1980). Male dominance, late capitalism, and the growth of instrumental reason. *Berkeley Journal of Sociology, 25,* 249-280.

12

Postmodernism and
the Interrogation of Masculinity

DAVID S. GUTTERMAN

The form is fluid, but the meaning even more so.

Nietzsche, *On the Genealogy of Morals*,
Second Essay, Section 12

Shifting Subjects, Indeterminate Identities, Ascribing Agency

Over the last hundred years, the Enlightenment concept of the transcendent subject (existing before and beyond the social realm) has been critiqued by theorists who maintain that subjects are culturally constituted. This shift has roots in Nietzsche's (1967) pronouncement in *On the Genealogy of Morals* that "there is no 'being' behind doing, effecting, becoming; 'the doer' is merely a fiction added to the deed—the deed is everything" (p. 45). This "deed" that constitutes individuals is often seen as social forces—from one's relation to the mode of production (in the Marxist tradition) to the public discourses that produce social systems of value (a perspective most often associated with postmodernism). Michel Foucault, a leading proponent of this latter direction of analysis, instructs that systems of power in a given society produce social subjects discursively.[1] "The individual," Foucault (1980b) writes, "is an effect of power" (p. 98).

219

If the social subject is discursively "produced" by "relations of power" (Foucault, 1988, p. 118), then a subsequent question is whether the subject represents the productive work of any one discourse or a plenitude of discourses. As Teresa de Lauretis argues, feminism and feminist theory have been, and must continue to be, must continue to be critical sites of argument and discussion with regard to this issue of singularly or multiply constructed subjects.[2] For example, conflicts within feminism between African American and white women concerning representativeness and goals have illustrated that individuals are produced by a variety of discourses.[3] Therefore the category of "women" will reflect differences between and among women of, for example, varying races, ages, classes, and sexualities. Indeed, rather than perceiving an individual in relation to a singular subject position, an individual ought to be recognized as being produced by a multitude of discourses. As Chantal Mouffe (1992) has asserted:

> We can then conceive the social agent as constituted by an ensemble of 'subject positions' that can never be totally fixed in a closed system of differences, constructed by a diversity of discourses among which there is no necessary relation but a constant movement of overdetermination and displacement. The identity of such a multiple and contradictory subject is therefore always contingent and precarious, temporarily fixed at the intersection of those subject positions and dependent on specific forms of identification. (p. 372)

Mouffe's conception of a "multiple and contradictory subject . . . contingent and precarious" has critical social and political implications that I will discuss in greater detail later. For now, suffice it to say that understandings of subjects produced by a multiplicity of discourses will necessarily lead to internal conflict and contradiction. These conflicts in turn create an arena where the governing conceptions of a particular discourse suffer a sort of slippage wherein predominant roles and values lose their claims to absolute authority and subsequently can be altered. Barbara Herrnstein Smith (1988) refers to the resulting personal heterogeneity as "our irreducible *scrappiness*" (p. 148).

Furthermore, one can think of this multiply constituted subject as having a multiplicity of identities. Accordingly, it is critical to examine the process of identification or identity formation by which individuals come to identify themselves and be identified by others. A framework of oppositional binarisms has historically provided the governing logic of identity formation in the West. This framework has grounded identity in a series of either/or categories within which individuals are expected to exist. Within these governing categories, Iris Marion Young (1990) asserts, "Any move to define an identity, a closed totality, always depends on excluding some elements, separating the pure from the impure" (p. 303). In this manner, individual identity says as much about who one is not, as it does about who one is.

The hazards of perceiving identity within such a framework of closed boxes of purity are manifold, particularly around the perception of difference. William Connolly (1991) asserts, "An identity is established in relation to a series of differences that have become socially recognized. These differences are essential to its being. . . . Identity requires difference in order to be, and converts difference into otherness in order to secure its own self-certainty" (p. 64). For example, the axis that serves as the fundamental basis of gender identity in the West clearly functions along this organization of the same/different. The perception that men and women are "opposite sexes" (with accompanying "genders"—masculine/feminine)[4] creates the expectation that one is either a man or a woman and that these two categories are essentially disparate. This sense of difference then becomes the demarcation of otherness when gradations of value are placed on the two distinct domains.

In Western culture, of course, that which is usually associated with men (activity, culture, reason) is usually held in higher esteem than that which is associated with women (passivity, nature, emotion). I say "usually" here for I want to assert that within broad cultural paradigms there are often localized situations where gendered attributes can be reversed. This inversion transpires in terms both of identity (i.e., women who drag men to the opera are sometimes seen as the bearers of culture) and of value (i.e., when male aggressiveness intersects with African-Americans in society, the assertive, forceful qualities of those men are demonized rather than valorized by portions of the white American population). In negotiating the obstacles to opening closed binary systems (grounded on difference as otherness), it is crucial to remember that not only are cultural norms socially constructed but so too are the values attached to those norms.

I accept that identity formation is relational (i.e., what I am or claim to be is rooted in making distinctions from what I am not). However, I also believe that this recognition of difference does not need to be perceived as indicative of otherness, or, in Connolly's words, "evil." Indeed, the goal I am advocating is an intervention in the process where difference is transformed into otherness or evil. Connolly suggests that the crucial step is moving away from the teleological project of trying to master the world and our "selves." That is, the effort to position oneself as a transcendent subject necessitates investment in difference. This difference implicitly challenges the claim to transcendency for it entails an eternal oppositional entity or identity. The transcendency is falsely maintained by inscribing difference with a negative cultural valuation in order to limit the capacity of "different" beings to become subjects. The critical step in the process of acknowledging and celebrating difference is a recognition of contingency—of the instability of our "selves" and the world. Connolly (1991) defines contingency as follows:

> By contrast to the necessary and the universal, it means that which is changeable and particular; by contrast to the certain and constant, it means that which is uncertain and variable; by contrast to the self-subsistent and causal, it means that which is dependent and effect; by contrast to the expected and regular, it means that which is unexpected and irregular; and by contrast to the safe and reassuring, it means that which is dangerous, unruly, and obdurate in its danger. (p. 28)

This definition of contingency provides a foundation from which one can understand both "individual scrappiness" and the complex identity of social groups. An appreciation of contingency enables an appreciation of difference. As Connolly (1991) explains, "The one who construes her identity to be laced with contingencies, including branded contingencies, is in a better position to question and resist the drive to convert difference into otherness to be defeated, converted or marginalized" (p. 180).

The notion of "branded contingencies" is an important one. I believe Connolly is suggesting here that specific facets of personal identity can be discursively inscribed on individuals so forcefully that an individual may have very little power or space in which to discursively challenge or reshape that particular aspect of his or her social persona. In a fascinating discussion of the socialization of her son, Kathy Ferguson (1993) addresses the process by which contingent identities are branded on to social subjects. Determined to raise her son in a nonstereotypical fashion, Ferguson paid careful attention to the adjectives she appended to the word *boy*: "I told him often that he is a sweet boy, a gentle boy, a beautiful boy, as well as a smart and strong boy" (p. 128). She could not, however, escape the gendered implications of the word *boy*. Indeed, when examining the cultural construction of identity, I believe it is useful to conceive words like *boy* not as nouns but rather as adjectives that describe a subject. By doing so one can more easily and deeply appreciate the contingency of the meanings attached to the word *boy*. Being a boy is different in different cultures/families/contexts and will mean different things to individuals as they grow older.

In the United States, where gender, racial, and sexual identities are so emphatically marked on individuals, there is often little discursive space to challenge these aspects of one's identity. I am reminded here of a line from Marlon Riggs' (1989) film *Tongues Untied* in which Riggs states, "Cornered by identities I never wanted to claim, I ran—fast—hard—deep—inside myself." In this case, Riggs was categorized and defined as the "governing culture" recognized his (racial) difference, branded the cultural meanings attached to race (gender and sexuality) onto him, and turned them into otherness. However, as Riggs recognizes the contingent, unstable state of the identities branded onto him, he is able to resist the limits placed on him by others while reveling in difference.

The metaphor of performance provides an explanatory framework for understanding the contingency of identity. Performance here should by no means be construed to signify falseness or unrealness. Rather, I am suggesting that "identity is something one *does,* an active corralling of practices, events, desires, contingencies, a regulatory semiotic and material operation" (Ferguson, 1993, p. 159). As members of any particular culture, community, or group, individuals are given a vast array of scripts that together constitute them as social subjects. Some scripts are branded onto individuals more emphatically than others. However, as we see in *Tongues Untied,* recognizing that identity is contingent, is a performance, provides the potential for rewriting the scripts of individual (and group) identity. The notion of rewriting leads to the critical question of agency.

A common critique of the postmodern subject is that by sacrificing stability and unity one also sacrifices agency. The transcendent subject was traditionally perceived as a fundamental precursor to agency. So, for example, the feminist movement initially focused on establishing a notion of woman that could serve as a prediscursive subject and thus enable women to attain political agency. Indeed, many feminist theorists respond skeptically to postmodern reconceptions of the social subject, asking, in the words of Nancy Hartsock (1990), "Why is it that just at the moment when so many of us who have been silenced begin to demand the right to name ourselves, to act as subjects rather than objects of history, that just then the concept of subjecthood becomes problematic?" (p. 163). As Hartsock's question indicates, this question of agency must be answered if postmodernism is to be able to support and sustain (no matter how ungrounded the ground) a politics of social change—a need obviously central to social movements seeking to reframe the implications of differences of sex, race, sexuality, and so forth.[5]

Judith Butler (1992) answers this question of agency in a world of postmodern subjects by stating:

> We may be tempted to think that to assume the subject in advance is necessary in order to safeguard the agency of the subject. But to claim that the subject is constituted is not to claim that the subject is determined. On the contrary, the constituted character of the subject is the very precondition[6] of its agency. (p. 12)

That is, although subjects are constituted, the process and content of their constitution provide the foundation for reformulating the terms of discourse which produce subjects. As Joan Scott (1993) has stated:

> Treating the emergence of a new identity as a discursive event is not to introduce a new form of linguistic determinism, nor to deprive subjects of agency. It is to refuse a separation between "experience" and language and to insist instead on the productive quality of discourse. Subjects are constituted discursively, but there are conflicts among discursive systems, contradictions within any one of them, multiple meanings possible for the subjects they deploy. And subjects do have agency. They are not unified autonomous individuals exercising free will, but rather subjects whose agency is created through situations and statuses conferred upon them. (p. 409)

Postmodern theories of subjectivity, identity, and agency, then, can be useful not only for rethinking governing cultural values but also as a framework for actively seeking social change. Indeed, postmodernism's focus on instability, multiplicity, and contingency, as well as its subsequent celebration of difference, provides an extraordinary basis for interrogating the cultural scripts of normative masculinity. For the remainder of this essay, I will first focus on two places of resistance to governing scripts of masculinity—the question of gay male gender identity and the efforts of profeminist men. I will then discuss two different strategies that can be employed in efforts for social change (including struggles to reimagine masculinity)—identity politics and coalition politics.

Resistance to the Heterosexual Matrix
and Normative Masculinity

The social construction of masculinity in Western culture provides a fascinating (and disturbing) example of the ways the "drive to convert difference to otherness" has functioned. Masculinity (and femininity) has long served as crucial social marker of individual identity. Masculinity has largely been produced and sustained by interwoven discourses of sexuality and gender—discourses themselves rooted in dualistic configurations. As Jeffrey Weeks (1985) has written, "masculinity or the male identity is achieved by the constant process of warding off threats to it. It is precariously achieved by the rejection of femininity and homosexuality" (p. 190). This definition of masculinity as a category maintained by making strict polar distinctions of gender and sexuality is consistent with the concept of the "heterosexual matrix" that Judith Butler maintains governs Western culture today. Drawing from the works of Monique Wittig and Adrienne Rich, Butler (1990) defines the heterosexual matrix as:

> [A] hegemonic discursive/epistemic model of gender intelligibility that assumes that for bodies to cohere and make sense there must be a stable sex expressed through a stable gender (masculine expresses male, feminine expresses female) that is oppositionally and hierarchically defined through the compulsory practice of heterosexuality. (p. 151, n. 6)

In other words, the cultural demand for heterosexuality creates the need for clear markers of gender so that sexual partners can be "correctly" chosen. In this way discourses of (hetero)sexuality establish the categories of gender, and these categories enable the perpetuation of that system of sexuality. Because this system is "oppositionally and hierarchically defined" any aberration from either the category of gender or that of normative heterosexuality is met with efforts to silence, change, or destroy the differences. This process epitomizes how gender is used to maintain heterosexuality, which is itself a "contingency branded into" men and women in our culture (Connolly, 1991, p. 176).

The concept of the heterosexual matrix (as well as Weeks' formulation of normative masculinity) illustrates how the discourses of gender and sexuality are entangled and mutually sustaining/informing. However, I agree with Eve Sedgwick (1990) that "gender and sexuality represent two analytic axes that may productively be imagined as being as distinct from one another as, say, gender and class, or class and race. Distinct, that is to say, no more than minimally, but nonetheless usefully" (p. 30). I believe that the importance of this separation lies in the consequent freedom to reimagine sexuality apart from gender. This freedom is "useful" for it can lead to a cultural valuation of sexual practices and perspectives that are only indirectly informed by gender. For example, as Samira Kawash (1993) points out, if the gender of a person's sexual object choice is given priority, cultural notions of sexuality will revolve around the axis of the same (homo)/different (hetero) binary (p. 28). One example of the ramifications in Western culture of this configuration of sexuality is the way "[i]t delegitimates non-gender-exclusive desires. Current struggles over the 'authenticity' of bisexuality illustrate this effect: if the world is divided into 'same' and 'different,' 'homo' and 'hetero,' then bisexuality is something which cannot exist, and individuals claiming a bisexual identity are confused or in a state of transition" (p. 28).

In *Epistemology of the Closet,* Eve Sedgwick (1990) presents a brief list of alternate ways of thinking about sexuality that offers clues into the possible openings provided by distinguishing between sexuality and gender.

> To some people, the nimbus of "the sexual" seems scarcely to extend beyond the boundaries of discrete genital acts; to others, it enfolds them loosely or floats virtually free of them; many people have their richest mental/emotional involvement with sexual acts that they don't do, or even don't *want* to do. (p. 25-26)

Among other potential openings is the denaturalizing of the relationship between sexuality, reproduction, and motherhood. The political implications of the fracturing of that triad are manifold—not the least of which is the proliferation of nonnormative heterosexual parental and familial structures. Ultimately rethinking the relationship and the distinctions between sexuality, gender, and the heterosexual matrix enables a reimagination of masculinity that is open to a cornucopia of contingent, shifting identities.

Gay Male Gender Identity

Gay male gender identity is an area where the scripts of the heterosexual matrix and normative masculinity are being interrogated and rewritten.[7] This issue invites conflicting forces of cultural discourses and personal identity. The cultural discourse on gender in the United States today still revolves around fairly clear notions of what it means to be male, and sexuality is a central facet of male gender identity. Sexual acts and desires—a sense of the "erotic" as D'Emilio and Freedman put it—have been a crucial element of the identity of many gay men (D'Emilio & Freedman, 1988, p. 323). The conflicts between individual nonnormative sexuality and cultural conceptions of normative maleness create interesting places of slippage where the standards of gender are undermined or contested. For instance, some facets of gay male culture in the United States are rooted in a "self-conscious 'effeminacy' " whereby gay men adopt mannerisms most often associated in our culture with women (Weeks, 1985, p. 190). The disposition has "played with gender definitions as they existed, accepting the limits of the apparently natural dichotomies, but in doing so sought to subvert them, treat them as inevitable but ridiculous" (Weeks, 1985, p. 191). This effeminacy achieves its clearest manifestation in drag and "genderfuck."[8]

Clothes and other accompanying accoutrements are commonly used to signify gender (and, at times, sexual) identity. How a person dresses says much about self-definition and identity formation. One self-identified "drag queen," Christopher Lonc (1991), explained his dress as follows:

It is my choice not to be a man, and it is my choice to be beautiful. I am not a female impersonator; I don't want to mock women. I want to criticize and to poke fun at the roles of women and of men too. I want to show how not-normal I can be. (p. 225)

This self-expression thus also serves as a political force of destabilization. As Judith Butler (1990) states, "In imitating gender, drag implicitly reveals the imitative structure of gender itself—as well as its contingency" (p. 137). Furthermore, the entanglements of the relationship between sexuality and gender in the culture can also be seen in drag. For instance, Lonc (1991) discusses how he initially adopted the "passive" role of a "woman" in sex in an effort to "mimic straight society" but eventually was able to adopt an active role in sex. He explains:

Looking back I can see that I did it because I too was trapped into thinking that the appearance of a person completely defined their sexual preference . . . [but after taking an active role in sex] I felt the fallacy of the traditional men's role . . . versus the traditional female role. I think it also made me understand drag and genderfuck more because it made visible and experiential the nonsense of clear-cut opposites. It made me see that what I had assumed were mutually exclusive roles were the same thing. (p. 226)

Both the entrenchment and the fragility of the binaristic logic that frames the predominant cultural notions of sexual and gender identity categories are evident in this testimony. The acknowledgment of this fragility is critical for the recognition of the overriding fluidity of sexual and gender identity.[9]

The fluidity and instability of the discourses of sexuality and gender (as well as the relationship between these discourses) can also be seen in what Weeks (1985) calls, "the macho-style amongst gay men" (p. 191). The emphasis on physical strength, blue jeans, muscle shirts, tank tops, motorcycles, and other conventional characteristics of normative male gender identity is frequent in gay culture. For example, the commonalities in gay male pornography and heterosexual male pornography[10] with regard to the focus on sexual performance, size of the penis, and perpetual male sexual desire reflect similarities in male gender roles and behavior. Moreover, a weight room, spa, or other physically-oriented environment often serves as a place for men to meet in gay male pornography. The adoption of such characteristics can be read as an effort at destabilizing predominant cultural constructions of masculinity. As Richard Dyer explains:

> By taking the signs of masculinity and eroticising them in a blatantly homosexual context, much mischief is done to the security with which "men" are defined in society, and by which their power is secured. If that bearded, muscular beer drinker turns out to be a pansy, how ever are they going to know the "real" men any more? (Dyer, as quoted in Weeks, 1985, p. 191)

Given this emphasis on conventional male gender characteristics, Weeks maintains that gay people have increasingly "defined themselves less as gender deviants and more as variants in terms of [sexual] object choice." As a result, "*sexual* identity, at least in the lesbian or gay subcultures of the west, has broken free from *gender* identity" (Weeks, 1985, p. 191). I do not agree with Weeks' conclusion that sexual identity for gay people is now independent of considerations of gender. Rather, as I have been arguing, sexual and gender identities are fluid, unstable, contingent, distinct, but also entangled. If there is a "break" as Weeks puts it concerning the identity of "macho" gay men, I would suggest that in this case male gender identity has broken free from the imperative of heterosexuality. This break is a space where the performative character of gender identity can clearly be seen—witness "genderfuck" and the "troublesome" (to the dominant culture) tangle of normative masculine gender identity and nonnormative sexuality. This break is a space where the scripts of normative masculinity can give way to a proliferation of masculinities.

The Subversive Potential of Profeminist Men

Another example of the way cultural scripts can be rewritten can be seen in the efforts of profeminist men. As Weeks explains, to be a "man" in our culture one is supposed to stalwartly reject homosexuality and what is considered feminine. Profeminist men not only resist these scripts but also move beyond the acceptance of that which is constructed as feminine to engage and involve themselves in feminist principles and actions. Indeed, rather than creating new categories of masculinity and femininity, or heterosexuality and homosexuality, at their best profeminist men challenge the "naturalness" of these divisions. Profeminists are often most effective when they use their culturally privileged status as men as a platform from which to disrupt categories of sexual and gender identity. (The privileges of race, class, education, etc., of course, also provide some profeminist men with access to other platforms.) This is often a delicate balancing act, but by contextualizing and critiquing the closed category of male, heterosexual identity, profeminist men pose a unique predicament for cultural discourses of power. Much as heterosexual transvestites (see note 8) and macho gay men are especially disturbing to normative standards of masculinity, the slipperiness of profeminist men provides them with opportunities to be extraordinarily subversive. Thus, whereas women and gay men often are forced to seek to dismantle the categories of gender and sexuality from culturally ordained positions of the "other," profeminist men can work to dismantle the system from positions of power[11] by challenging the very standards of identity that afford them normative status in the culture.

One illustration of this subversiveness is the ability of profeminist men to gain access to audiences of men who otherwise would be hostile to feminist women or gay and lesbian individuals. I believe that engaging heterosexual men in the ongoing discussion concerning the instability of categories of sexuality and gender, as well as various issues such as rape, sexual harassment, and homophobia, is critical for the continuing success of feminist and gay and lesbian movements. Diverse yet complementary strategies need to be employed to meet this end.[12] This process of gaining access to male audiences is, however, quite complex. If profeminist men openly and confrontationally display their political allegiance when speaking about sexuality and gender issues to nonfeminist men, they often face the same hostility as feminist women (if not more hostility because of violating an unspoken, assumed "brotherhood"). One strategy for gaining access to nonfeminist men is for profeminist men to "pass" as "normal" (nonfeminist) men.[13] Such behavior is similar to selectively being closeted. Eve Sedgwick's comments about the destabilizing potential of "relations of the closet" are particularly poignant here. She states, "relations of the closet—the relations of the known and the unknown, the explicit and the inexplicit around homo/heterosexual definition—have the potential for being peculiarly revealing. . . . 'Closeted-ness' is itself a performance . . ." (Sedgwick, 1990, p. 3). Viewing "closeted-ness as performance" enables one to recognize the instability of closeted positions.

The metaphor of cross-dressing provides another way of conceiving this sort of ambiguity that profeminist men can create and utilize. In Western culture two basic presumptions about men are that they are straight and that they are not feminist. Men who seek to destabilize notions of sexual and gender identity (including these two presumptions) will often position themselves against these two normative markers of masculinity (i.e., as queer and/or feminist). But by "cross-dressing as normal men" (and here I mean cross-dressing both in physical appearance and in overt attitude), these profeminist men can "pass" as "normal men" and can then move among other men, strategically subverting social demarcations of sexuality and gender. In one typical scenario a profeminist man can pass long enough to be heard by nonfeminist men and then frame the discourse in such a way that questions designed to destabilize cultural constructions of sexuality and gender are prominently entertained. Undoubtedly raising these questions will reveal the profeminist man's political beliefs, but by this time the crucial first step of gaining access to nonfeminist men will have been achieved. Moreover, this public expression of feminist beliefs by profeminist men will also be disruptive of governing attitudes to sexuality and gender in much the same way as macho gay men. To paraphrase Richard Dyer: If that man in the corner is drinking beer and talking about basketball and then starts espousing feminist ideas, how can one tell who the "real men" are anymore?

Indeed, I believe that given cultural presumptions of normative behavior, individuals are all often moving in and out of closets, are all often "cross-dressing" based on cultural norms and expectations. This consequence of cultural presumptions of normalcy ought to be utilized in efforts to destabilize categories of sexuality and gender. As Judith Butler (1990) says:

> Inasmuch as "identity" is assured through the stabilizing concepts of sex, gender and sexuality, the very notion of "the person" is called into question by the cultural emergence of those "incoherent" or "discontinuous" gendered beings who appear to be persons but who fail to conform to the gendered norms of cultural intelligibility by which persons are defined. (p. 17)

Profeminist men can actively become such "incoherent and discontinuous gendered beings" by adopting a strategy I will call the "politics of ambiguity." By utilizing the fluidity of identity and the shield provided by cultural presumptions of normalcy, profeminist men can thereby gain access to other men and then reveal the "rewrites" they have made in the cultural scripts of masculinity, as well as encourage, challenge, and nurture other men to rewrite the scripts of their own identity.

Strategies for Change:
Identity Politics and Coalition Politics

I am not content to discuss theoretical aspects of identity without addressing the political and activist implications of postmodern subjectivity. Accordingly, I want to conclude this chapter by examining two different strategies often employed in efforts for social change: identity politics and coalition politics. Identity politics is generally organized around subject positions or identity markers that are prominent demarcations of difference in a given culture. These demarcations of difference are so central to the organization and value systems of a culture that they become naturalized and thus perceived as stable categories (or "forms" in the words of Nietzsche) with stable meanings. For instance, although sexuality has long played a central role in the constitution of identity in the West,[14] Eve Sedgwick (1990) argues that:

> What was new from the turn of the century was the world-mapping by which every given person, just as he or she was necessarily assignable to a male or a female gender, was now considered necessarily assignable as well to a homo- or hetero-sexuality, a binarized identity that was full of implications, however confusing . . . [and] that left no space in the culture exempt from the potent incoherences of homo/heterosexual definition. (p. 2)[15]

That is, the binary of heterosexual/homosexual has in the past hundred years become an ossified marker of identity and difference.[16] With this broad change in mind, it is important to recognize that the more central an element is to a system in power (in this case sexuality as a component of individual identity) and the more fundamental that system is in the grander scheme of structures of cultural order (categories of "sexed" people in the United States), the more the "deviant" identification or behavior will be contested and ostracized. Thus as sexuality became a more central element of individual identification, the boundaries between normative sexuality and aberrant sexuality became more precisely demarcated. In this case, the vast multiplicity of sexuality became reduced to heterosexual (normative, extremely highly valued) and homosexual (deviant, negative cultural valuation)—categories that are presumed to be stable in U.S. culture.[17]

Given the increasing centrality of sexuality as a defining element of individual identity and the constitution of the social subject, it is no surprise that identity politics has been central in feminist and gay movements. For example, Jeffrey Escoffier (1985) asserts, "The fundamental ambivalence of homosexuals originating in their being raised to be heterosexuals made the discursive process of identity formation central to gay and lesbian politics" (pp. 119-120). The centrality of identity politics in gay activism in the United States today is illustrated by the emphasis placed on "coming out" (and to some extent "outing") as a critical political strategy.[18] Beyond the political ramifications, "Coming out of the closet was incorporated into the basic assumptions of what it meant to be gay. As such, it came to represent not simply a single act, but the adoption of an identity in which the erotic played a central role" (D'Emilio & Freedman, 1988, p. 323). In *Epistemology of the Closet,* Eve Sedgwick (1990) mentions a "T-shirt that ACT-UP sells in New York bearing the text, 'I am out, therefore I am' " (p. 4). This play on Descartes's dictum concerning the essential constitutive facet of the human subject illustrates the manner in which coming out is perceived as central to individual identity. The centrality of coming out is reinforced by the political statement made by the wearer of the T-shirt, demonstrating the importance of identity politics in the strategies employed by many gay activists.

However, a danger lies in the assumptions often made in politics grounded on identity. Just as it is important to question whether "thinking" is a fixed state on which to ground human subjectivity, in this case one must address the stability of "being out." Indeed, being out has highly contingent implications—meaning different things to different people and different things to the same person in different contexts. Moreover, just as " 'closeted-ness' is a performance" (Sedgwick, 1990, p. 3), so too is being out—and as such, there are a multiplicity of scripts available to be performed and even more to be written.

Examining the problems of grounding social movements on identity politics, feminist theorist Christina Crosby (1992) asserts that such formulations run the risk of not interrogating the stability of identity itself. Crosby cautions against assuming "that ontology is the ground of epistemology, that who I am *determines* what and how I know" (p. 137, emphasis added). Remember Judith Butler's earlier assertion that the social subject is constituted but *not* determined by cultural forces. This distinction is critical and cannot be overstated. As a result, identity politics is never innocent or complete. For as Donna Haraway (1991) makes clear, "We are never [even] immediately present to ourselves,"[19] and thus any politics grounded predominantly on a presumed stable aspect of individual identity will be limited in its ability to create fundamental changes in social discourse and thus the systems and institutions of social power (p. 192).[20] So the acknowledgment that identities are partial and unstable must be continually foregrounded to avoid an identity politics that remains rooted in value-laden demarcations of self and other. By maintaining an awareness that the self is unstable and partial, one can escape from closing categories of identity and subjectivity definition; rather, a fluidity is maintained that ideally will allow for a pleasurable disunity, a proliferation of difference.

This fluidity is crucial for a political strategy that is also central to struggles for social change: coalition politics. Coalition politics is rooted in the capacity of individuals and groups to come together in order to achieve a common goal. However, the members of the coalition, as well as the goal itself, are neither unified or stable. Much as individual subjectivity is contingent and multiple, so too is the subjectivity of a coalition. Much as a stable subject is not needed for personal agency, so too is coalitions' capacity for action drawn from the multiple discourses and identities that constitute its subjectivity. Coalitions "are not utterly groundless, but their grounds are shifting, provisional, passionately felt yet unreliable. Coalition politics makes sense for mobile subjectivities, which can feel empathy with many different perspectives but find themselves fully at home in none" (Ferguson, 1993, p. 178). Acceptance of such a formulation enables a group to come together across differences to struggle for a common goal.

The recognition that mobile subjectivities do not provide a place where one can be "home" is vital for postmodern concepts of the subject and coalition politics. Describing postmodern "eccentric subjects," Teresa de Lauretis (1990) asserts that such subjectivities entail "leaving or giving up a place that is safe, that is 'home'—physically, emotionally, linguistically, epistemologically—for another place that is unknown and risky . . . a place of discourse from which speaking and thinking are at best tentative, uncertain, unguaranteed" (p. 138). Similarly, Bernice Johnson Reagon (1983), in her classic speech on coalition politics, states:

> Coalition work is not work done in your home. Coalition work has to be done in the streets. And it is some of the most dangerous work you can do. And you shouldn't look for comfort. . . . In a coalition you have to give, and it is different from your home. (p. 359)

So, one is faced with the question of who is prepared and able to take such risks. These risks are ameliorated if the contingency and fluidity of identity are recognized. As I have argued, gay/bisexual and profeminist men who interrogate and rewrite the cultural scripts of masculinity are often aware of the fluidity of identity. By perceiving themselves as "mobile subjectivities . . . [which] are ambiguous: messy, multiple, unstable but persevering" (Ferguson, 1993, p. 154), such individuals are able to honor and profit from the differences they will be sure to encounter in a coalition (as well as in themselves). Moreover, the appreciation of difference enables a coalition, for example, not to try to figure out what *a* new cultural script for masculinity ought to be. Instead, the coalition could focus on destabilizing and denaturalizing the scripts in place and create the space for a variety of different masculinities to be performed. Focusing on the creation of such space is consistent with the recognition that "in coalition politics acceptance of incompleteness is crucial" (Ferguson, 1993, p. 35). If individuals embrace such ambiguity, they can perform fluidly—and work in coalitions with others—in a contingent world.

Notes

1. See, for example, Foucault (1980b, pp. 93, 97-98).

2. de Lauretis (1990, pp. 115-116, 131-135).

3. See, for example, bell hooks, *Talking Back: Thinking Feminist, Thinking Black* (1989) and *But Some of Us Are Brave.* (1982). Hull, Scott, and Smith, eds.

4. My understanding of the relationship between sex, gender, and sexuality is rooted in the work of Judith Butler and Michel Foucault. See Butler (1990, chap. 1)., and Foucault (1980a, pp. 24-25, 155).

5. See Butler (1990, p. 143) for a discussion of the "embarrassed, etc." that ends lists of identity categories such as this one. Butler sees in this "etc." an inability to find closure that reaffirms the multiplicity and variability of identities and subject positions.

6. It is perhaps curious that the antifoundationalist Butler uses the term *precondition* in this formulation of agency. It seems appropriate to me, nonetheless, for Butler's commitment to the cultural construction of subjectivity necessitates that individual agency cannot be otherwise but derived from the constituted identities of the subject. A person employs the capacities for agency that are a function of identity.

7. I am not trying to generalize here what "gender" is for all gay men. Indeed, "the idea that there are homosexualities rather than homosexuality is now a familiar one" (Weeks, 1985, pp. 196-207) and thus demands that male gender be conceived of as plural as well.

8. I want to make clear that I am here talking about only gay men who dress in drag. I am not at all suggesting that all men who cross-dress identify as gay. On the subject of cross-dressing, I recommend Marjorie Garber, *Vested Interests: Cross-Dressing and Cultural Anxiety.* For instance, on the pervasive cultural association between cross-dressing and gay men she states:

In mainstream culture it thus appears just as unlikely that a gay man will be pictured in nontransvestite terms as it is that a transvestite man will be pictured in non-gay terms. It is as though the hegemonic cultural imaginary is saying to itself: if there is a difference (between gay and straight), we want to be able to *see* it, and if we see a difference (a man in women's clothes), we want to be able to interpret it. In both cases, the conflation is fueled by a desire to *tell the difference,* to guard against a difference that might otherwise put the identity of one's own position in question. (If people who dress like me might be gay, then someone might think I'm gay, or I might get too close to someone I don't recognize as gay; if someone who is heterosexual like me dresses in women's clothes, what is heterosexuality? etc.) Both the energies of conflation and the energies of clarification and differentiation between transvestitism and homosexuality thus mobilize and problematize, under the twin anxieties of *visibility* and *difference,* all of the culture's assumptions about normative sex and gender roles. (Garber, 1993, p. 130)

9. Judith Butler describes drag as an effort in parody that she sees as a fundamental political strategy in the struggle to deconstruct conventional categories of sexuality and gender. Discussing drag, she states, "This perpetual displacement constitutes a fluidity of identities that suggests an openness to resignification and recontextualization; parodic proliferation deprives hegemonic culture and its critics of the claim to naturalized or essential gender identities" (Butler, 1990, p. 138).

10. I do not want to categorize genres of pornography as gay or heterosexual too exclusively. Individuals of any sexual or gender identity may find stimulation in various pornographic materials that are not necessarily created with them in mind.

11. The normative status is, of course, more available for heterosexually identified men in U.S. culture than for queer men, but queer profeminists still have access to some elements of normative gender identity.

12. This is a very delicate issue, which was addressed in feminist circles in Elaine Showalter's 1983 essay, "Critical Cross-Dressing: Male Feminists and the Woman of the Year." In this important, but problematic piece, Showalter analyzes the film *Tootsie* and concludes that it is not a feminist film in part because it contains an affirmation of the message "feminist ideas are much less threatening when they come from a man" (Showalter, 1987, p. 123). For critiques of Showalter's essay see Craig Owens (1987), "Outlaws: Gay Men in Feminism," and Marjorie Garber (1993, pp. 6-7). Though it is troubling, I believe

that this message still requires consideration in U.S. culture today, particularly for men. The fault lies not with feminist women, but with the acculturation of men who are taught not to take women's voices seriously and that feminists are social deviants. As a result profeminist men have an important role to play in speaking to other men.

13. The historical roots of passing in the West primarily concern issues of race, gender, and sexuality. For a compelling examination of the politics of passing and the nature of passing as performance, see the film *Paris Is Burning* (Livingston, 1991) as well as bell hooks' critique of the film, "Is Paris Burning?" (hooks, 1992, p. 147). hooks critiques director Jennie Livingston for her silencing of the racial elements of African-American gay male ball culture, especially the unaddressed assumption that the highly valued and highly sought femininity is a femininity "totally personified by whiteness."

14. As Foucault asserts, "Since Christianity, the Western world has never ceased saying, 'To know who you are, know what your sexuality is' " (Foucault, 1988, p. 111).

15. On the issue of why heterosexual/homosexual became the central axis of sexual identity amid all other possible options, see Sedgwick (1990, pp. 8-9).

16. Recall Foucault's much cited assertion about the turn-of-the-century shift in Western understandings of homosexuality, "The sodomite had been a temporary aberration; the homosexual was now a species" (Foucault, 1980a, p. 43).

17. As I discussed earlier, given the governing dualistic framework of identity, bisexuality was all but obliterated.

18. On the role of coming out as a political strategy see D'Emilio and Freedman (1988, pp. 322-323).

19. Nietzsche also recognizes both the opaqueness and instability of individual identity. In *The Gay Science* he states, "Now something that you formerly loved as a truth or probability strikes you as an error; you shed it and fancy that this represents a victory for your reason; but perhaps this error was as necessary for you then, when you were still a different person—*you are always a different person*—as are all your present 'truths' " (Nietzsche, 1974, p. 307; emphasis added).

20. Nevertheless, identity markers can be helpful in locating one's positions in a cultural framework (Haraway, 1991, pp. 192-195). These positions are not necessarily locked boxes (unless one allows them to be). I offer here the advice of William Connolly (1991) on the process of self-identification:

> To come to terms with one's implication in these strategies [the consolidation of identity through the constitution of difference], one needs to examine established tactics of self-identity, not so much by engaging in self-inquiry into one's deep interior as by exploring the means by which one has become constituted as what one is, by probing the structures that maintain the plausibility of those configurations, and by analyzing from a perspective that problematizes the certainty of one's self-identity the effects these structures and tactics have on others. (pp. 9-10)

Rather than denying my own implication in the discourses of sexuality and gender that predominate in U.S. culture, I want to acknowledge my own struggles to understand the breadth and depth of the limits imposed on my identity. Thus although I am hesitant but willing to label myself as a profeminist, heterosexual male for purposes of providing markers for readers to analyze and deconstruct my own work, I want to emphasize that as I write, play, and live, I am trying to open up these categories of identification rather than close them around me like a protective shield.

References

Butler, J. (1990). *Gender trouble: Feminism and the subversion of identity*. New York: Routledge.

Butler, J. (1992). Contingent foundations: Feminism and the question of "postmodernism." In J. Butler & J. W. Scott (Eds.), *Feminists theorize the political* (pp. 3-21). New York: Routledge.

Connolly, W. E. (1991). *Identity\difference: Democratic negotiations of political paradox*. Ithaca, NY: Cornell University Press.

Crosby, C. (1992). Dealing with difference. In J. Butler & J. W. Scott (Eds.), *Feminists theorize the political* (pp. 130-143). New York: Routledge.

de Lauretis, T. (1990). Eccentric subjects: Feminist theory and historical consciousness. *Feminist Studies, 16*(1), 115-150.

D'Emilio, J., & Freedman, E. B. (1988). *Intimate matters: A history of sexuality in America*. New York: Harper & Row.

Escoffier, J. (1985, July-October). Sexual revolution and the politics of gay identity. *Socialist Review,* Numbers 81 & 82, *15*(4 & 5), 119-153.

Ferguson, K. E. (1993). *The man question: Visions of subjectivity in feminist theory*. Berkeley: University of California Press.

Foucault, M. (1980a). *The history of sexuality: Volume one*. New York: Vintage.

Foucault, M. (1980b). Two lectures. In C. Gordon (Ed.), *Power/knowledge: Selected interviews and other writings* (pp. 78-100). New York: Pantheon.

Foucault, M. (1988). Power and sex. In L. D. Kritzman (Ed.), *Politics, philosophy, culture: Interviews and other writings, 1977-1984* (pp. 110-124). New York: Routledge.

Garber, M. (1993). *Vested interests: Cross-dressing and cultural anxiety*. New York: HarperPerennial.

Haraway, D. (1991). *Simians, cyborgs and women: The reinvention of nature*. New York: Routledge.

Hartsock, N. (1990). Foucault on power: A theory for women? In L. Nicholson (Ed.), *Feminism/postmodernism* (pp. 157-175). New York: Routledge.

hooks, b. (1989). *Talking back: Thinking feminist, thinking black*. Boston: South End Press.

hooks, b. (1992). *Black looks: Race and representation*. Boston: South End Press.

Hull, G. T., Scott, P. B., & Smith, B. (Eds.). (1982). *But some of us are brave: Black women's studies*. New York: The Feminist Press.

Kawash, S. (1993). Feminism, desire and the problem of sexual identity. In C. M. Baker (Ed.), *Proceedings from "Engendering Knowledge/Engendering Power: Feminism as Theory and Practice"* (pp. 27-30). Durham, NC: Duke University Women's Studies Program.

Livingston, J. (Producer & Director). (1991). *Paris is burning* [Video]. USA: Academy Entertainment.

Lonc, C. (1991). Genderfuck and its delights. In W. Leyland (Ed.), *Gay roots: Twenty years of gay sunshine: An anthology of gay history, sex, politics, and culture* (pp. 224-227). San Francisco: Gay Sunshine Press.

Mouffe, C. (1992). Feminism, citizenship and radical democratic politics. In J. Butler & J. W. Scott (Eds.), *Feminists theorize the political* (pp. 369-384). New York: Routledge.

Nietzsche, F. (1967). *On the genealogy of morals and ecce homo* (W. Kaufmann & R. J. Hollingdale, Trans.). New York: Vintage.

Nietzsche, F. (1974). *The gay science* (W. Kaufmann, Trans.). New York: Vintage.

Owens, C. (1987). Outlaws: Gay men in feminism. In A. Jardine & P. Smith (Eds.), *Men in feminism* (pp. 219-232). New York: Methuen.

Reagon, B. J. (1983). Coalition politics: Turning the century. In B. Smith (Ed.), *Home girls* (pp. 356-368). New York: Kitchen Table Women of Color Press.

Riggs, M. (Producer, Director, Photographer, & Editor). (1989). *Tongues untied* [Video]. San Francisco: Frameline.

Scott, J. W. (1993). The evidence of experience. In H. Abelove, M. A. Barale, & D. M. Halperin (Eds.), *The lesbian and gay studies reader* (pp. 397-415). New York: Routledge.

Sedgwick, E. K. (1990). *Epistemology of the closet.* Berkeley: University of California Press.

Showalter, E. (1987). Critical cross-dressing: Male feminists and the woman of the year. In A. Jardine & P. Smith (Eds.), *Men in feminism* (pp. 116-132). New York: Methuen.

Smith, B. H. (1988). *Contingencies of value: Alternative perspectives for critical theory.* Cambridge, MA: Harvard University Press.

Weeks, J. (1985). *Sexuality and its discontents: Meanings, myths & modern sexualities.* London: Routledge & Kegan Paul.

Young, I. M. (1990). The ideal of community and the politics of difference. In L. Nicholson (Ed.), *Feminism/postmodernism* (pp. 300-323). New York: Routledge.

13

The Male Body and
Literary Metaphors for Masculinity

ARTHUR FLANNIGAN-SAINT-AUBIN

[T]he male issue is to accept our genitals the way they are most of the time rather than . . . holding onto exaggerations of what the penis is like at erection as the proper image of masculine self-definition [. . .] we males need to honor and celebrate our personal experience with our genitals. We men have often reduced women to their biological sexuality [while avoiding or denying] the truth of our own biological sexuality. We have fabricated a steel fig leaf. . . . (Haddon, 1988, p. 23)[1]

Masculinity, in its psychologic and cultural manifestations and implications, is assumed to be the homologue of the phallic genitality of the male with, at the very least, metaphoric connections to it—in part, aggressive, violent, penetrating, goal-directed, linear. Lacking in this perspective in particular is what I shall call the *testicular* and *testerical* aspect of male sexual anatomy and physiology. If the testicles are entered into the equation, therefore, an entirely different metaphoricity emerges, stemming from testicular/testerical characteristics: passive, receptive, enclosing, stable, cyclic, among others—qualities that are lost when male equals penis. Men need to rehabilitate the testicular/testerical mode and thereby the fullness of the experience of the male body and male biologic sex. Of course, everything that is not phallic and in line with traditional masculinity is automatically considered other, that is, feminine; as a result, as I shall argue, these other components of and metaphors for masculinity, although they are authentically and intrinsically male, are not viewed or perhaps even *experienced* consciously as male. A fuller appreciation of the form and function of the male body can be the starting point for a fuller knowledge of the complexity of masculinity, thus challenging the masculine stereotype at the very level of the body where in fact it appears to originate (Haddon, 1988, p. 8). In this chapter I shall begin by (re)turning to the locus of the male body as a metaphoric springboard to offer some reflections on the construction and experience of masculinity; I shall conclude by suggesting that the phallic ideal (in the guise of Superman, for example) occludes the complexity and perhaps the contradiction inherent in any representation of masculinity within patriarchy.

Given the intriguing parallels that exist between biologic maleness at the chromosomal, embryological, and postnatal levels and masculinity as psychologic and cultural constructs, it would seem logical to (re)turn to the body, and in particular to the adult male body, for a more comprehensive and consciously constructed frame of reference. Sexual anatomy and physiology can provide a rich frame indeed and has provided a starting point for many women writers and theorists to explore femininity.[2] Men too can, must, and, I contend, *do* use their bodies to read and to write, to construct and deconstruct the world. Because a sense of maleness and an experience of the body as male are so pervasive in the evolution of consciousness (and Western civilization in particular) (Ong, 1981), it seems important to pursue the issue. Yet this very pervasiveness renders it impossible to give a full account of its significance to the individual male psyche and to the culture as a whole.

Patriarchal ideology takes the male body, or rather a fantasied version of the male body, as its metaphoric basis, as the metaphor for its generating and structuring principle. In other words, patriarchy homologizes human existence with man's corporeality and man's experience of his bodily nature as male. The organization of social and cultural life within patriarchy mirrors this fantasied collective male experience and the individual man's experience of himself and his relationship to his surroundings. The individual male who poses the most basic question of his identity, of who he is, concludes that he is different from his (female) birther/nurturer. Just as male identity (and subsequently masculinity)[3] is predicated on separation from an original, feminine source, within patriarchy, knowledge in general is achieved through differentiation, through separation, and through a polarization of opposites that can be experienced only as conflictual and hierarchical: other/self, feminine/masculine, human/divine, Evil/

Good, among others. Any difference is necessarily comparative: inferior/ superior.

Because masculinity, within this perspective, is other than or different from femininity (the source), it develops oppositionally to nature. Masculinity is a "becoming," a process as opposed to a perceived feminine "being" or state. Like "progress" within patriarchy, it is something to be achieved and to be experienced as triumph over nature, and therefore it seeks to penetrate and appropriate virgin frontiers. It is linear in orientation and directed toward goals. Competition and power are the watchwords. That this is metaphorically connected to the male body, to the individual man's experience of his body, is evident: Masculinity is (like) progress, the patriarchal ideal; so to be masculine is to be like the penis or phallus: "potent, penetrating, outward thrusting, initiating, forging ahead into virgin territory, opening the way, swordlike, able to cut through, able to clear or differentiate, goal-oriented, to the point, focused, directive, effective, aimed, hitting the mark, strong, erect" (Haddon, 1988, p. 10).

Because a man's most basic sense of self necessarily stems from or at least must necessarily include a conception and image of the body as male, it would be surprising if biologic maleness did not entrain a particular self-identity and therefore an entire psychoculture distinct from those that would be engendered by biologic femaleness. Yet as I have suggested, patriarchy's primal metaphor is anchored by a particular version of the male body. For when examined carefully, that is, by teasing out the internal contradictions and blindspots within patriarchy, it is clear that masculinity and therefore patriarchy—or rather masculinity as it expresses itself within patriarchy—derives from a very selective and partial conception and experience of the male body. Patriarchal polarization of opposites skews the male's experience of his bodily nature and it makes masculinity monolithic, seemingly without internal contradiction. But masculinity must not be confused with masculinity within patriarchy, and the experience of the male body must not be reduced to or confused with patriarchy's conscious account of the experience of the male body. Though this masculinity may indeed be partially correct, it is, at the very least, incomplete.

Like Haddon, I maintain that biologic gender can be explored as symbolic or emblematic of the ontology of masculinity. The symbolic meaning that men attach to the form and function of male organs suggests the metaphoric connections between the experiences of the male body and psychologic masculinity: In other words, the experiences of the male body constitute indices, albeit lacunary ones, of masculinity. This symbolic meaning and metaphoric connection can be discerned, I contend, in male fantasies including myths, dreams, daydreams, and male readings and writings of history and fiction. I too shall suggest a complex masculinity for which there is only symbolic as opposed to direct knowledge: Trapped within patriarchal logos, masculinity ultimately may be unknowable, but it can be broached or inferred from the symbolic secret code of the male body. In this chapter the question that I shall pose periodically and in different guises is the following: How might a more conscious experience and comprehensive account of the experience of the male body serve as a metaphor for understanding masculine psychology and culture in general and for understanding male/masculine discursive practices or interpretive strategies in particular?

This is not to be confused with biodeterminism. This is not to suggest, nor do I believe, that anatomy is destiny or that biologic structures and functions produce psychologic or cultural manifestations. I am suggesting rather that biology on the one hand and psychic and psychologic processes (psychology/culture) on the other are connected and are reinforced in a complex, symbiotic relationship: Consciously, men internalize and theorize masculinity filtered, on the one hand, through the experiences of the male body and, on the other hand, through the "psyche's evolving representation of aspects of itself as male" (Haddon, 1988, p. 9) or as somehow part and partial to male anatomy. In other words, masculinity, like femininity, has a biologic component; although neither is dependent on biologic forces, they are not purely social constructs with no physiologic component.

In moving beyond patriarchal thinking, a new construction and a different experience of masculinity seem to emerge and, therein, the possibilities of a new psychoculture. Of course, the crucial questions remain to be posed and explored: Is and how is a nonpatriarchal conception of masculinity possible? Is it possible to predict how masculinity would construct itself nonpatriarchally? How are patriarchal ideology and discourse inflected by displacing the concept of the phallus from its central position? Can one conceive of masculinity as if one were no longer constrained by the contingencies of socialization and cultural biases? These are challenging questions with far-reaching implications; I cannot attempt, of course, to address any of them in a comprehensive manner within the scope of this chapter. At the very least, however, the locus of the male body and biologic maleness are promising places to begin to address these issues because the physiologic differences between men and women mirror how people differentiate between masculinity and femininity as inherent divisions within the human psyche and thus how people differentiate and understand all "genderized" polarities, whether real or imagined and whether in the body, mind, or culture. I maintain that sexual physiology and therefore male and female bodily differences provide the most apt, albeit imperfect, basis from which to construct metaphors that will allow the envisioning of femininity and masculinity in a way that would effectively counter, as Haddon (1988) writes, "both Freud's reductive and patriarchally determined view of anatomy and destiny and the abstract notion of 'unisex' as an ideal"(pp. 6-7).

Minding and Mining the Male Body

Because at every stage of ontogenetic development biologic maleness consists of a rerouting, so to speak, of the encoded female and because it consists of imposing a male pattern that interrupts an original process, it might indeed be said that the Y chromosome and the male gonad that it engenders are homologues of the structuring forces within patriarchy. They create the male/masculine specificity by establishing an all-important differentiation between an unmatched pair and by posing themselves and developing counter to the original (and, from a masculinist position, deemed "inferior") female/feminine source.[4] If, however, metaphors are constructed based on chromosomal patterns and hormonal metabolism and, in particular, if the Y chromosome is taken as a metaphor for the masculine impulse and principle as they are manifested at the intrapsychic, interpersonal, and sociocultural levels, what becomes of the male X chromosome? How might it enter into the generation of metaphors or the metaphoricity? While concentrating on the XX pair and the Y in the XY pair, researchers have virtually ignored the disposition and function of the male X chromosome, Although in the XY pair it is genetically male, the X chromosome is referred to as "female." As will become clearer in the discussion to follow, the privileging of the Y chromosome and the tendency to dismiss the male X chromosome as "female" correspond to the tendency to privilege phallic masculinity at the expense of testicular/testerical masculinity and to dismiss everything else as nonmasculine and therein feminine. Therefore, in addition to constructing metaphors for masculinity—metaphors with which and through which one might experience, contemplate, and theorize masculinity—that would reinsert the X into the XY pair, I shall also suggest ones that would attribute to this gene locus, in addition to its differentiating *compulsion,* its binding/bonding *impulsion,* that is, its impulse to seek a pairing, a twin, a bond—its compensatory reaction to the condition of being uniquely, in all of mammalian life, without a double.

Moreover, it is evident that what the experts, beginning with Freud, label "postnatal masculinity" is indeed a process, a "becoming"; it is equally evident that masculinity, like maleness, is a high-risk process as there is so much that can go awry.[5] Therefore, psychologically as well as biologically, and contrary to Freud's contention, femininity is the natural condition of which masculinity is a modification. Masculinity, like maleness, has to be developed in a way and to an extent that femininity does not. All infants are necessarily "feminine"; the male has to "grow out of" or "away from" his first encounter with mother's female body and feminine qualities. The infant has to become masculine by proving that he is not feminine and by erecting "intrapsychic barriers that ward off the desire to maintain the blissful sense of being one with mother" (Stoller, 1979, p. 33); and, indeed, clinical studies demonstrate that unless this merging is interrupted, males develop "femininity." Because nature itself is envisioned to be female—it is, after all, Mother Nature—to become masculine is to become different from nature, to oppose nature, to become unnatural.

Indeed, contest/opposition appears to be the masculine modality par excellence and the obvious masculine route to self-identity: I come to know myself only by knowing that something else is not me and is to some extent opposed to or set against me. Etymologically, *contest* derives its root from the Latin *testis* (witness) and, as I indicate below, so does *testes/testicle*; it derives from *trei* (three) and *sta* (stand); it relates to *tri-st-i,* a third person standing by to bear witness in a dispute. "Thus a testis or witness, a 'third stander,' implies an agonistic situation between two persons which the testis or third person reports from the outside" (Ong, 1981, pp. 15, 45).

In many species in the animal world, including humans, opposition, *agon,* and adversativeness seem to play a significantly more determining role in the existence of males than females (Newmann, 1954). But as any male in this culture can confirm, masculinity has constantly to be proved and can at any time be taken away because genitals provide no assurance. In fact, in most cultures in which the issue has been investigated, men are more concerned about threats—real or imagined—to their masculinity than are women about threats to their femininity. This insecurity and sense of inferiority can be seen, for example, in the precariousness of the male claim to paternity—whereas maternity is never an uncertainty for women—

which results in male demands for female chastity and fidelity (Ong, 1981, p. 4). This insecurity seems also to be the initial impetus to male bonding in all-male groups and seems to be associated with the tendency toward gynophobia, femiphobia, misogyny, and homophobia, a tendency that is found in both males and females and that, some theorists conclude, results from a defensive reaction against uterine and postuterine maternal control (Money, 1974).

For the little boy, masculinity is experienced as constant insecurity in face of the threat of feminine absorption; the ubiquitous fear that one's sense of maleness and masculinity are in danger, what theorists label "symbiosis anxiety," is a major factor in the creation and experience of masculinity. When compared to girls, boys, therefore, appear to experience more stress as they develop and mature. This stress can be witnessed in the higher rates of learning disabilities (such as dyslexia), speech disorders (such as stuttering), and personality disorders in males. Boys and men seem frequently driven to create and to re-create this stress: Are daredevils like Evel Knievel, for example, paragons of masculinity as some would claim (Haddon, 1988)?

Masculinity within patriarchy is a temporal, linear "program" (left to the caprice of Father Time), and a male must find it outside of the self; masculinity is not easily interiorized. One sees homologues again with biologic maleness, for when the male matures sexually, the testicles descend outside the body cavity proper. Why this evolved remained unclear for a long time because the physiological reasons are not especially apparent—the testicles play no role in intromission; how this evolved is still not understood. Finally, though, the accepted symbol for man, Mars's spear ($\male$), is especially appropriate: it is the symbol of exteriority, conflict, stress, partition, and change.

The individual male who successfully completes the perilous process that patriarchy programs for him reaps his rewards: phallic masculinity and, as suggested later, heterosexuality. But rather than considering his "unsuccessful" brother as mired in perversions and neuroses, one might question implicitly, first, the explicit claims of the desirability of phallicism and, second, the explicit claims of the naturalness of heterosexuality. In a word, one might reclaim and acclaim the *testicular* and *homosexual* options as male/masculine postures or articulations. I shall turn my attention presently to the issue of a testicular/testerical masculinity while considering implicitly two related questions: Is it impossible to imagine a construction of masculinity that is nonphallic? Is it equally impossible to imagine an experience of masculinity that is not homophobic?

Another Bio-logic:
Displacing the Penis/Phallus[6]
and Toward the (Re)inscription of the Testicles

There is indeed another bio-logic, another logic of and to the male body; one might well ask if studies of the Y chromosome and male hormones reflect the biology of masculinity or the masculinity of biology. I am suggesting, of course, that biology, all knowledge, all civilization is "engendered"; that is, reading, writing, thinking cannot be exercised neutrally, without passing through the sieve of gender. The very manner of exploring the biological and psychological sciences bears the mark of patriarchal ideology because, as Evelyn Fox Keller (1985) indicates, a masculine conception of scientific investigation has shaped the conception of nature, including human nature.

However, to re-pose the basic question that interests me presently: How does living in a physical body that is male contribute to self-identity and a conception of the world? In exploring the male body, one must attempt to transcend certain patriarchal or rather masculinist patterns, the first of which is a mode of thinking that associates the very notion of body with woman and with the feminine. The second is that "male" equals penis/phallus, that is, the visible, simple, straightforward as contrasted to "female," that is, the hidden, complicated, cyclic. When the male body, in and of itself at the mature adult sexual level, is considered as metaphoric locus, one must indeed begin to relinquish many of the stereotypes about gender. Particular attention to male anatomy and physiology in all its complexity leads, as I have already suggested, to the generation of new metaphors and a conception of masculinity that goes counter to many of the traditional generalizations and stereotypes. When all of the complex and seemingly contrariant aspects of the male body are considered, what emerges, in particular, is a metaphor for masculinity that seems illusory and self-contradicting; what emerges is a metaphor that suggests that masculinity is *de rigueur* multifaceted and plastic; and what emerges ultimately is a metaphor that confirms that phallic masculinity is indeed factitious.

Psychoanalysts are rather convincing in revealing how the genitals play a role in gender identity and how an awareness of the organs' dimensions, the spontaneous sensations and the sensations produced from self-exploration, and the visualization of one's own genitals and those of others contribute to the developing body ego and "help to define the psychic dimensions of one's sex to oneself" (Stoller, 1979, p. 41; Stoller, 1974-

1976, p. 39). As far as the male is concerned, psychoanalytic theory, for the most part, explains the development of male sexuality and accounts for the developing male body ego in terms of how the little boy manages the fantasied pleasures and dangers of having a penis. The penis, the theory goes, endows the boy with a sense of pride and power and subsequently with the anxiety from knowing that not all beings are so endowed. In other words, the little boy's sense of himself is coextensive with the physicality of the penis and thus with the meaning that he gives it. The exclusive (and some would contend obsessive) emphasis on the penis in psychoanalytic theory—at the expense of the testes for the man and the clitoris and vagina for the woman—and what indeed seems to be ubiquitous phallocentrism and phallogocentrism are scripted into patriarchy and are seen in the purest form in the masculinist myth as Freud himself inflected it.

Freud concluded that the little boy, when compared to the little girl, is privileged and superior: He is born with genitals that are visible, easily accessible, and easily manipulated to produce pleasure. Although his prized possession can be threatened, he is still ahead of the little girl because threat of loss is not as traumatic or ultimately debilitating as the girl's original deprivation. The little boy's other crucial advantage is that his first relationship is (appropriately or "naturally") heterosexual as his initial love object (Mother) is of the opposite sex. Yet despite his advantages—or rather because of them—the little boy's very maleness (penis) and heterosexuality (desire) eventually will be the cause of his trauma: His natural desire (for Mother) will provoke the threats (of castration) from a formidable rival (Father); moreover, his anxiety augments when he sees that others (penisless girls) are lacking or have lost the prized object. If he does not successfully negotiate these threats to his masculinity and heterosexuality, the little boy finds refuge in perversions and neuroses.

But one must ask, where are the testicles (not to mention the sphincter) in this familiar scenario?[7] Although recognized as a locus of erotic pleasure and thus, I would contend, subject to the same kind of symbolic investment as the penis, the testicles are rarely considered in explanations of the genesis of the male body ego, in the explications of male sexuality, or in the development of masculinity. Although some psychoanalysts have long acknowledged that the physical possession of the penis does not appear to account for all of the dimensions of male identity and a sense of maleness, they do not look elsewhere for clues to these other dimensions or even attempt, in some cases, to specify them.[8]

In all of the case histories of boys born without a penis, these boys do possess testes in a normal scrotum—a fact that analysts remark without according it much importance. They proceed as though the penis alone constitutes male genitalia and therefore as though this organ alone, in conjunction with mysterious uterine and postuterine hormonal forces, contributes to a sense of maleness and masculinity. Even when it is allowed that the scrotum and testes might play a role in the development of a sense of maleness and masculinity, it is thought to be a secondary, indirect role; they are dismissed simply as substitutes for the absent penis. Most analysts do not think that they contribute directly to a sense of maleness and perhaps only indirectly through the attitudes of parents and others. It is significant, I believe, that in all of the clinical cases reported in the literature on testicular abnormality—for example, Klinefelter's syndrome or other male hypogonadism in which males who appear physically normal at birth are discovered in adolescence to possess testes that do not produce sufficient levels of androgen—the subjects were considered pathological in gender identity or gender role behavior or as perverted in sexual practice, whether or not they possessed a functioning penis. The point I wish to make is that one man's pathology or perversion might very well be another's nonphallic masculinity. Finally, it is remarkable that, given the privileged position that the complex occupies in psychoanalytic theory, neither Freud nor his disciples have ever commented on the paradox that castration literally means the removal of the testicles.

The privileging of the penis results, of course, in phallocentrism and the phallic metaphor for masculinity, which, though an incomplete symbol or index, has both negative and positive articulations. To be phallic in the positive sense is, for example, to be penetrating: inquisitive, persistent, steady, objective, courageous, discriminating, dominant. To be phallic in the negative sense is, for example, to be intrusive: violent, unyielding, discriminatory, exploitive, domineering. Traditionally, as I have already noted, everything not within these categories is taken to be nonmasculine and feminine. In particular, what are thought to be vagina- or womblike qualities— enclosing, protective, gestating, stable—are considered to be foreign, unnatural, and undesirable in the male. But if a man's experience of his body predisposes him to view the world through the filter of a phallic archetype, what metaphors and what masculinity emerge when he reclaims his testicular/testerical nature? How do possession of the testes and the production of sperm, for example, affect the developing body ego? What metaphoricity might be attached to what is now recognized to be male biologic rhythms and cycles? What are the intraphysic and interpersonal implications?

These are difficult questions to answer. As indicated above, very little study has been conducted by psychologists or psychoanalysts on the symbolic or metaphoric meaning that men attach to the testes and scrotum; but neither has there been extensive study by biologists, physiologists, neurologists, or psychoendocrinologists on the form and function of the testes, such as spermatogenesis—especially when compared to the number of studies focused on female anatomy and sexuality and on phallic male sexuality.[9] One can only speculate as to how the individual man, no longer dispossessed of the testicular, will experience and verbalize his bodily experience as male and as a male.

But one might begin with a return to etymology. Because the Latin *testes* is the plural of *testis,* a witness, the testes were thought perhaps to bear witness to the truth—which is the meaning of *testify* and *attest;* and the truth of patriarchy is manhood, virility. *Testicle* derives from *testiculi,* little witness. *Testicle* is also related to *testa,* which designates both an earthen pot for seed storage and the skull that protects the brain. In botany, the testa is the protective outer encasing of a seed. On the other hand, and as I have already suggested, testes/testicles are also related to contest, testiness, and thus to opposition and *agon* in general. This gives a first indication of the two directions into which a metaphoricity based on the testes will lead.

First, and obviously:

> The testicular component of a man's sexuality has very different qualities than the penis or phallus. Physiologically, the testicle is a reservoir, a holding place, where seed is nurtured to maturation. Unlike the penis, whose power manifests itself through intermittent erection and ejaculation, the testicle is stable and abiding. It quietly and steadily undergirds the man's sexuality. It "hangs in there." The testicle is the germinal source, the vessel from which is poured forth the sap or water of life. (Haddon, 1988, p. 11)

On the basis of these qualities, if one were to imagine the masculine prototype as uniquely or predominantly testicular, it would indeed fall within the realm of the traditional feminine. I realize, as others have pointed out, that to call this masculine nature "testicular" is a bit misleading because it seems to suggest that that part of male anatomy commonly referred to as the "balls" is one, simple organ. Anatomically, it refers in fact to a number of structures that include more than just the testicles proper.

However, if taken together, the phallic and what I am calling the testicular offer a rather intriguing emblem for masculinity. Just as the phallic masculine can be both positive and negative, so too can the testicular masculine. Whereas Haddon postulates three testicular possibilities—wholesome, exaggerated, and atrophied—I maintain that there are two. The positive encompasses what she labels wholesome and the negative what she labels as exaggerated and atrophied. In fact, it is only this positive aspect—"characterized by sourcefulness, resourcefulness" and relating to "staying power, patience, steadiness, steadfastness, abiding presence, and providing of an undergirding, supportive base" (Haddon, 1988, p. 15)—that I designate as *testicular.* I too maintain then that a man is experiencing the testicular mode when he is nurturing, incubating, containing, and protecting. The testicular masculine is characterized by patience, stability, and endurance.

I postulate and label as *testerical* the negative potential deriving from the testicle, evident already in the contest/opposition associations of testes. For just as one might exaggerate the positive phallic traits, one might do the same with the nonphallic: Staying power and steadfastness might become stubbornness or intractability and might lead to holding on when letting go would be preferable; incubation might become, in an exaggerated state, stagnation. The testerical masculine then is characterized by testiness and all that being testy implies: petulant, fretful, insolent, temperamental, morose, and so forth. It is characterized also by lack of direction and by inertia. Evidently, most of the testerical, like the testicular, is considered effeminate and is therefore usually considered undesirable in man. It is important, however, to resist conceiving or theorizing the testicular/testerical as nonmasculine by subsuming it under the feminine.

The patriarchal ideal is unequivocally phallic; there are few nonphallic role models. I maintain that in fact within patriarchy, the construction of a masculine identity and the experience of masculinity are indeed contingent upon a denial of the testicular/testerical; they are contingent on a man's projecting this aspect of the self onto woman. Yet the phallic need not be normative. Men need to return to the body to attest (to) their testicular/testerical nature, which for too long now has been protested, contested, detested, and projected onto women. As stated in the epigraph to this chapter, the male issue is to abandon the long-cherished notion that the erect penis is the proper and unique image and index of masculine identity; the male issue is to accept and to experience fully the biosexual, the body, the genitals the way that they are most of the time:

nonerect but "hanging in there." Men, who have often reduced women to their biologic sexuality, must indeed acknowledge the truth of their own bodies, of their own sexuality. Men must indeed dare to remove the steel fig leaf.

When men reclaim this testicular and testerical nature, a new conception of the body and of the world as filtered through the body becomes accessible. If, as I have suggested, men have tended to reduce women to biology while denying their own corporeality and corporeal reality, it is to a large extent because of the regularity and what has been considered (in folklore and myth) the magical quality of the female menstrual cycle, a biologic rhythm that men lack. Although there are other biologic rhythms— both male and female—the female menstrual cycle is the one that has received the most intensive scientific inquiry: One has only to point out, for example, the myriad of studies devoted to the biologic origins of the cycle, "the physiologic actions occurring during the cycle, the morphologic changes associated with these changes, and the psychologic concomitants of the cycle" (Persky, 1987, p. 115).[10] As is the case with the female menstrual cycle, through science and folklore one has extensive knowledge of as well as many misconceptions about the female menopause, but relatively little knowledge about the corresponding male climacteric. Nevertheless, there is clinical evidence of the male climacteric with both physiologic and psychologic manifestations including decreased memory, irritability, and depression. Moreover, male hormonal profile is connected to psychologic stress and disturbances and is therefore implicated in mental processes and in the etiology of mental disease (Persky, 1987, pp. 17, 80; Werner, 1979, p. 1141).

Despite the scientific evidence, men have thought of and continue to think of themselves as somehow less connected to or dependent on the body; that is, men, when compared to women, are thought of as having fewer if any psychologic processes related to bodily functions and metabolism. Why else, to cite one obvious example of this, is there a clinical and a colloquial *hysteria* but no *testeria*? However, the more important question to pose is the following: What *metaphors* for masculinity impose themselves when one reconsiders and reexperiences the male body consciously through its cycles and rhythms? To repeat, however, the importance for me is not to be found in the biologic origins of male rhythms and cycles or even in their psychologic concomitants per se. It is to be found rather in how a fuller awareness of male bodily function might serve as metaphors for understanding and experiencing masculinity in general and therefore for deconstructing or decoding masculine discursive practices in particular. How, for example, might this help to diagram male language? How might this masculinity be implicated in literary structures, in both the reading and writing of texts? Moreover, might there be literary or textual homologues to male stuttering, male dyslexia, and other male disorders, as there are surely discursive homologues to male masochism, for example?[11]

Although the predominately (or occasionally the uniquely) testicular/testerical male role models are invariably depicted as nonphallic—Pee Wee Herman, Uncle Remus, Santa Claus, and Mr. Rogers, for example—to experience the testerical or to be predominantly testicular is not to be penisless. The masculine modes are not mutually exclusive. Perhaps one can best sense the distinction and yet the interarticulation between the phallic and the testicular/testerical in male fantasies, as seen, for example, in pornography and erotica; this interarticulation can be seen in male discursive practices and interpretive strategies, such as in male humor and in rap music.[12] The modes are occasionally depicted as interarticular in the homosexual thematic and are at least suggested as potentially interfluent in the myth of the androgynous male.

This interarticulation of the masculine modes in male discursive practices and interpretative strategies—which might be viewed as homologous to the biologic interconnection between penile and testicular tissue—has still to be specified and analyzed in detail, of course. The modes have been historically depicted as complementary in varying degrees in male "couples" in fiction and myth, from Gilgamesh and Enkidu in this early literary epic and from Achilles and Patroclus in the *Iliad* to Jonathan and David in the Judaic and Christian tradition and to Roland and Oliver in the medieval chivalric tradition (Woods, 1987). In popular culture they are seen more often as successfully combined in the "odd couple": the "buddy" cops, attorneys, and doctors of television and cinema such as Starsky and Hutch and Butch Cassidy and the Sundance Kid. This is, of course, within the same narrative tradition that is also found in contemporary fictional friendships, twinships, and male rivals in the works of such diverse writers as Jean Genet, Michel Tournier, Manuel Puig, and James Baldwin.[13]

One of the more interesting, if not particularly seamless, interfacing of the masculine modes is found in the Superman/Clark Kent couple. Whereas Superman is the phallic "Man of Steel," it is Clark Kent who has "balls." He is testicular and potentially testerical; he is mild-mannered, enduring, ever present. Superman is episodic; he "rises" to the occasion "like a speeding bullet" and then disappears with only a trace of his former self. Clark Kent "hangs in there" until the Man of Steel, driven by crises, springs into action. Although it is Superman who possesses X-ray (or is it Y-ray?) vision and who is all powerful, it is Clark who is actually sensitive to and therefore responds to the slightest change in his environment; moreover, Clark alone is sensitive to and responds to the charm and beauty of Lois Lane because Superman, true to his Man of Steel nature, cannot allow himself to be distracted from his duty to protect Truth, Justice, and the American Way. Women, including Lois, therefore, leave him cold (as steel).[14]

The Reemergence of the Prototypical Testicular/Testerical Hero

At the time of this writing, Superman is dead. After having previously announced that the hero (Clark) would marry Lois Lane, the editors and writers of the Superman comics created quite a stir among their (overwhelmingly male) readers and within the popular press with the publication of "The Death of Superman" in January 1993. Of course this constitutes merely a narrative device to spark interest in the hero in order to sell comics; nevertheless, this turn of events is hardly surprising. Superman must be read as emblematic of an inevitable and periodic shift from a phallic to a testicular/testerical posture. The particular manner in which this masculine prototype has evolved suggests the possibilities of a non- or postpatriarchally toned male/masculine posture. In other words, within a very paragon of (phallic) masculinity, one can discern already the schemata of a nonphallic, perhaps homoerotic, testicular/testerical masculinity.

First, although his world, like ours, is unmistakably and arrantly heterosexual, Superman himself is not unequivocally heterosexual. Frequently the hero has to react against or camouflage his unwanted homosexual desire.[15] Second, although he is trenchantly phallic, Superman's creators, Jerry Siegal and Joe Shuster, were never able to imagine the Man of Steel with a penis (Greenberger, Byrne, & Gold, 1987); the notion that he could have an erection would be ludicrous and undoubtedly offensive to most readers. This is true in part because his powers are his penis; his very body, his muscles, his height, and even his attire are phallic, so the organ would be superfluous. But more important, this is true because as the legend and the hero have evolved since 1938, it is not the phallic Man of Steel who is the hero and who comes to occupy the center of the stories. It is rather the testicular and testerical Clark Kent who emerges finally in 1986 as the real hero in the Superman legend.

In the more than 50 years since his inception, Superman's double subjectivity has become problematic and untenable and therefore he has undergone numerous modifications, as the writers explain, to "improve" him and to make him more interesting. However, after stripping the hero of one third of his powers in 1971, the writers and editors finally took away his godlike capabilities in 1986 and debuted a new superman. In fact, he was not new at all but was thematically closer to the original 1938 Superman than he had ever been. As a consequence of or in conjunction with this change, there was a revolutionary and, I believe, irreversible change: "In a major philosophical reversal, Clark Kent had become the 'real' character, who posed as Superman, instead of the reverse" (Greenberger, Byrne, & Gold, 1987, p. 12). Superman reemerged as Clark Kent, that is, in the post-1986 episodes, Clark no longer depends on the existence of Superman; he stands on his own. The narrative no longer anticipates the emergence of Superman with the same preambular insistence; therefore the reader does not await this emergence with the same single-mindedness as with the previous episodes. Were he not to appear at all, the events would be, with few exceptions, just as compelling. The recognition of the testicular/testerical Clark as the center of the narrated events is significant indeed. This supporting and dependent character has become the main, independent character; the emphasis and implicitly the valuation has shifted from the dynamic, extraordinary, and episodic actions of the super man to the undergirding, supporting, and ordinary qualities of the man. Clark might very well come to represent the prototypical testicular/testerical hero.

"Why should Superman, this paragon of every masculine attribute (all those muscles, brains, X-ray vision and the power of flight), have room for improvement? Is it because this ideal of masculinity falls short even on its own terms?" (Middleton, 1992, p. 5). The Superman fantasy suggests in fact the plasticity of masculinity, and it exposes, moreover, the factitious phallus and its *hard-(w)on* masculinity, that precarious and ephemeral power that has to put itself constantly on the line to prove itself and to merit its status. Although the patriarchal ideal is a phallic one and even though there are few testicular/testerical role models, the phallic, as I have suggested, need not be normative. Men have only to remove the steel fig leaf, not to expose the penis, but to touch the testicles, to get in touch with their testicular/testerical masculinity. To paraphrase E. Ann Kaplan (1983), to raise questions about the testicular/testerical—and implicitly therefore to raise questions about the desirability and naturalness of phallicism (and heterosexuality)—is a first step toward moving beyond patriarchal imagination and in establishing a male posture and masculine discourse that transcend the phallic without denying its reality. At this particular juncture in knowledge, it may very well be that formulating questions, the simple interrogative mode, constitutes the only discourse available to men as a resistance to patriarchal hegemony.

Notes

1. Haddon is citing an unnamed "male colleague." In the first sections of this essay, I have been enormously influenced by her observations concerning the experiences of gender and the human body. A version of this essay was first presented in 1991 at the 16th Annual Conference on Men and Masculinity in Tucson. I am indebted to David Eckman, Judy White, and Harry Brod, who have read and commented on different versions of the essay.

2. This is especially true for certain French theorists and writers (see, e.g., Cixous, 1981; Irigaray, 1985) who equate gender and reading and writing specificity. From a psychoanalytic perspective, for example, they postulate that women's desire differs from men's desire and that the manifestation/transformation of this desire—whether in phantasms, texts, or speech—is different. It is a difference, they contend, grounded in a particular relationship to the body. Women, it is maintained, speak and write differently than men; in particular, it is theorized, they write and speak from and through the body (Flannigan-Saint-Aubin, 1992).

3. I am, of course, drawing a distinction between a sense of maleness ("I am male") and masculinity or masculine identity ("I am manly"). A sense of maleness is thought to be in part the result of certain hormonal and chromosomal forces. A boy's sense that he is masculine or manly is the result of a complicated, social process that depends on the attitudes and actions of parents and of the culture at large.

4. The human embryo is protofeminine, that is, it has a genetic biologic tendency toward femaleness and a countermand toward maleness. Accordingly, all fetal organs, including the fetal brain and sexual organs, are feminine and will develop as female unless there is a deviation from the naturally occurring process/state. As far as scientists understand the process of sex differentiation, in the genetic male (XY), the Y chromosome prompts the cell in which it is found to produce a protein that then makes it impossible to be combined with cells that do not contain the Y chromosome (i.e., genetically XX or female cells). Because this same protein is what prompts the fetal gonad to develop into the male testicle (as opposed to the female ovary), this single gene locus is responsible for the two most fundamental ways in which individuals are differentiated and identified: as male or female; as self or other—which replicate in effect the two most fundamental differentiations within patriarchal culture (Haddon, 1988).

5. For maleness to occur, for example, the necessary androgens have to be present at the right time and in the right amounts, and they must be of the right chemical structure. Moreover, the human male embryo, like that of all mammalians, begins existence in an environment that is both supportive and nurturing and yet, to a certain extent, hostile. The male embryo's own gonad has to produce the appropriate quantity of testosterone to continue progress toward maleness and to counter the effects of its mother's hormones.

(These same maternal hormones pose no danger to the female embryo.) Almost from the beginning of conception then the potentially male organism must react against its environment on which it nevertheless completely depends; furthermore, as psychoanalysis confirms, this uterine pattern continues psychically as well in postuterine life in such a way that the male (in order to achieve masculinity) has to oppose the maternal and distinguish himself from the maternal differently and to a different degree and with different consequences than the female.

6. I employ *penis* essentially to designate the male organ itself and *phallus* to specify the erect penis and, more significantly, to designate the symbolic meaning with which it is invested.

7. I have explored elsewhere the significance of the anus and the dimensions of "sphincteral" masculinity: "The Mark of Sexual Preference in the Interpretation of Texts," delivered at the University of Delaware, 1987. See also Hocquenghem (1978).

8. Some psychoanalysts, without negating the importance of the phallic stage in male ontogeny, theorize nevertheless that the actual physical possession of the penis is not essential to a sense of maleness and masculinity in boys; that is, boys born without a penis can and do develop "normally" (Stoller, 1974-1976).

9. One very suggestive study (Bell, 1961) that seems to constitute an exception to the traditional view on the relative importance of the testes and scrotum was published over 30 years ago; but to my knowledge, there has been no significant follow-up.

10. The male body quite obviously produces hormones—such as testosterone in the gonad or testes, to cite one example—that affect bodily functions and metabolism, which in turn can and do affect psychologic processes. Male testosterone level is subject to pulsatile or episodic secretions, circadian or daily variation, and cirannual or seasonal fluctuations.

11. Some of the recent efforts to identify or theorize male masochism are unsuccessful, I believe, because most theorists seem to conclude a priori that men do not and cannot speak from the body, or through the body. See, for example, Silverman (1988) and Deleuze (1967). This appears to be an implicit assumption in much of Jardine and Smith (1987) as well.

12. This interarticulation is implicit in some feminist-informed analyses of pornography (see, e.g., Kappeler, 1986); in the modalities of male humor as seen in the persistence of transvestism and cross-dressing jokes in male comics and comedians from Milton Berle and Flip Wilson to Martin Lawrence and the "Men On" characters in Fox television's "In Living Color," and in what I call the "male swagger" in contemporary urban music, especially rap, considered the male music genre par excellence. See, for example, George (1992).

13. Consider, for example, the following couplings: Molina and Valentin in *Kiss of the Spider Woman* (Puig, 1979); David and Giovanni in *Giovanni's Room* (Baldwin, 1956); John and Paul in *Gemini* (Tournier, 1975); Robert and Querelle in *Querelle* (Genet, 1974). In each case there are phallic traits in one partner and testicular/testerical traits in the other that together would form a more nearly complete whole in terms of efficiency and beauty.

14. I should specify that I am referring to Superman as he appeared originally and as he appears currently in comic book form. I realize, of course, that the Superman myth has extended well beyond his comic book version into newspaper comic strips, novels, radio, television, and movies. But as the editors at D. C. Comics have pointed out, "before all of this, during all of this, and after all of this, there was Superman—the Comic Book" (Greenberger, Byrne, & Gold, 1987, p. 16).

15. See, for example, the suggestion and the implication of Superman's homophobia and homosexual desire in Middleton (1992); within this perspective his homosocial

relationships, on the one hand, with his nemesis Lex Luthor and, on the other hand, with his superhero friend Batman take on a particular significance. It is Sedgwick (1985) who explains the distinction between *homosocial* and *homosexual* in a way that reveals the social, political, and sexual implications of the two terms as well as the paradox implicit in this distinction.

References

Baldwin, J. (1956). *Giovanni's room.* New York: Dell.

Bell, A. I. (1961). Some observations on the role of the scrotal sac and testicles. *Journal of the American Psychoanalytic Association, 9,* 261-286.

Cixous, H. (1981). The laugh of the Medusa (K. Cohen & P. Cohen, Trans.). In E. Marks & I. de Courtivron (Eds.), *New French feminisms: An anthology* (pp. 245-264). New York: Schocken.

Deleuze, J. (1967). *Présentations de Sacher-Masoch: Le froid et le cruel* [Introduction to Sacher-Masoch: Coldness and cruelty]. Paris: Les Editions de Minuit.

Flannigan-Saint-Aubin, A. (1987, January). *The mark of sexual preference in the interpretation of texts.* Lecture at the Foreign Language Forum, University of Delaware, Newark.

Flannigan-Saint-Aubin, A. (1992). Reading and writing the body of the *négresse* in Françoise Ega's *Lettres à une noire. Callaloo, 15,* 49- 65.

Genet, J. (1974). *Querelle.* New York: Grove Press.

George, N. (1992). *Buppies, b-boys, bops, & bohos: Notes on post-soul black culture.* New York: HarperCollins.

Greenberger, R., Byrne, J., & Gold, M. (Eds.). (1987). *The greatest Superman stories ever told.* New York: D. C. Comics.

Haddon, G. P. (1988). *Body metaphors: Releasing god-feminine in all of us.* New York: Crossroads.

Hocquenghem, G. (1978). *Homosexual desire* (D. Dangoor, Trans.). London: Allison & Bushby.

Irigaray, L. (1985). *This sex which is not one* (C. Porter, Trans.). Ithaca, NY: Cornell University Press.

Jardine, A., & Smith, P. (Eds.). (1987). *Men in feminism.* New York: Methuen.

Kaplan, E. A. (1983). Is the gaze male. In A. Snitow, C. Stanwell, & S. Thompson (Eds.), *Powers of desire: The politics of sexuality* (pp. 309-327). New York: New Feminist Library, Monthly Review Press.

Kappeler, S. (1986). *The pornography of representation.* Minneapolis: University of Minnesota Press.

Keller, E. F. (1985). Reflections on gender and science. New Haven, CT: Yale University Press.

Middleton, P. (1992). *The inward gaze: Masculinity & subjectivity in modern culture.* New York: Routledge.

Money, J. (1974). Prenatal hormones and postnatal socialization in gender identity differentiation. *Nebraska Symposium on Motivation, 21,* 221-295.

Newmann, E. (1954). *The origins and history of consciousness* (F. Hull, Trans.). New York: Pantheon.

Ong, W. J. (1981). *Fighting for life: Contest, sexuality, and consciousness.* Ithaca, NY: Cornell University Press.

Persky, H. (1987). *Psychoendocrinology of human sexual behavior.* New York: Praeger.

Puig, M. (1979). *Kiss of the spider woman.* New York: Knopf.

Sedgwick, E. K. (1985). *Between men: English literature and male homosocial desire.* New York: Columbia University Press.

Silverman, K. (1988). Masochism and male subjectivity. *Camera Obscura, 17,* 31-66.

Stoller, R. (1974-1976). *Sex and gender.* New York: Jason Aronson.

Stoller, R. (1979). *Sexual excitement: Dynamics of erotic life.* New York: Pantheon.

Tournier, M. (1975). *Gemini.* New York: Doubleday.

Werner, H. (1979). Male climacteric. *Journal of the American Medical Association, 112,* 1441-1443.

Woods, G. (1987). *Articulate flesh: Male homoeroticism and modern poetry.* New Haven, CT: Yale University Press.

14

Weekend Warriors

The New Men's Movement

MICHAEL S. KIMMEL
MICHAEL KAUFMAN

Held up as the end-all of organization leadership, the skills of human relations easily tempt the new administrator into the practice of a tyranny more subtle and more pervasive than that which he means to supplant. No one wants to see the old authoritarian return, but at least it could be said of him that what he wanted primarily from you was your sweat. The new man wants your soul.

William H. Whyte, *The Organization Man*, 1956

Across the United States and Canada men have been gathering in search of their manhood. Inspired and led by poet Robert Bly, the *éminence grise* of this new men's movement—and whose book *Iron John* topped the best-seller lists for more than 35 weeks in 1991—dozens of therapists and "mythopoetic" journeymen currently offer workshops, retreats, and seminars to facilitate their "gender journey," to "heal their father wounds" so

AUTHORS' NOTE: An earlier version of this essay appeared in *Feminist Issues* Volume 13:2 (Fall 1993) as "The New Men's Movement: Retreat and Regression with America's Weekend Warriors" by Michael S. Kimmel and Michael Kaufman. We are grateful to Tim Beneke, Bob Blauner, Terry Boyd, Harry Brod, Joseph Dunlop-Addley, Kay Leigh Hagan, Gil Herdt, Arlie Hochschild, and Iona Mara-Drita for comments and criticism.

that they may retrieve the "inner king," the "warrior within," or the "wildman." Hundreds of thousands of men have heeded the call of the wildman, embraced this new masculinity, and become weekend warriors.

The movement has certainly come in for its share of ridicule and derision. Countless magazine articles, newspaper stories, and even several TV sitcoms have portrayed the movement as nothing more than a bunch of white, upper-middle class professionals chanting and dancing around bonfires, imitating Native American rituals, and bonding. Recently, feminist women have indicated their suspicions that this men's movement is patriarchy with a New Age face, a critique that is explicitly political. To date, the new men's movement has received virtually no serious analytic scrutiny from men. This chapter is an attempt to make sense of that movement, to subject the new men's movement to serious analysis.

Like any other social movement, the new men's movement can best be examined through a set of analytic frames, each designed to illuminate a specific part of the movement. Through an analysis of the major texts of the movement, as well as through participant observation at several men's retreats, we will attempt to make sense of this phenomenon. Specifically, we want to pose four sets of questions:

1. *Historical and political context:* What specific historical conditions have given rise to this new men's movement? What does the movement have to do with the women's movement? Why now?

2. *Social composition:* To what specific groups of men does this new men's movement appeal? Why these men? What is the class, racial, and ethnic composition of these weekend retreats?

3. *Ideology of masculinity:* What is the vision of social change that the new men's movement embraces? From what sources do they derive their vision? What is their diagnosis of the causes of malaise among contemporary men?

4. *Organizational dynamics:* What are the organizational vehicles by which the men's movement will accomplish its aims? What does the evocation of ritual, chanting, drumming, and initiation mean in the context of the movement?

By exploring these four aspects of the mythopoetic men's movement, we will be able to assess the consequences of the movement, both for men and women individually and for the larger framework of other movements for social change. In talking about this men's movement, we see it as distinct from the profeminist men's movement, even though at least some of the men attracted to Robert Bly also consider themselves profeminist. It is also distinct from the self-consciously antifeminist and misogynist men's rights movement, although, again, some other mythopoetic men wander into this camp.

The Men's Movement and the Real World

Contexts and Composition

The first two dimensions of the new men's movement can be fairly briefly summarized. In the past two decades, masculinity has been seen increasingly as in "crisis," a widespread confusion over the meaning of manhood. (Much of this discussion applies specifically to the United States and Canada, although there are some points of contact with Australia and Western Europe.) From the earliest whines of "men's liberation" in the mid-1970s, to the current "Great American Wimp Hunt," and the preoccupation with the diets and fashion tastes of "Real Men," questions of the definitions of masculinity have been contested. That men are confused over the meaning of masculinity has become a media cliché, and hundreds of advice books and magazine columns today advise men on gender issues.

The contemporary crisis of masculinity has structural origins in changing global geopolitical and economic relations and in the changing dynamics and complexion of the workplace. Traditional definitions of masculinity had rested on economic autonomy: control over one's labor, control over the product of that labor, and manly self-reliance in the workplace. The public arena, the space in which men habitually had demonstrated and proved their manhood, was racially and sexually homogeneous, a homosocial world in which straight, white men could be themselves, without fear of the "other." Economic autonomy, coupled with public patriarchy, gave men a secure sense of themselves as men. If they should fail, they could always head out for the frontier, to the boundaries of civilization, where they could stake a new claim for manhood against the forces of nature.

That world is now gone. The transformation of the workplace—increased factory mechanization, increased bureaucratization of office work—means that fewer and fewer men experience anything resembling autonomy in their work. This century has witnessed a steady erosion of economic autonomy: from 90% of U.S. men who owned their own shop or farm at the time of the Civil War to less than 1 out of 10 today. The continental frontier was declared closed at the turn of the century, and since that time a succession of frontiers has been invented to take its place—from the Third World, to outer space (the "final frontier"), to the corporate "jungle." The current global restructuring finds many former outposts on that frontier demanding inclusion into the economy; decolonization and movements for regional or ethnic autonomy destabilize American hegemony.

Perhaps nothing has had a larger cultural impact in this crisis of masculinity than the recent rise of the women's movements and also the gay and lesbian movements. By the late 1960s, the civil rights movement had already challenged the dominant view that the public arena and the workplace were virtual preserves for whites. With the rise of the women's movement, there was a challenge to older and even more fundamental beliefs about men's place in society. Old certainties and gender divisions were questioned, a process augmented by the gay and lesbian movement, which challenged the heterosexual assumptions of those old gender arrangements.

Although these economic, political, and social changes have affected all different groups of men in radically different ways, perhaps the hardest hit *psychologically* were middle-class, straight, white men from their late 20s through their 40s. For these were not only the men who inherited a prescription for manhood that included economic autonomy, public patriarchy, and the frontier safety valve but also the men who believed themselves *entitled* to the power that attended on the successful demonstration of masculinity. These men experienced workplace transformation as a threat to their manhood and the entry of the formerly excluded "others" as a virtual invasion of their privileged space.

As a result, many middle-class, white, middle-aged heterosexual men—among the most privileged groups in the history of the world—do not experience themselves as powerful. Ironically, although these men are everywhere in power, that aggregate power of that group does not translate into an individual sense of feeling empowered. In fact, this group feels quite powerless. Entitled to partake in the traditional power of masculinity, these men feel besieged by new forces outside of their control and somewhat at a loss as they observe the women in their lives changing dramatically while they feel increasingly helpless.

It should come as no surprise, then, to observe that the overwhelming majority of the men who are currently involved in the new men's movement are precisely middle-class, middle-aged, white, and heterosexual. The men who feel most besieged, and who have the resources with which to combat that siege, are the most frequent weekend warriors. Attendance of men of color ranged, over a variety of retreats and conferences in various parts of the United States that we attended, from zero to less than 2%, while never greater than 5% of the attendees were homosexual men. The majority of the men were between 40 and 55, with about 10% over 60 and about 5% younger than 30. Professional, white-collar, and managerial levels were present in far greater proportion than blue-collar and working-class men, in part because the expense of the weekend retreats (usually $200 to $500 for a weekend) and the day-long seminars ($50 to $200) makes the retrieval of deep manhood a journey open only to the economically privileged.

The men's movement is the cry of anguish of privileged American men, men who feel lost in a world in which the ideologies of individualism and manly virtue are out of sync with the realities of urban, industrialized, secular society. It retells the tales of overdominant mothers and absent fathers who have betrayed the young boy and deprived him of his inheritance of a sense of personal power. The men's movement taps a longing for the lost innocence of childhood and a cry for certainty about the meaning of manhood in a society where both men's power and rigid gender definitions are being challenged by feminism. These themes, trumpeted by Bly and his followers, link up with the experiences of predominately white, heterosexual, middle-class, and middle-aged readers who have made his book and the movement that surrounds it such a success. Movement leaders speak directly and with compassion to men's uneasiness and discomfort; eloquently to their grief about their relationships with their fathers, to their despair over their relationships with women, their pain, and sense of powerlessness and isolation. What exactly does the men's movement say? What is its diagnosis of the masculine dilemma?

The Search for the Deep Masculine

The men's movement has many different voices, drawing on many different traditions. Some rely entirely on Greek and Roman mythologies for images of heroic manhood; others use Jungian archetypes or Eastern religions as the foundation for new visions of masculinity. But certain themes are constantly sounded, especially essentialist assumptions about gender distinctions, a contemporary diagnosis of feminization of American manhood, the search for lost fathers (and father figures), and a vision of retrieval of heroic archetypes as models for men. Bly's argument rests on the fusion of (a) a psychological analysis of Jungian archetypes, in which fairy tales and myths serve as illustrations; (b) a historical interpretation of the progress of industrialization and modernization on men's lives; and (c) an anthropological survey of nonindustrial cultures and their rituals of initiating men into society and providing secure identities for adult men. These are sandwiched between a political critique of contemporary men and a vision for the future of manhood that reclaims lost rituals and grounds men's identities more securely. Because *Iron John,* based on a explication of a Grimm fairy tale, is the touchstone of the men's movement, we can explicate its ideology by deconstructing its seminal text. The fable goes as follows:

> Once upon a time, a hunter volunteers to go into the woods and find out why the King had lost several of his men. The hunter returns with a Wild Man, who has lived at the bottom of a lake and has apparently been devouring the others. The King puts the Wild Man in an cage in the courtyard. One day, the King's 8-year-old son is playing near the cage with a ball. The ball rolls into the cage. To get it back, the Wild Man makes the boy promise to get the key to his cage and free him. The key is under the boy's mother's pillow. The boy steals the key from under his mother's pillow and opens the cage. The Wild Man walks off into the woods with the boy. (They have set each other free.)
>
> In the woods with Iron John, the boy fails to follow Iron John's instructions, so he is sent off to work, first as a cook's apprentice, later as a gardener. Here, he meets the daughter of the king. He goes off to war, proving himself in battle, although he doesn't take credit for it. At a post-bellum festival, he catches three golden apples tossed by the king's daughter in a competition, but the boy rides off in a different suit of armor, after catching each one. Eventually, he is brought before the king and asks for the girl's hand in marriage. The big wedding celebration is suddenly interrupted by the entrance of a great King, who walks up to young man and embraces him. "I am Iron John, who through an enchantment became turned into a Wild Man. You have freed me from that enchantment. All the treasure that I won will from now on belong to you."

Bly uses the Iron John fable to several ends—to suggest manhood as a quest, to heal the split between the dutiful son and the Wild Man, to imply that the son's healing of his own wound will simultaneously heal the father's own wounds, to suggest the possibilities of manly nurture and initiation of men by other men, and, most central, to launch his critique of contemporary men.

The New Man as Wimp

The mythopoetic men's movement agrees that something is dramatically wrong with American manhood; "the male of the past twenty years has become more thoughtful, more gentle. But by this process he has not become more free. He's a nice boy who pleases not only his mother but also the young woman he is living with," Bly writes (1990, p. 2). The evidence of feminization is abundant, as Bly points to:

> the percentage of adult sons still living at home has increased; and we can see much other evidence of the difficulty the male feels in breaking with the mother: the guilt often felt toward the mother; the constant attempt, usually unconscious, to be a nice boy; lack of male friends; absorption in boyish flirtation with women; attempts to carry women's pain, and be their comforters; efforts to change a wife into a mother; abandonment of discipline for "softness" and "gentleness"; a general confusion about maleness. (1990, p. 43)

The new man is incapable of standing up to women, so eager is he to please. "If his wife or girlfriend, furious, shouts that he is 'chauvinist,' a 'sexist,' a 'man,' he doesn't fight back, but just takes it" (p. 63). In short, the new man turns out to be a wimp; he is the problem, not the solution, and manhood needs to be rescued from such sensitive Mama's boys.

The men's movement assumes a deep, essential manhood, and its retrieval is the solution. Manhood is seen as a deeply seated essence, an ingrained quality awaiting activation in the social world. Intrinsic to every man, manhood is transhistorical and culturally universal. "The structure at the bottom of the male psyche is still as firm as it was twenty thousand years ago," observes Bly (p. 230), while Moore and Gillette (1992) claim that the deep elements of manhood have "remained largely unchanged for millions of years" (p. 49). It is the exact opposite of the essence of woman:

> Male and female make up one pair. . . . One can feel the resonance between opposites in flamenco dancing. Defender and attacker watch each other, attractor and refuser, woman and man, red and red. Each is a pole with its separate magnetic charge, each is a nation defending its borders, each is a warrior enjoying the heat of extravagant passion, a distinguished passion which is fierce, eaglelike, mysterious. (Bly, 1990, pp. 174-175)

Though masculinity is seen as an inner essence diametrically opposed to femininity, individual men do not inherit manhood through their biological composition. Manhood must be achieved. It must be validated by other men; women cannot validate manhood. "It takes work to become a man," write Moore and Gillette (1992). "Achieving adult male status requires personal courage and the support and nurturing of older men" (p. 234). It is the task of the larger society to facilitate this achievement, because when the actualization of manhood is thwarted, dire consequences result. "If a culture does not deal with the warrior energy . . . it will turn up outside in the form of street gangs, wife beating, drug violence, brutality to children, and aimless murder" (p. 179)—all of which sounds remarkably similar to the words of right-wing ideologue George Gilder (1974). The route to manhood is perilous, but the consequences of failure are far worse.

What then are the appropriate stages of manhood, the stages that each man should follow if he is to activate his deep, essential masculinity? In sum, there are four stages of manhood, each with an accompanying scholarly and mythical apparatus to facilitate its passage: (a) bonding with the mother and breaking away from her (psychological level); (b) bonding with the father and breaking away from him (historical critique of modernity); (c) finding the male mother (anthropological reclamation of initiation ritual); and (d) the reentry into adult heterosexual union (reproduction of heterosexuality, gender roles). Each of these is central to the mythopoetic vision.

Bad Deals From Moms and Dads

The men's movement embraces a traditional, and rather conservative, rendering of psychoanalytic theory. The task of becoming men requires a break from the initial identification with the mother. In today's world this is not simple; men's repudiation of the feminine is thwarted. More than one man "today needs a sword to cut his adult soul away from his mother-bound soul" (Bly, 1990, p. 165). There are two reasons why men have not broken the bond with mother. First, mothers won't let them, remaining locked in somewhat incestuous flirtations with their sons. (This is why the young boy must steal the key from under his mother's pillow—she will not voluntarily give it, and thus him, up.) Second, fathers are not there to facilitate the transfer of identity. Separation from mother is traditionally facilitated by father who provides a role model for his son and presents to him an alternative to femininity. But sadly, men are not doing their job as fathers. It is not entirely men's fault but rather a consequence of modern society. Here, the men's movement adopts a

somewhat mythic history of the Industrial Revolution and its consequences for male development.

If we state it as another fairy tale, this myth goes something like this:
Once upon a time, the division of labor was fully gendered, but both father
and mother remained closely bound to the home and children. Fathers
were intimately involved with the development of their sons. As artisans,
they brought their sons to their workplaces as apprentices; the sons had
an intimate appreciation for the work of the father. But the Industrial
Revolution changed all that; the separation of spheres imprisoned women
in the home, as feminists have long argued, and it exiled men from the
home (a fact curiously absent from feminist analysis, Bly seems to think).
Now fathers are nowhere to be found in the lives of their sons. The "love
unit most damaged by the Industrial Revolution has been the father-son
bond," writes Bly (1990, p. 19). Mythopoets label this the "father wound."

The consequences of the father wound are significant, including adolescent male rebellion:

> The son does not bond with the father, then, but on the contrary a magnetic
> repulsion takes place, for by secret processes the father becomes associated
> in the son's mind with demonic energy, cold evil, Nazis, concentration camp
> guards, evil capitalists, agents of the CIA, powers of world conspiracy. Some
> of the fear felt in the 1960s by young leftist men ("never trust anyone over
> 30") came from that well of demons (Bly, 1990, p. 45);

feminism, because father absence:

> may severely damage the daughter's ability to participate good-heartedly in
> later relationships with men. Much of the rage that some women direct to the
> patriarchy stems from a vast disappointment over this lack of teaching from
> their own fathers (p. 97);

and feminist-inspired male bashing:

> The emphasis placed in recent decades on the inadequacy of men, and the evil
> of the patriarchal system, encourages mothers to discount grown men. . . . Be-
> tween twenty and thirty percent of American boys now live in a house with
> no father present, and the demons have full permission to rage. (pp. 186, 96)

(The reader is left to figure out exactly which demons those might be.)

The absence of the father leaves a void in the center of every adult man,
a psychic wound that yearns for closure. Without healing the father

wound, men are left only with mother, left literally with women teaching them how to become men. But Bly and his followers argue that only men can really teach men to be authentic men, validate masculinity, and provide a male with a secure sense that he has arrived at manhood.

Masculinity as Praxis

Fortunately, the men's movement has discovered such a mechanism, developed in nonindustrial cultures over thousands of years, that can substitute for the absent father and provide the young male with a secure grounding in gender identity. It is the male initiation ritual, symbolically reproduced by thousands of weekend warriors across the nation, men who flock to male-only retreats to tell stories, beat drums, and recreate initiation rituals from other cultures. These nonindustrial cultures are seen as providing a mechanism for young boys to successfully pass through an arduous rite, at the end of which they are secure in their manhood. It is never again a question. There is no "man problem."

In each case, initiation centers around separation from the world of women and rebirth into the world of adult men. This is achieved in spatially separate men's huts or retreats and during specific temporally demarcated periods. As with baptism, there is symbolic death of the boy (the profane self, the self born of woman) and rebirth. Bly (1990) recalls one Australian culture in which the adult men construct a 20- to 30-foot-long tunnel of sticks and bushes and push the young boys through, only to receive them with much ceremony at the other end, having now been reborn ("born out of the male body") (p. 47). He also describes the Kikuyu, who take young boys who are hungry after a day-long fast and sit them down by a fire in the evening. Each adult male cuts his arm and lets the blood flow into a gourd that is passed to the young boys to drink "so that they can see and taste the depth of the older males' love for them." This represents a shift from "female milk to male blood" (p. 47).

The purpose of the initiation has a long theoretical legacy. Mircea Eliade argued that initiation "is equivalent to a revelation of the sacred, of death, of sexuality, and of the struggle for food. Only after having acquired these dimensions of human experience does one become truly a man" (Eliade, 1962). Sociologist Max Weber commented on the consistency of these ritual structures in his epic *Economy and Society.* "He who does not pass the heroic trials of the warrior's training remains a 'woman' just as he who cannot be awakened to the supernatural remains a 'layman,'" (1978, vol. 2, p. 1144).

At the conclusion of the initiation ritual, the young male is socially a man. He has been prepared psychically by separation from mother and identification with father and sociologically by leaving the individual father and becoming one of the band of brothers. Now he is ready to reconnect with woman in spiritual and sexual union, seeking joyous connection, not neurotic demonstration of manhood or narcissistic self-pleasuring. He is ready for marriage.

Thus the spiritual quest for authentic and deep manhood reproduces traditional norms of masculinity and femininity, of heterosexuality, and, in Western culture, monogamous marriage; in short, the men's movement retrieval of mythic manhood reproduces the entire political package that Gayle Rubin (1975) called the "sex-gender system." In the present, as in the mythical past, the demonstration of manhood becomes associated with a relentless repudiation of the feminine. Because, in today's era, the father's absence makes this separation difficult, weekend retreats offer an emotional substitute for real fathers. At these retreats, men can heal their father wound—the grief men feel that their fathers were not emotionally or physically present in their lives. They can feel a sense of intimacy and connectedness to other wounded and searching men. They can discover the depths of their manhood. This is the men's movement's promise for masculine renewal.

False Promises

It is a false promise. In this section of the chapter we will develop a broad-based critique of the mythopoetic men's movement, bringing to bear a variety of social scientific literature to understand the limitations of each phase of the men's movement's promise. We will discuss (a) the limitations of essentialism, (b) the psychoanalytic misdiagnosis, (c) the anthropological context of male bonding, (d) the historical search for masculinist solutions, and (e) the sociology of regression. We conclude with an analysis of the value of the feminist critique of masculinity as a blueprint for men's transformation.

The Construction of Essentialism

The central assumption in the mythopoetic vision is an ontological essential difference between women and men. For all theorists of the movement, the male-female difference is not socially constructed and does not vary cross-culturally. Whether based on Jungian archetypes, bowdlerized readings of Eastern religions, or the selection of myths and fairy tales, the men's movement claims that men and women are virtually different species. The mythopoetic search for the "deep masculine" and the psychically "hairy man" is a search for something that exists as a natural, biological reality. Moore and Gillette (1992) claim that the central elements of manhood are the "hard wired components of our genetically transmitted psychic machine"—without a hint of awareness of how gendered and mechanistic is their language (p. 33).

The men's movement, therefore, misses one of the central insights of social science—that gender is a product of human action and interaction, that definitions of masculinity and femininity are the products of social discourse and social struggle. Being a man is distinct from being biologically male. Essentialism leads the men's movement to adopt a version of manhood that corresponds rather neatly with this society's dominant conception of masculinity—man as warrior and conqueror—and to suggest that this represents the quintessence of manhood. Thus Moore and Gillette venerate Ronald Reagan's courage during the hostage crisis and vilify Jimmy Carter as a wimp: "Emblematic of his weak thinking was his absurd attempt to dramatize energy conservation by not lighting the national Christmas tree, an ancient symbol of eternal life and ongoing vigor. Of more consequence was his impotent reaction to the Iran hostage crisis . . ." (p. 166). That this definition of masculinity rests on men's gender power does not have to enter into the equation—rather, the mythopoetic warrior's quest is to rediscover his masculine core and experience a bond with his psychic ancestors.

Healing the Mother Wound

These essentialist assumptions lead Bly and others to an inversion of feminist psychoanalytic insights of the past three decades. Following Chodorow (1978), Dinnerstein (1976), Rubin (1975), Benjamin (1985), and others, we think that the core psychological problem of gender formation for men is, in a sense, not too little separation from mother but too much. In societies where men do little parenting, both young boys and girls have a primary identification with mother. However, the establishment of a boy's identity and his individuality is a psychic process in which the boy struggles to renounce identification with mother, and the nurturing she represents, and embrace identification with father. It is a process with enormous costs. "Boys come to define themselves," writes

Chodorow (1978), "as more separate and distinct, with a greater sense of rigid ego boundaries and differentiation. The basic feminine sense of self is connected to the world, the basic masculine sense of self is separate" (pp. 174, 169). Such a process has political ramifications:

> Dependency on his mother, attachment to her, and identification with her represent that which is not masculine; a boy must reject dependence and deny attachment and identification. Masculine gender role training becomes much more rigid than feminine. A boy represses those qualities he takes to be feminine inside himself, and rejects and devalues women and whatever he considers to be feminine in the social world. (Chodorow, 1978, p. 181)

Manhood is defined as a flight from femininity and its attendant emotional elements, particularly compassion, nurturance, affection, and dependence. This does not mean that men completely lose these capacities. Rather it means that these things become more or less muted and often experienced as inimical to male power. Though the definition of manhood varies by class and culture, by era and orientation, hegemonic definitions of masculinity (Connell, 1988) are based on independence, aggression, competition, and the capacity to control and dominate. This helps to explain men's rage at women, men's rage at their own dependency and weaknesses, and the rage of so many straight men at gay men (whom they misperceive as failed men).

As a result, most men are afraid of behavior or attitudes that even hint at the feminine. So many men are willing, even eager, to engage in all manner of high-risk behavior, lest they be branded wimps or tainted with the innuendo that they might be homosexual. The whole quest for masculinity is a lifelong set of high-risk behaviors. The costs to men may be on a different level than the costs to women, but men's lived experience involves considerable alienation and pain. Men remain emotionally distant, aggressively risk-taking, preoccupied with power, status, money, accumulating sexual partners, because these are all badges of manhood. We call this obsessive flight from the feminine the "mother wound." Through the mother wound the boy internalizes the categories of gender power of a patriarchal society. The social project of suppressing women and their social power is internalized and unconsciously recreated in the psychic life of the young boy.

The men's movement claims that the root psychological problem for men is that men have not yet cut the psychic umbilical cord. By contrast, we see the problem as the opposite: the relentlessness by which men consciously and unconsciously demonstrate that the cord is cut. From this difference comes the men's movement's prescription for retrieving manhood: to wrench men away from the home, off to the woods with other men, into a homosocial space where men can validate one another's masculinity. It is a feel-good response, but it does little to address the roots of the problem of either a father or a mother wound. Men breaking down their isolation and fears of one another is important, but to get to the core of the problem requires men to play a role in domestic life through equal and shared parenting. Boys would experience men as equally capable of nurture, so that they would not associate nurturing with only one gender, leaving "people of both genders with the positive capacities each has, but without the destructive extremes these currently tend toward" (Chodorow, 1978, p. 218). Men would find their defensive shells pierced by affection and interdependence, thus transforming the definition of masculinity itself, no longer "tied to denial of dependence and devaluation of women." Politically, shared parenting would "reduce men's needs to guard their masculinity and their control of social and cultural spheres which treat and define women as secondary and powerless" (p. 218).

Perhaps more than anything else, it is through the social practices of parenting that men may connect with the emotional qualities that they have rejected in real life—nurturing, compassion, emotional responsiveness, caring. These emotional resources will not be adequately discovered reading a book or stomping through the woods hugging other men who have taken totemic animal names. They are to be found in the simple drudgery of everyday life in the home. Cleaning the toilet, ironing, or washing dishes is not romantic—you don't have to be a "golden eagle" to keep your nest clean. But they are the everyday stuff of nurture and care. They are skills that are learned, not received by divine revelation after howling at the moon in the forest. We need more Ironing Johns, not more Iron Johns.

Although men's entry as equal parents becomes a key part of intergenerational solutions, it is not only biological fathers who can rediscover their capacity to nurture. Gay men, largely in response to the AIDS crisis, have developed inspiring formal and informal social networks of caregiving, nurturance, and support.

The route to manly nurture is through doing it in the everyday way that women nurture in current society, the ways mothers—and not usually fathers—nurtured them. If mothers embody responsibility, care, and nurture, why would Bly suggest that men's project is to reject mother and run away from her? Men need to heal the mother wound, to close the gap between the mother who cared for them and the mother men have tried to leave behind as they struggled to get free of her grasp. What men have lost in that process is precisely what men are currently searching for. Healing the mother wound would allow men to feel that their manhood was not inextricably linked to repudiating mother and all she stands for, but rather in reclaiming, as men, a positive connection to the pre-oedipal mother, the mother who represented to them all those emotions men currently seek: connectedness, interdependence, nurture, and love.

In a distorted way, this is what is at the core of all the pseudorituals in the men's movement. Isn't this what getting in touch with the earth is all about? When workshop leaders encourage men to smear dirt on themselves or take off their shoes and feel the earth under their feet (even when they happen to be in a carpeted meeting room), they hook into a fierce longing for reconnection with the earth and with their mothers who physically embodied their most visceral connection with life and its origins.

Anthropological Androcentrism

The desire to heal men's wounds leads the men's movement to a survey of initiation rituals and rites of passage, as the mechanisms by which traditional cultures established manhood as praxis. But here is one of the chief failings of the movement. Even the most cursory glance at the same myths, archetypes, and anthropological borrowings reveals that all the cultures so celebrated by the men's movement as facilitating deep manhood have been precisely those cultures in which women's status was lowest. Because male domination is not a category of thought to the movement, it need not be a category of history. But its absence creates a major analytic and strategic problem.

Bly and the others wander through anthropological literature like postmodern tourists, as if the world's cultures were an enormous shopping mall filled with ritual boutiques. After trying them on, they take several home to make an interesting outfit—part Asian, part African, part Native American. Moore and Gillette snatch theories from Native American cosmology, Jungian archetypes, and images from ancient Egypt, seventh-century Tibet, Aztecs, Incas, and Sumerians. All are totally decontextualized. But can these rituals be ripped from their larger cultural contexts, or are they not deeply embedded in the cultures of which they are a part, expressing important unstated psychological and metaphysical assumptions about both the males and females of the culture as well as reflecting the social and economic realities of life, including structures of hierarchy and domination?

Bly argues that these men's rituals helped men achieve stable and secure senses of themselves as men, and that these rituals had nothing to do with the hierarchical relations between women and men. In fact, he hints that where men are secure in their gender identity, life is actually better for women. But what we actually learn from nonindustrial cultures—as opposed to what we might wish we had learned—is that these initiation ceremonies, rituals, and separate spheres have everything to do with women's inequality. One survey of over 100 nonindustrial cultures found that societies with separate men's huts are those in which women have the least power. Those cultures in which men sleep separately from women are those in which women's status is lowest. "Societies with men's huts are those in which women have the least power," writes geographer Daphne Spain (1992). In short, "institutionalized spatial segregation reinforces prevailing male advantages" (p. 76). Anthropologist Thomas Gregor agrees; men's clubs of all kinds are "associated with strongly patriarchal societies" (Gregor, 1982, p. 27).

Gregor's work on the Mehinaku of central Brazil illustrates the selectivity in the men's movement's mythic anthropology. The Mehinaku have well-institutionalized men's houses where tribal secrets are kept and ritual instruments played and stored. Spatial segregation is strictly enforced. As one man told Gregor: "This house is only for men. Women may not see anything in here. If a woman comes in, then all the men take her into the woods and she is raped. It has always been that way" (in Gregor, 1982, p. 27).

The men's movement is quite selective about which societies and which of their customs they should appropriate. The initiation rituals were ones through which men symbolically appropriated women's power of reproduction and childbirth. Such rituals had a central place in early patriarchal cultures. After all, how could men possibly claim to be all-powerful when it was women who had the ultimate power of bringing life into the world? Men thus devalued women's power of reproduction and asserted that only men could give birth to men, symbolized in elaborate rebirthing rituals to bring men into the world.

If the goal is not to reassert male power but to ensure gender equality, then the best approach is not to champion the initiation of men into separate mythic spheres:

When fathers help take care of children and women control property, boys are apt to grow up with fewer needs to define themselves in opposition to women, and men are less inclined toward antagonistic displays of superiority. When wives are not required to defer to husbands, and men are not encouraged to display bravado and fierce hostility, then cultural ideologies are unlikely to portray men as superior and women as inferior. (Coltrane, 1992, p. 105)

Interestingly, the interpretations of the myths themselves are asserted to be unambiguous, always leading men away from the home and from women, off into the company of other men. But to take but one example of the dozens of ambiguous readings that might emerge from a confrontation with the original texts, one is reminded that throughout the Odyssey, Odysseus spends his time yearning to be home with his wife and child, looking longingly out at the sea and weeping every night he is away. In Book 11, he returns home, following his prophesy to stop wandering. He takes his oar to a place where men do not salt their food (inland) and where they do not recognize the oar (mistaking it for a thresher), and there he plants the oar in the ground and offers a sacrifice. Then his wanderings will be at an end, and he will be at peace. To us, the quest is, as E.T. said, to go home.

What is more, the evocation of some mythic figures as unambiguous heroes is also problematic. Although some mythopoetic leaders advocate the retrieval of Zeus energy, they willfully forget that Zeus was "an incessant rapist, molesting both mortal women and ancient goddesses," whose reign ushered in a terrible era for women, according to Robert Graves—"the hitherto intellectually dominant Greek woman degenerated into the unpaid worker and breeder of children wherever Zeus and Apollo were the ruling gods" (cited in Caputi & MacKenzie, 1992, p. 72; see also Brod, 1985). Loading up on "Zeus juice" may make compelling myth, but it makes for bad gender politics.

These rituals also have consequences for race relations that their purveyors either ignore or disguise as "respect for traditional cultures." To see a group of middle-class white men appropriating "Indian" rituals, wearing "war paint," drumming and chanting, and taking on totemic animal names is more than silly play, more even than "a bunch of boys playing games with the cultures of people they don't know how to live next door to" (Gossett, 1992, p. 21). It is politically objectionable, similar to the "tomahawk chop" of Atlanta Braves baseball fans. But then again, how wise is the storyteller who asserts, as Bly does, that golden hair is a universal sign of beauty? Perhaps, as Braves fans asserted, participants believe that their behavior honors these Native American traditions. In the postmodern, New Age supermarket of the mythopoetic men's movement, though, it feels more like boys playing cowboys and Indians, and letting the Indians win for a change.

There is another, deeper level at which the racism of the new men's movement is even more deeply troubling. Here we will make a brief historical analogy. During the late 19th century, minstrel shows were enormously popular among white working-class men. These shows were particularly popular with young Irish men, and later, in the first decades of the 20th century, among young Jewish men. Performers in "blackface" would imitate black men, singing and dancing in racial send-ups. But what did these blackface performers sing about? They sang of their nostalgia, their longing for home, for the comforts of family, especially Mammy. In a sense, as historians understand it now, these young Irish and Jewish performers and audiences projected their own anxieties and longings—the ones that they could not express for fear of feminization—and projected them onto newly freed black migrants to the cities. Blackface was more about the longings of white immigrants than about the real lives of black people.

Of course, today, blackface would be immediately transparent as racist. So men's movement leaders encourage what we might call "redface"—the appropriation of Native American rituals and symbols—the drum, chants of "ho," war paint, animal names, and so on. They imagine that these Native cultures expressed a deep spirituality, an abiding love and respect for nature, and a palpable sense of brotherhood. What they are really doing, we believe, is projecting onto these cultures their own longings and their own needs. Such a project relies upon racial, and racist, stereotypes.

Some of the faux-religious iconography of the mythopoetic men's movement gets pretty silly. Moore and Gillette (1992) suggest a small crystal pyramid be carried around as "a useful portable icon," and that the soundtrack albums for *Spartacus* or *Ben Hur* provide good background music to access the inner King, because they are "particularly evocative of King energy" (pp. 215, 217). As Joseph Conwell (1896) wrote in *Manhood's Morning,* a turn-of-the-century advice manual for how to grow up and be a real man, "[r]ot is rot, and it is never more rotten than when it is sandwiched between religious quotations and antiquated poetry" (p. 155).

Historical Hokum[1]

This brief historical analogy of racist tropes in ritual appropriation leads to a larger historical contextualization of the mythopoetic quest. Bly and his followers claim that the current male malaise is the result of the confluence of several factors that have produced the overdominance of women and absence of fathers in a young man's life. The mythic search is initiated in a historically unique situation in which routine forms of male bonding have been delegitimated or disappeared. Only men can validate other men's manhood, but the possibilities for this are limited. Thus, they claim, the search for the authentic male represents a step forward, into historically uncharted waters, where men will come face to face with their grief and their pain. On the contrary, we believe that the mythopoetic men's movement is a step backward in two distinct temporal senses—historical and developmental. It augurs a social return to turn-of-the-century masculinist efforts to retrieve manhood and a personal effort to recreate a mythic boyhood. These two temporal retreats, we believe, require a spatial retreat from women's equality, to which we shall turn in the next section.

The concern that modern culture feminizes men, turning the heroic warrior into a desk-bound nerd, is not a very new idea at all. The late 19th century witnessed an equally potent critique of the enervation of modern manhood and the sources of feminization. Then, as now, the causal sequence of this enervation was seen as a consequence of the Industrial Revolution, which demanded more and more of men's time away from home. This father absence left a void in a young boy's life, which mothers rushed to fill. Thus mothers, and later women in general, as public school and Sunday school teachers, became the validators of manhood. When fathers did return to the home in the evening, they found an utterly feminized domestic sphere, against which they chafed as they squirmed to find some deep bonding with other men.

Such diagnoses echoed across the country in a variety of settings. Here's the dashing Basil Ransome's indictment of the age in Henry James's *The Bostonians* (1885/1966), a sentiment that could have been written by Robert Bly today:

> The whole generation is womanized; the masculine tone is passing out of the world; it's a feminine, a nervous, hysterical, chattering, canting age, an age of hollow phrases and false delicacy and exaggerated solicitudes and coddled sensibilities, which, if we don't soon look out, will usher in the reign of mediocrity, of the feeblest and flattest and the most pretentious that has ever been. The masculine character, the ability to dare and endure, to know and yet not fear reality, to look the world in the face and take it for what it is . . . that is what I want to preserve, or rather, as I may say, to recover; and

I must tell you that I don't in the least care what becomes of you ladies while I make the attempt! (p. 293)

From pulpits to editorial pages, from gymnasiums to classrooms, men appeared concerned about the feminization of American culture and sought remedies that would cure men of their culturally induced enervation.

Structurally, the traditional definitions of masculinity were rapidly eroding at the turn of the century. The closing of the frontier meant that no longer would men have that literal-geographic space to test their mettle against nature and other men. The rapid industrialization of American manufacturing meant that individual men were no longer the owners or proprietors of their own labor. As noted earlier, at the time of the Civil War, 90% of men in the United States were independent farmers or self-employed businessmen or artisans. By 1870 that number had dropped to two of three, and by 1910 less than one third of U.S. men were economically autonomous. At the same time, the northward migration of newly freed slaves, the dramatic immigration of Southern Europeans, and the emergence of visible homosexual enclaves in major cities all signaled new competitors for white, middle-class men's power in the public domain. What is more, women were demanding equality in the public sphere in unprecedented ways—not only in the ballot box or the classroom, but in the workplace and in the bedroom, as social "feminists" argued for the right to birth control and "sex rights."

Suddenly men felt themselves to be on the defensive and launched a multifaceted critique of turn-of-the-century culture. A health and fitness craze swept over the country, as more and more men sought the tonic freshness of the outdoors to offset the daily routine of "brain work." Bernarr Macfadden and other promoters of "physical culture" rode a wave of interest that saw dramatic increases in sports such as boxing, football, and weight lifting as methods to develop real manhood.

Child-rearing manuals promoted a dichotomous separation of little boys and little girls. Parents were instructed to dress boys and girls differently from birth and to follow that separation through to youth, where boys were to be encouraged to do certain activities (sports, rough play) and prevented from doing others (reading, sleeping on feather beds, going to parties) for fear of possible contamination by feminizing influences. Separate child rearing continued into the schoolroom. Coeducation was feared because women would sap the virility of male students. By adolescence, "boy culture" was to be organized and disciplined under male supervision, but strict separation of the sexes was to be maintained to ensure that boys would grow up to be real men. The reorganization of the Young Men's Christian Association in the 1880s and the organization of the Boy's Brigades and Knights of King Arthur in the 1880s and 1890s indicated an effort to provide young boys with adult male role models, simultaneously disciplining and controlling boy culture and demarcating male space from female space in a highly ritualized and mythopoetic setting. The founding of Boy Scouts of America in 1910 by Ernest Thompson Seton provides a graphic indictment of contemporary manhood. Women, he argued, were turning "robust, manly, self-reliant boyhood into a lot of flat chested cigarette smokers with shaky nerves and doubtful vitality" (cited in Macleod, 1983, p. 49).

Cultural feminization was challenged by religious leaders, who sought to reinvest the cultural images of Jesus with virile manhood. The Muscular Christianity movement sought to transform religious iconography, which often portrayed Jesus as soft and gentle. Jesus was "no dough-faced, lick spittle proposition," proclaimed evangelist Billy Sunday, but "the greatest scrapper who ever lived." "Lord save us from off-handed, flabby cheeked, brittle boned, weak-kneed, thin-skinned, pliable, plastic, spineless, effeminate, ossified, three carat Christianity" Sunday pleaded (cited in McLaughlin, 1955, pp. 179, 175).

Adult men could retreat to their fraternal lodges. Fraternal orders were enormously popular at the turn of the century; slightly less than one of four American men belonged to an order (Harwood, 1897). The lodge was a homosocial preserve, celebrating a purified, nurturant masculinity. James Laird of the Nebraska Grand Lodge endorsed a Masonic war against "destructive effeminacy" in 1876. "What Masons want, what the world wants, is not sympathy, not cooperation, not reform, not redemption, but strength" (cited in Carnes, 1989, p. 141).

These fraternal orders are the turn-of-the-century precursor to contemporary mythopoetic retreats. Here men's initiation rituals took on a systematic, routinized character: With up to 50 different levels of status, one could be reasonably certain that an initiation was going to take place at each meeting. Such rituals followed a similar appropriation of tradition. The profane man, the man born of woman, is symbolically killed and reborn into the band of equal brothers, imitating what these men knew of initiation in non-Western cultures. (Like baptismal priests, the fraternal elders often wore long robes and aprons—literally appropriating women's dresses as they symbolically appropriated women's reproductive power.)

There is one interesting difference in the images of these turn-of-the-century men from their 1990s progeny. The earlier movement reflected the 19th-century fascination with the classical era. Mythical views of ancient Egypt, Greece, and Rome provided the icons. Bly and the mythopoetic men's movement fall very much within the New Age iconography: The classical past is no longer in vogue. Rather there is a retreat to an even more distant mythical past, that of repackaged images of native societies.

The masculinist efforts to retrieve authentic manly adventure resonated in American literature as well. Following the Freudian axiom that the objects that give meaning to life that people lose in reality are recreated in fantasy, writers sought to recreate what had already been lost. The first "western," Owen Wister's *The Virginian* (1902), Jack London's *The Call of the Wild* (1903), and Edgar Rice Burroughs's Tarzan series returned men to the frontier and the jungle, even as they receded from men's grasp. Wrenched from effete civilized life, Tarzan and Buck hear the call of their primitive instincts and return to become, respectively, apes and wolves. Mythic heroes who stood for untamed manhood, capable of beating back rapid industrialization and feminization, abounded in artisanal heroes like Paul Bunyan (collected 1914-1916), John Henry (ca. 1873), and Casey Jones (1900).

Most troubling of all these masculinist efforts to revive a recharged manhood is the turn-of-the-century cult of the warrior, embedded within the new militarism that contributed to the Spanish American War in 1898. The soldier was seen as a moral exemplar, none more than Theodore Roosevelt, whose triumph over youthful frailty and illness and subsequent robust aggression served as a template for a revitalized social character. Roosevelt fused compulsive masculinity (the strenuous life) with military adventurism (imperialist intervention) into a powerful synthesis. Evocations of the warrior in the era of Operation Desert Storm clearly made Robert Bly uneasy; he attempted, unsuccessfully, to organize a group of writers against the war in the Gulf, just as he earlier had worked to organize writers against the Vietnam War. But many of his followers uncritically embrace warrior images, without any trace of discomfort.

The weekend warriors join a host of contemporary masculinists who search for the masculine primitive among the shards of advanced industrial culture.[2] How different are they from the wealthy members of the Bohemian Club in San Francisco who go off to Bohemian Grove retreats every summer—retreats that are drenched with ritualized male bonding, dancing partially naked in front of campfires, "full of schmaltz and nostalgia"—with corporate CEOs, legislators (and presidents), and other members of the American ruling class (cf. Domhoff, 1974)? or who take part in the occasional Wild Man retreat if they felt the creeping enervation of having to deal with adult women on an equal basis? But in case the impact on women is lost to our dreaming senior, let him hear the voice of one of his brothers, another member of Yale's Skull and Bones club. "I would predict an increase in date rape," he prophesied, should the club be forced to admit women (cited in *Newsweek,* 23 September 1991, p. 41).

Boys' Town

The image of the eternal fraternity reveals a partially hidden longing that lies just beneath the surface of Bly's appeal. The search for the deep masculine is actually a search for lost boyhood, that homosocial innocence of preadolescence, at once rough and tumble and sweetly naive. It is an effort to turn back the clock to that time before work and family responsibilities yanked men away from their buddies, from a world of fun. Leslie Fiedler noticed this nostalgic yearning for lost boyhood, a world of homosocial intimacy, as the dominant theme in American literature. Unlike the European novel, in which the action revolved around adult men and women in domestic entanglements, the American novel allows the young man to escape domesticity by being kidnapped, running away, enlisting in the army, or being shipwrecked. The American romantic couple is Natty Bumppo and Chingachgook, Ishmael and Queequeg, Huck Finn and Jim, the Lone Ranger and Tonto. These couples "proffer a chaste male love as the ultimate emotional experience" revealing an "implacable nostalgia for the infantile, at once wrong headed and somehow admirable," he writes. The authors' "self congratulatory buddy-buddiness" also reveals an "astonishing naivete" (Fiedler, 1966, p. 144). "I reckon I gotta light out for the country," says Huck, "cuz Aunt Sally, she's gonna civilise me, and I can't stand that."

The mythopoetic men's retreats recall the clubhouse with the sign reading "No Gurls Allowed" or the movie *Stand By Me,* which captures that last summer before junior high school, before having to posture to impress girls will forever distort the relationships among the boys. What Kenneth Keniston calls the "fallacy of romantic regression" appeals not to men who want to be men, but rather to men who want to rebecome boys; thus their antipathy toward women and work is so easily displaced onto mothers who have not been part of their lives for decades. "No one is going to catch me lady and make me a man. I want always to be a little boy and to have fun." So said Peter Pan. So say the men at wild man retreats.

This search for lost boyhood as the search for the authentic masculine helps explain several of the paradoxes that emerge at the men's retreats. Men's movement leaders speak to men not as fathers but as sons searching for their fathers. But curiously, the attendees at the workshops are middle-aged men, many of whom are, themselves, fathers. They rarely speak of their own children (and when they do, it is almost exclusively their sons; it is as if daughters do not exist in this world). They speak as sons, of their pain as sons estranged from fathers. That is, they would rather complain about something they can barely change than work toward transforming something that they can: their relationships with their own children and the structured inequalities of power between men and women, adults and children, and one man and another.

However, at the retreats, they are also asked to honor the elders, the older men at the weekend retreats, who are seen to embody a certain deeply male wisdom. Leaders invite participants to admire the wisdom of older men, to listen to their stories, to learn from the wisdom they have gained through the years. But wait, are these not the same elder men (fathers) who abandoned their sons? Thus when Bly or his followers speak as fathers, they criticize contemporary men as having followed mother, having been dutiful little boys (having been feminized). But when they speak as sons, they are angry and hurt by fathers who behaved exactly as they have.

How do we explain this shift in focus? "I'm not sure why they want to be back in the good old days," observed a woman therapist in 1967. "Do they want to be back there as the father, or do they want to be back there as the child?" (cited in Brenton, 1967, p. 107). When men speak as sons, men are angry and wounded by their fathers. When men speak as fathers, men expect veneration and admiration from sons. Men are thus going to have it both ways, particularly whichever way allows them to feel like the innocent victim of other people's disempowering behavior, the victim of what others (fathers or sons) have done to them. This is again the lost (false) innocence of mythic boyhood.

But it is also more than that—it is staking a claim for victimhood and entitlement at the same time. This is what explains the emphasis on the role of the little prince in the Iron John story and explains the way that these men, feeling like boys, want to claim their inner King. The prince is actually not the central figure in Iron John's story; it is Iron John himself, who is liberated by the young boy's quest. As the title indicates, he is the star. But male readers see themselves as the king's son, the prince, and not as Iron John.

But who is the prince? The prince is the rightful heir to power; he will be the King. He is literally *entitled* to power, but he is not yet ready for it. So too for manhood. Men's movement participants believe themselves entitled to that power, the power that comes from being a man, the power one might call patriarchy, or male privilege. They do not feel that power yet—but they want to, and they feel themselves entitled to it. This is why the men at the mythopoetic retreats find it so much easier to imagine themselves as sons, to call themselves "adult children"—as if the word *adult* was an adjective, modifying the word *child*—rather than as fully adult, responsible to others, and refusing to claim their privileged inheritance.[3]

Whispers of the Heart

We believe that the mythopoetic quest is misguided because it reproduces masculinity as a power relation—the power of men over women and the power of some men over other men. But there is no reason to doubt Bly or his followers' sincerity or their desire to recreate a world of gender certainty. The appeal of this message is in response to feminism, but not only in the negative sense we have been describing. It is also an indication that millions of men have been forced to grapple with what it means to be a man. Men are searching, looking for a new sense of meaning. That they have been looking under every possible stone and crystal is no surprise, nor is it a surprise that the most popular solution so far is one that offers a quick and comfortable fix. Although the mythopoetic solution may not bring real change, the enthusiasm with which it has been greeted represents, at least in part, part of a process of change.

A key aspect of that process, a progressive whisper within a reactive structure, is that mythopoetic groups and gatherings can be means for men to break their isolation from other men. Part of patriarchy's interpersonal cement is an isolation that keeps each man fearful of his own masculinity and forces him to go to lengths to prove to the other guys that he is a real man. By breaking the isolation, by setting up opportunities for men to express a range of feelings among themselves and to talk about their fears and loves and challenges, men can take steps toward disassociating manhood and domination and reestablishing it on the basis of connection and harmony with those around them.[4]

This activity of redefinition is seen in the nostalgia for boyhood. We have talked about the regressive side of this nostalgia, but we also must ask why this nostalgia is so powerful. Perhaps it is part of what Barbara

Ehrenreich (1983) described as men's flight from commitment symbolized by the magazine that extolled a male inhabiting an adult body but acting like a boy at play, literally a Play-boy. But there is more: It is a longing for what men have given up in order to fit into the tight pants of masculinity. Becoming a man required a suppression of a range of human capacities, capabilities, and emotions. But these capacities maintain a nagging presence in men's own lives. Few completely or effortlessly fit into the dictates of male gender power, particularly in a society where women have demanded equality and have challenged men to examine their own lives. As men attempt to expand their emotional repertoire, as they learn to reach out to brothers, sisters, and children, it reawakens a childhood voice that has long been buried. Playing in the woods recalls the days when men were less preoccupied with maintaining gender barriers, when men felt more at home with the bodies and the tears of other males, and when men felt more at home with themselves. It is not that any moment of their lives men were completely free of the rigors of gender acquisition, but rather that gender demands did not yet so completely overwhelm a range of other human characteristics and possibilities. Of course, part of the yearning for the past is a nostalgia for a past that did not completely exist.[5]

The alternative is not to reject personal change and personal growth. It is not for men to start a political movement in the image of other political movements: "Alright men, let's get out there and get this job done no matter what the cost." It is to hear what women have been telling men for the past two and a half decades—that personal change is an indispensable element of, and tool for, social change, and that structural social change is an indispensable element for personal change. It is a personal vision of political change and a political vision of personal change that we propose as an alternative to the men's movement that will allow men's wild and progressive impulses to blossom.

The Flight From Feminism

What keeps Bly and his followers from taking this radical course of personal and social change are his protests that his work has nothing to do with women or feminism. Bly (1990) writes that his book "does not constitute a challenge to the women's movement," that he "does not seek to turn men against women, nor to return men to their domineering mode that has led to repression of women and their values for centuries" (p. x). But such claims are disingenuous.

Though Bly is careful to hedge his comments, the book is full of inferences that reveal how he embraces traditional gender roles:

A mother's job is, after all, to civilize the boy (p. 11);

or

A man who cannot defend his own space cannot defend women and children (p. 156);

or

As more and more mothers work out of the house, and cannot show their daughters what they produce, similar emotions may develop in the daughter's psyche, with a consequent suspicion of grown women (p. 96).

Alone with other men, Bly gives this antifeminist tendency fuller play. Journalists Steve Chapple and David Talbot describe an encounter between Bly and his campers at a retreat: "'Robert, when we tell women our desires, they tell us we're wrong,' shouts out one camper. 'So,' says Bly, 'then you bust them in the mouth because no one has the right to tell another person what their true desires are'" (cited in Chapple & Talbot, 1990, p. 196).

If Bly sidesteps the issue, his followers do not. One leader of retreats to heal the father wound argues:

A lot of men feel hung out to dry by the women's movement. A lot of men feel that they, personally, are being held responsible for everything that's macho and wrong in the world today: rape, wife-beating, war. They've been feeling very bad about themselves, and so they're overjoyed to recover their maleness and feel proud about themselves as men. (cited in Chapple & Talbot, 1990, p. 195)

Ray Raphael (1988) celebrates men's ability to do anything women can:

At a time when an enlightened feminism has taken away many of our traditional props, at a time when many of our manly roles have become virtually obsolete, at a time when we have been placed on the defensive in what we perceive as a never-ending competition between the sexes, we have countered by aggressively usurping the roles once played by women. (p. 172)

Journalist Trip Gabriel reports from the gender front that "more than the men's movement cares to admit, it is a reaction to the decades of feminism, a reclaiming of prerogatives that men have long been made to feel defensive about" (Gabriel, 1991, p. 31).

Note how each of these men couch the reaction against feminism in terms of men's defensiveness. Men have been made to feel bad about traditional masculinity, about men's violence, rape, pornography, battery, and a litany of other feminist accusations. Their response is not to enlist in the feminist struggle against these excesses of manly behavior but to declare themselves tired of listening.

The retreat to find a revitalized and recharged manhood, embodied in the new men's movement, is most definitely a retreat. It is a retreat from the mother, who embodies, in the practices of mothering, precisely the positive qualities of caring and nurturing that men are running away from her to find. It is a retreat from the historical specificity of the present era, a retreat from political responsibilities to confront male excesses that daily manifest themselves on the streets, in the schools, in the workplaces, in the bedrooms—excesses such as rape, violence, spouse abuse, gay bashing, high-risk sexual behavior, drunk driving. It is a retreat to a highly selective anthropological world of rituals that reproduce men's cultural power over women and that are now used to facilitate a deeper nostalgic retreat to the lost world of innocent boyhood. It is thus a retreat from women, from adult men's responsibilities to embrace women's equality and struggle against those obstacles that continue to lie in the path of gender equality. Male bonding, hailed as the positive outcome of these weekend retreats, is double sided. Bonding implies connection with others and also implies constraints, responsibilities. The deep masculine will never be retrieved by running away from women. Only by fighting for equality, side by side, as equals, can men realize the best of what it means to be a man.

Notes

1. The material in this section is drawn primarily from Kimmel's *Manhood: The American Quest* (in press).

2. Masculinists, as distinct from either profeminist men or self-conscious antifeminists, are more concerned with what they see as the feminization of men than the feminism of women. In response to this fear of feminization, they attempt to carve out homosocial environments in both the public and private spheres in order to celebrate male bonding

and fantasies of escape from women. See Michael Kimmel, "Men's Responses to Feminism at the Turn of the Century," *Gender & Society,* vol. 1, no. 3 (1987).

3. It has also been suggested that movement participants are princes because there can be only one King, Bly himself, the symbolic "good" father who facilitates, through traditional analytic transference, the healing of the father wound. But we believe that the mythopoetic men's movement is more than Freudian psychoanalysis on a mass scale; it is also political and ideological.

4. An alternative approach to breaking this isolation but within a profeminist perspective is addressed in Kaufman's *Cracking the Armour: Power, Pain, and the Lives of Men* (1993).

5. Our thanks to Harry Brod for suggesting this final point, the sense of nostalgia for something that did not fully exist.

References

Benjamin, J. (1985). *The bonds of love.* New York: Pantheon.

Bly, R. (1990). *Iron John: A book about men.* Reading, MA: Addison-Wesley.

Brenton, M. (1967). *The American male.* London: Allen & Unwin.

Brod, H. (1985, April). Reply to Bly. *AHP Perspective.* New York: Association for Humanistic Psychology.

Caputi, J., & MacKenzie, G. O. (1992). Pumping *Iron John.* In K. L. Hagan (Ed.), *Women respond to the men's movement* (pp. 69-81). San Francisco: HarperCollins.

Carnes, M. C. (1989). *Secret ritual and manhood in Victorian America.* New Haven, CT: Yale University Press.

Chapple, S., & Talbot, D. (1990). *Burning desires.* New York: Simon & Schuster.

Chodorow, N. (1978). *The reproduction of mothering.* Berkeley: University of California Press.

Coltrane, S. (1992). The micropolitics of gender in nonindustrial societies. *Gender & Society, 6*(1), 86-107.

Connell, R. W. (1988). *Gender and power.* Stanford, CA: Stanford University Press.

Conwell, J. A. (1896). *Manhood's morning; or, "go it while you're young": A book for young men between 14 and 28 years of age.* Vineland, NJ: The Hominis Book Company.

Dinnerstein, D. (1976). *The mermaid and the minotaur.* New York: Harper & Row.

Domhoff, G. W. (1974). *The bohemian grove and other ruling class retreats.* New York: Harper & Row.

Ehrenreich, B. (1983). *The hearts of men.* New York: Anchor.

Eliade, M. (1962). *The sacred and the profane.* Chicago: University of Chicago Press.

Fiedler, L. (1966). *Love and death in the American novel.* New York: Stein & Day.

Gabriel, T. (1991, September 22). In touch with the tool belt chromosome. *New York Times.*

Gilder, G. (1974). *Naked nomads.* New York: Quadrangle.

Gossett, H. (1992). Men's movement??? a page drama. In K. L. Hagan (Ed.), *Women respond to the men's movement* (pp. 19-25). San Francisco: HarperCollins.

Gregor, T. (1982). No girls allowed. *Science, 82* (December).

Harwood, W. S. (1897). Secret societies in America. *The North American Review, 164,* 620-623.

James, H. (1885/1966). *The Bostonians*. New York: Signet.

Kaufman, M. (1993). *Cracking the armour: Power, pain, and the lives of men*. Toronto: Viking Canada.

Kimmel, M. (forthcoming, 1994). *Manhood: The American quest*. New York: HarperCollins.

Macleod, D. (1983). *Building character in the American boy*. Madison: University of Wisconsin Press.

McLaughlin, W. (1955). *Billy Sunday was his real name*. Chicago: University of Chicago Press.

Moore, R., & Gillette, D. (1992). *The king within: Accessing the king in the male psyche*. New York: William Morrow.

Raphael, R. (1988). *The men from the boys: Rites of passage in male America*. Lincoln: University of Nebraska Press.

Rubin, G. (1975). The traffic in women: Notes on the "political economy" of sex. In R. R. Rieter (Ed.), *Toward an anthropology of women* (pp. 157-210). New York: Monthly Review Press.

Spain, D. (1992). *Gendered spaces*. Chapel Hill: University of North Carolina Press.

Weber, M. (1978). *Economy and society* (2 vols.). Berkeley: University of California Press.

Whyte, W. (1956). *The organization man*. New York: Anchor.

Name Index

Subject Index

About the Contributors

Harry Brod is a part-time teacher of gender-related courses at the University of Southern California, the University of California at Los Angeles, and Antioch University at Los Angeles and of Philosophy for Children through the Los Angeles Unified School District. He is the editor of *The Making of Masculinities: The New Men's Studies, A Mensch Among Men: Explorations in Jewish Masculinity,* and the forthcoming *Can(n)ons of Masculinity: The Hidden History of Masculinities in Western Political Theory.* He is the author of *Hegel's Philosophy of Politics: Idealism, Identity, and Modernity.*

David L. Collinson is Lecturer in Industrial Relations and Organizational Behavior, University of Warwick, U.K. He is the author of *Managing to Discriminate* (with David Knights and Margaret Collinson) and *Managing the Shopfloor* and coeditor of *Job Redesign.*

Scott Coltrane is Assistant Professor of Sociology at the University of California, Riverside. His research on gender, families, and social change has appeared in *Sociological Perspectives, American Journal of Sociology, Social Problems, Gender & Society, Journal of Marriage and the Family, Journal of Family Issues,* and *Men's Studies Review.* He is coauthor (with Randall Collins) of *Sociology of Marriage and the Family: Gender, Love, and Property* (3rd edition). His forthcoming book *Family Man* focuses on the changing role of fathers and the implications of domestic labor sharing for gender equity.

R. W. Connell is Professor of Sociology at the University of California, Santa Cruz. His books include *Gender & Power, Schools and Social Justice,* and *Class Structure in Australian History.* His recent research focuses on poverty and education, AIDS prevention and gay sexuality, changes in masculinity, and historicity and politics in social theory.

Don Conway-Long has taught courses on men and masculinity in the Women's Studies Program at Washington State University since the early 1980s. He is now pursuing a doctorate in anthropology. He spent the 1992-1993 year in Morocco on a Fulbright grant studying masculinity patterns and beliefs among men in Rabat.

Arthur Flannigan-Saint-Aubin teaches French at Occidental College. His articles on race, gender, and sexuality have appeared in *The Journal of the History of Sexuality, Callaloo, The French Review,* and *L'Esprit Createur.* He is author of *Mme de Villedieu's Les Desordres de L'Amour: History, Literature, and the Nouvelle Historique.*

David S. Gutterman is a graduate student in Political Science at Rutgers University. His current research interests include investigating concepts of courage in the work of Nietzsche and analyzing social change and the "politics of ambiguity."

Jeff Hearn is a Reader in Sociology and Critical Studies on Men and Co-Convenor of the Research Unit on Violence, Abuse, and Gender Relations, University of Bradford, U.K. He is the coauthor of *"Sex" at "Work"* (with Wendy Parkin), *The Gender of Oppression,* and *Men in the Public Eye,* and he is coeditor of *The Sexuality of Organizations, Taking Child Abuse Seriously,* and *Men, Masculinities, and Social Theory* (with David H. J. Morgan).

Pierrette Hondagneu-Sotelo is Assistant Professor in the Department of Sociology at the University of Southern California. Her forthcoming book is *Gendered Transitions: The Lives of Mexican Undocumented Immigrants in a California Community.*

Michael Kaufman lives in Toronto, Canada, and since the early 1980s has been active working with men to challenge sexism and to redefine masculinity. His books include *Jamaica Under Manley: Dilemmas of Socialism and Democracy* (1985), *Beyond Patriarchy: Essays by Men on Pleasure, Power, and Change* (1987), *Cracking the Armour: Power, Pain, and the Lives of Men* (1993), and *Community Power and Grass-Roots Democracy* (coedited with Haroldo Dilla, in press). Previously he held the position of deputy director of the Centre for Research on Latin America and the Caribbean at York University in Toronto. He is a founder of the White Ribbon Campaign, which works to end men's violence against women. He taught from 1979 to 1992 at York University and now works full-time writing and doing educational and training work on gender issues.

Michael S. Kimmel is Associate Professor of Sociology at SUNY at Stony Brook and the editor of the Sage Series on Research on Men and Masculinities. His books include *Men Confront Pornography* (1990), *Men's Lives* (coedited with Michael A. Messner, 1990, 3rd edition in press), *Against the Tide: Pro-feminist Men in the United States, 1776-1990,* with Tom Mosmiller (1992), and the forthcoming *Manhood: The American Quest,* a history of the idea of manhood in America. As a Visiting Professor, Kimmel was voted "Best Professor" by the students at University of California at Berkeley.

Mairtin Mac an Ghaill teaches in the Department of Education at the University of Birmingham, U.K. He is author of *Young, Gifted, and Black: Student-Teacher Relations in the Schooling of Black Youth.* He is presently preparing a book for publication titled *Acting Like Men: Masculinities, Sexualities, and Schooling.*

Michael A. Messner is Associate Professor in the Department of Sociology and the Program for the Study of Women and Men in Society at the University of Southern California. He is coeditor (with Michael S. Kimmel) of *Men's Lives* and (with Donald F. Sabo) *Sport, Men, and the Gender Order: Critical Feminist Perspectives.* He is author of *Power at Play: Sports and the Problem of Masculinity.*

David H. J. Morgan is a Senior Lecturer in the Department of Sociology at the University of Manchester, U.K., where he has been more or less continuously since 1962. He is the author of *Discovering Men* and is the coeditor (with Jeff Hearn) of *Men, Masculinities and Social Theory* and (with Sue Scott) of *Body Matters.* He has been an active member of the British Sociological Association and is currently joint editor of its journal *Sociology.*

7198